# Handle
## With
# Care

# Rochelle Bugg

# Handle With Care

My life as a young carer,
the loss of my parents and how
I learned to live again

**JB**

First published in the UK by John Blake Publishing
An imprint of Bonnier Books UK
80–81 Wimpole Street, London, W1G 9RE
Owned by Bonnier Books
Sveavägen 56, Stockholm, Sweden

www.facebook.com/johnblakebooks ⊙
twitter.com/jblakebooks ▢

First published in paperback in 2021

Paperback ISBN: 978-1-78946-035-3
Ebook ISBN: 978-1-78946-036-0
Audiobook ISBN: 978-1-78946-399-6

British Library Cataloguing-in-Publication Data:
A catalogue record for this book is available from the British Library.

Design by www.envydesign.co.uk

Printed and bound in Great Britain by Clays Ltd, Elcograf S.p.A.

1 3 5 7 9 10 8 6 4 2

Text copyright © Rochelle Bugg 2021

John Blake Publishing is an imprint of Bonnier Books UK
www.bonnierbooks.co.uk

This is for anyone who has cared, is caring,
or will one day care for someone they love through
a chronic or terminal illness.

And for Mum and Dad.
Look what your little girl did.

# Contents

# Introduction

Peeling off my rubber gloves, I popped the Mr Muscle back under the sink and gave a satisfied nod as I looked around the place I'd called 'home' for the past four years. It had been a productive – albeit tiring – Saturday morning.

The night before, after a hectic first week at my new job in London, I'd rushed straight from work to King's Cross station. M&S gin-in-a-tin in hand, I caught the train back up to Leeds, where I'd lived since finishing uni there, then woke up early to clear out my old flat.

After scrubbing and polishing everything to Mrs Hinch levels of perfection, I locked up for the last time, handed my keys back to the estate agent and headed to my boyfriend Kunle's house, letting myself in with the spare key while he was still at work.

*Now for an afternoon nap,* I thought to myself.

To be honest, I needed it. Not only was I exhausted from my first week in a new job and cleaning out my old flat, but I still had to sit down with Kunle tonight and finish talking about where things stood between us, now that I'd moved down south. I'd just signed the lease on a new place with my middle sister, Hannah, who was twenty and in her second year of uni in London, but Kunle's career plans didn't look like they were going to bring him down to the big smoke with me, so it was time to make some decisions.

Flopping onto the bed, I grabbed my phone to set an alarm, but as I did, it started ringing in my hands, its shrill tone almost causing me to toss it in the air. I looked at the screen.

*Olivia.*

It was my other sister who, at sixteen years old, was the youngest of us three.

I rolled my eyes. What did she want this time? She lived at home with Mum in Ipswich and was forever calling for help with her homework as if I was her own personal Google.

'Hi Liv,' I said flatly. 'What's up?'

'Ummmm, Ro...' she started, in a tone that caused me to sit bolt upright. Something was wrong.

'Yeah? What is it?' I asked, slightly panicked.

'Mum told me not to call you but I'm worried...' she replied. 'She went to the doctor and they sent her to the hospital. They did some tests and said she's had a ... wait, I can't remember the long name, let me check the leaflet they gave her. OK, it says it's called a TIA, a Transient Ischaemic Attack, also known as a mini-stroke. I'm upstairs in my room so she doesn't know I've called you—'

'Is she OK?' I asked so quickly that I hardly gave her a chance to finish her sentence.

'She said she's fine, but I went downstairs before and I think she's been crying,' Olivia went on.

I rambled for a few minutes trying to reassure her that everything would be OK, but I barely managed to convince

2

myself. Then I hung up and – completely ignoring Olivia's pleas not to – called Mum straightaway.

'Mother! What's all this about you being an attention seeker today?' I asked in a pretend posh voice that I hoped would lighten the mood. 'What's going on? Fancy going to perv on some hot doctors or something, did you?' I mocked, deciding that bad jokes were the best way to play it if I was going to get the full story out of her.

'Ro, baby. I'm fine. It's not even anything,' she said. 'Do NOT worry about silly old me.'

'Yeah but what did they say exactly, Mum? Do you need me to come home?' I asked, reeling off question after question.

'Nooo, no, no,' she insisted. 'Go out for a nice meal tonight and have a glass of wine. Actually, have one for me as well. They've given me some tablets and told me to lay of the old vino for a bit.'

Then she paused.

'I just … I don't get … I don't get how it h-happened. I mean, a-a stroke…' she stuttered.

As the words tumbled out of her mouth and down the line to me, her voice cracked. Despite her being hundreds of miles away, I instinctively knew that her brow was furrowed and her lips were pressing down hard together in a feeble attempt to hold back the tears that were pricking at her eyes. In typical Mum style, she didn't want to cause a fuss, but I could tell that she needed me there with her.

Especially without Dad around.

My mum, Shirley, and my dad, James, were true sweethearts. The ultimate team. They did everything together – from running several businesses, to bringing us three girls up in a home filled with love and laughter.

Mum had always dreamt of a fairy-tale wedding on an exotic beach but having three kids, building up a number of businesses and managing tight finances meant it got pushed to the back-burner year after year. Eventually, her and Dad were in a position where they had the time and money to start planning. I still remember the pile of brochures on the kitchen table and the folded corner on the page of a resort in Mexico which Mum had picked as her favourite.

But it wasn't to be.

Soon after they started planning, when I was fourteen, and my dad just forty-seven, he fell ill, losing a lot of weight very suddenly and suffering from excruciating abdominal pain. Dad quickly became too poorly to travel to the bathroom, let alone the other side of the world.

He went back and forth to the doctors countless times before they eventually found what was wrong. At one point they said he had irritable bowel syndrome (IBS), then thought it might be gallstones. But when they finally gave him his prognosis, it was far worse.

Cancer of the pancreas.

Stage IV.

By the time he was diagnosed, the cancer had already started spreading through his body, meaning there were no treatment options. In short, he was screwed.

In July, on the last day of term, Dad had collected me and my sisters from school and driven us home. Nothing out of the ordinary. Little did I know that by the time the summer holidays were over, his time with us would nearly be over, too.

Instead of a sun-filled ceremony, Mum and Dad got married in a dingy hospital chapel on an autumn afternoon. By that point, he was just about strong enough to make it out of his bed for a few hours, saying 'I do' from a wheelchair, skin jaundiced and attached to a drip. My eyes still fill with tears when I think of how they were forced to trade a serene sunset celebration for some soggy sandwiches in a disused hospital office.

Just six weeks after finding out he had cancer, he was gone for ever.

To call it a shock would be to understate the cataclysmic way his death ripped through my life. That September, as my friends settled into the new school year with new hair and new pencil cases, I settled into a new reality – one without my dad.

The pain was so intense, so overwhelming, that it felt surreal.

It was clear we would never get over losing Dad, but it did bind us together more tightly. We'd always been a close family, but after he died, it was different. Even as we scattered across the country, living our own lives, every few weeks, without fail, we'd take it in turns to meet up and spend time together – in Leeds, or London, or back in Ipswich. Friends would comment, 'Oh I wish my family was that close', and it was true. We shared a bond that allowed us to speak without words – which is how I *knew* that Mum needed me back home right now.

'Right Mum. Listen to me, please. Make that youngest child of yours wait on you hand and foot until I get there,' I instructed. 'I'm gonna get the next train to Ipswich and come and give you a big hug. OK?'

'OK,' she replied, weakly.

As I said goodbye and hung up, Olivia's words were still ringing in my ears.

*A mini-stroke.*

How? This was my mum we were talking about. The woman who was always on the go.

My world was spinning and I needed Kunle to steady me.

5

Scrolling to his number on my phone, I pressed 'call' – oblivious to the fact the shock was about to wear off at the precise moment he answered. As he picked up, my calmness dissipated, replaced by hysterical sobbing and gasps for air as I struggled to get my words out.

'Roch, is it asthma? Do you need an ambulance?' he shouted down the phone. 'Can you not breathe?'

The stupidity of his questions snapped me out of my sobbing.

'Why would I be having an asthma attack when I don't have bloody asthma?' I snapped. 'No, it's my mum. She's had a stroke. I need to go home.'

'I'm leaving work now. Fifteen minutes and I'll be there,' he promised.

As soon as Kunle walked through the door, I collapsed into his arms and started wailing hysterically, accidentally leaving a trail of snot on his leather jacket. In a teary blur, I frantically packed my stuff, booked my ticket and made a mad dash to the train station to get back to Ipswich.

My plan was always to return to London as soon as I felt sure Mum was OK. That Saturday, I took the train to Ipswich fully intending to be back at work a few days later once we'd got to the bottom of what had happened. Thankfully, my manager was understanding when I explained I wouldn't be back in until Wednesday – and again when I phoned to say we'd better make that *next* Wednesday.

Something wasn't quite right, I just couldn't put my finger on it. Despite the doctors saying Mum was making good progress, I couldn't bring myself to leave her. So after a fortnight in Ipswich, I handed my notice in at my new job, cancelled the flat in London and moved back home.

Mum was treated for the 'mini-stroke' straightaway, but two months down the line, she was still tired all the time, still struggling to use her right side, and weirdly couldn't stop hiccupping. I kept a diary of her strange symptoms – but whenever I mentioned them to doctors, they'd assure me they would ease as her rehabilitation progressed. But then one consultant suggested they were down to depression, brought on by the shock of having a stroke so young.

That just didn't sit right.

I understood that depression would have been a perfectly valid response considering what had gone on. I knew you didn't even need a reason to be depressed, sometimes it just happened. But I also knew my mum. I had seen her angry and sad, but never depressed.

The more time passed, the more uncertainty bubbled up inside of me. I *knew* something wasn't right – and I knew it was down to me to find out what.

'I'm going to get a second opinion at a private hospital,' I told my sisters, a couple of months after Mum was first diagnosed with the stroke.

I remembered how long had been wasted sending Dad from pillar to post, so I knew that when it came to your health, there was no time to waste. We weren't going to make the same mistake twice. Being wary was worth it.

One appointment, thirty minutes, and £250 later, Mum was whisked away and admitted to hospital for more tests. It turned out the consultant shared my concerns – he could tell something wasn't right, too.

*I knew it.*

But nothing could have prepared me for what happened next. Less than twenty-four hours later, after a few rounds of poking, prodding, testing and scanning, the consultant's verdict was in.

Mum hadn't had a TIA. Her symptoms had been misdiagnosed. She had cancer.

*A brain tumour.*

A biopsy was taken and on 10th February, just shy of three months since I'd received that first phone call from Olivia, we went to collect the results. Bundling Mum into the car, we drove to Addenbrooke's Hospital in Cambridge to find out what type of tumour she had and how they planned to treat it.

After arriving, Hannah and Olivia helped Mum into the wheelchair she now needed to get around, while I went to pay for our parking. The machine spat out a small slip of paper and I noticed the bold printed numbers indicating when we needed to leave.

16:04.

As we made our way towards the hospital entrance, my mind began to wander. By the time our parking was up, we'd have the news. Good or bad.

*What would my world look like at 16:04?*

Half an hour early for the appointment, we sat together in the characterless waiting room. Suddenly I felt Hannah's hand on my knee.

'Stop,' she said, holding it down firmly.

I didn't even realise that I'd been bouncing my leg up and down anxiously.

'Sorry,' I whispered. But before long it started again. Unable to calm my nervous energy, I pretended to need the loo, walked to the nearest toilets and locked myself in a cubicle. Perched on the lid, I squeezed my hands together and decided to pray.

*I haven't done this since mumbling along to the Lord's Prayer in school assembly*, I thought.

Back then I didn't really know what I was saying. But I did now. Over the next few minutes, hands clasped and eyes shut, I recited a hundred variations of one silent prayer.

*Please let my mum be OK.*

Finishing with a hasty 'Amen' – the universal full stop of prayer – I had no idea if it would work, but I was willing to try anything to guarantee good news. I didn't want to go through what we'd been through with Dad all over again.

It didn't even bear thinking about.

Forty minutes of waiting and wondering passed, then a man's head finally bobbed out of a blue door marked Consulting Room 2.

'Shirley Bugg,' he called.

My stomach flip-flopped, part-excited for good news, wholly terrified at the prospect of bad, as we sprang into action and piled into the consultant's office.

'Mrs Bugg is it?' he asked, looking at Mum as if someone else might have accidentally found themselves being wheeled into his office for a fun afternoon out.

'Yes,' she said, matter-of-factly, with no hint of emotion.

There might have been some more small talk, I'm not sure. I can't remember because my brain went into free fall as I watched the consultant scribble two long words on a piece of paper, tear it off his pharmaceutical-branded notepad, and push it across his desk, under the four sets of beady eyes opposite him.

I forced my eyes to focus on his scrawl, taking in each letter.

*Anaplastic astrocytoma.*

Then, as he drew his hand away, he opened his mouth and delivered the bombshell.

'It's a very aggressive tumour I'm afraid, so there's nothing we can do,' he said. 'There's around a 25 per cent chance of surviving up to two years.'

In that split second, my world imploded.

It did not explode as you might expect. No, an explosion might have meant there was something spectacular about the situation, but there wasn't. It was just an utterly hopeless collapse. Life immediately deflated into a sorry pool of nothingness and I felt the world physically shift.

Every other worry I'd ever had suddenly seemed insignificant. It was as if I'd spent my life worrying about plant pots being knocked over by a gentle breeze, not knowing that a hurricane was about to hit and tear out every last tree from its roots.

This couldn't be happening.

'There must be something,' I managed to say eventually, my voice so panicked and desperate that I didn't even recognise it. 'There's got to be something, or someone, or somewhere we can go. Our dad died, you see. He had cancer, too. He died when we were all young. So we can't lose our mum as well. There's got to be something. Are there clinical trials? A new type of treatment? It doesn't matter what it is, but there has to be something. Anything.'

I don't know how long I pleaded manically with the consultant, but when I finally stopped, all he did was shake his head.

'I understand this must be a lot for you to take in but I'm afraid there really is nothing we can do. I am sorry,' he said. 'If you want a moment to gather yourselves before leaving, you can use the next room. It's empty and there are tissues in there if you need them.'

Blindsided by his lack of empathy, I turned to look at Mum. A lone tear was falling down her face, the sight causing me to break down into sobs all over again.

I was sure I could feel the walls closing in on us.

*I had to get her out of there.* Away from this man, telling her she had no hope. Away from the news we'd just been given. Away from the threat of history repeating itself.

*This couldn't be happening – not again.*

From the moment of her terminal diagnosis, Mum became my one and only focus. Overnight, I went from a carefree young professional in my mid-twenties, to my mum's carer and substitute parent for my two sisters – the weight of their three worlds landing squarely on my shoulders.

It was surprising how quickly I displaced myself from the centre of my own universe, rapidly beginning a new orbit with Mum in the middle. Just like a parent with a newborn, I slept around her schedule, ate around her schedule, and went to her whenever she called. My body may not have been stretched or marked by the physical changes of pregnancy, but just like a new mother, I too was a shape-shifter. Contorting around the cancer, morphing and moulding myself around Mum.

It was relentlessness.

My life was controlled by the ruthless routine of treatment and endless emails, red tape and admin. The deeper I was pulled into my role of carer, the more my personality slipped away from me, along with friends, hobbies and any semblance of my old life.

But while it was by far the hardest thing I'd ever done, it was equally the most important and most rewarding. It was my chance to return the love and care that Mum had *literally* spent her life giving to me and my sisters and an opportunity to keep the promise I'd made to my dad the day before he died, when he told me: 'Look after your mum for me.'

Despite scouring every corner of the internet for a magic

cure or pioneering clinical trial that might keep Mum with us, the tumour was too aggressive. While we never lost hope for a miracle, as her illness progressed the focus of our daily fight soon shifted to finding ways to make the most of the time we had left. And that's exactly what we did!

I was determined not to let the fact we couldn't do everything, stop us from anything.

There were the grand gestures, like our final holiday to Sorrento, a place Mum had always wanted to visit but hadn't had the chance; the surprise party where Mum's friends came together from all over the country; and 'recreating' America at home when Mum was too sick to travel but itching to see the States.

Then there were the smaller, more intimate things, like Triple T duty – where one of us would take Mum's tablets, tea and toast up to her on a tray each morning. It soon became a legendary daily ritual in our house, each of us girls taking it in turns. Of all the jobs involved in being a carer, this was the one none of us minded. Not only would we get to snuggle up next to Mum in bed in the hushed quiet of the early morning, but we got to watch the world's first professional biscuit dunker in action.

Even though her right side had pretty much stopped working, Mum turned tea and biscuits into an art form. The cross-body stretch to get the tin she kept on her bedside table. The way she clenched it between her thighs so she could take the lid off with her one good hand. She timed the 'dunk to mouth' manoeuvre to perfection, ensuring her favourite Rich Tea fingers never dropped in, and always finished with a dramatic twist of the wrist, executing her move with the skill and grace of an Olympic gymnast.

It was the little things like that which kept us going. Especially towards the end.

Before long, we had to rearrange the house to create a makeshift bedroom for Mum on the ground floor, because she couldn't keep climbing the three flights of stairs to her bedroom. She started sleeping more and her ability to communicate with us slowly slipped away.

As cancer whittled down the final parts of our mum and her care needs intensified, we turned to help from St Elizabeth Hospice. It was on their recommendation that we requested a Marie Curie nurse to start sitting with Mum overnight, so that someone was watching her 24/7.

That spring, we knew the end was near. We just didn't know how near.

When Mum's Marie Curie nurse arrived for her first shift, she looked at her notes, looked at Mum and then looked at me.

'I think it's likely it will be tonight or tomorrow morning,' she said.

*It* being death.

I was still in denial as I passed on the news to Hannah and Olivia, but when I heard the nurse's footsteps coming up the stairs to my room later that night, I knew what it meant. The three of us gathered around Mum's bedside talking, laughing, crying and holding her hand until it happened. The tranquillity of the room only breaking briefly as Mum took one deep, desperate gasp for air. Then another.

As she did, we snuggled in more closely to her, whispering soothing words as her piercing blue eyes stared at us. Then suddenly, she winked.

Three times.

One for each of us girls.

Then she was gone.

Just seventeen months after first falling ill, our darling mumma had gone back to be with her sweetheart – and we were alone. The three of us against the world.

Throughout Mum's illness, and in the years that followed her death, I was on a quest for answers – always wondering why things happened the way they did and why people cope so differently to having a terminally ill loved one. Time and time again I doubted myself, wondering if I was going mad and questioning the way I was dealing with things.

Blogging soon became a sanity check for me. A way to make sense of the whirlwind of events and emotions I was experiencing – as well as keeping friends and family updated on Mum's progress.

When I became a carer, there were no guidelines, no instructions, and no textbook that I could turn upside down and flick to the back for answers when I was struggling. I had to navigate the journey of caring alone, steering a course for me and my two sisters. It was scary, overwhelming and heartbreaking.

I constantly felt on the verge of losing my mind.

It wasn't until three or four years after Mum died that I was able to reflect and realise that everything I'd experienced was a natural part of becoming a carer, of grieving and of learning to live again.

I looked back and thought about *that* train journey – the one I made from Leeds to Ipswich right after Olivia's call to tell me about Mum's 'mini-stroke'. I didn't realise at the time, but sitting on that train was the last point in my life that anything would be familiar or 'normal'. Unbeknown to me, I wasn't going *back* to Ipswich; I was heading – completely unprepared – *towards* a whole new reality.

Sometimes I would daydream, replaying that journey in my

mind as if it were a Hollywood film. Only in the Tinseltown version of events, I would sit down on that train, look across and find a book on the seat next to me. Abandoned by a stranger in a hurry, in a magical twist of fate, it would tell the story of someone who had been through everything I was about to go through. After gobbling up every last page on the long journey home, in the months to come, I would draw comfort from knowing that someone else had already made it through the hellish ordeal I was only just embarking on. Time and time again, I would dig out that book, referring back to it for emotional support, practical guidance and simply to feel understood, in a world where it seemed no one 'got' what I was going through.

But nobody *was* talking about how being a carer affects you as a young person. Nobody *was* talking about whether it was normal to not want to socialise after a loved one's diagnosis. Nobody *was* talking about what is a normal amount to cry after your dad dies. Nobody *was* talking about whether it's normal that you can't stop obsessively thinking about how your dying mum won't see you get married.

There was *nothing* to act as a guide. And that made me feel even more isolated than I already did. It didn't seem right – not for me, and not for any other carer ever again.

There wasn't a book for me, but I wanted there to be one for you.

So I decided to write it.

I wrote it *for us*.

I wrote it for the people who have to grow up before they're ready. For the people that want a reassuring hug from their loved one, only to realise it's them who now has to give that hug. For the people who find themselves in a role they never asked for, but who are nevertheless determined to do a good job.

If your dad was diagnosed a couple of months ago and you don't know whether to quit uni and move home or carry on studying – *This book is for you.*

If you've just found out your mum's cancer is terminal and now you can't stop thinking about the grandchildren she will never meet – *This book is for you.*

If you care for your brother in the evenings and find it hard to get your college work done in between helping him – *This book is for you.*

If it's been six months since your best friend passed away and nobody seems to understand why you can't face going out for your birthday – *This book is for you.*

Whatever your experience of caring for or coping with the loss of a loved one – *This book is for you.*

I can't promise a one-size-fits-all, foolproof plan to take away the pain. Experience has taught me there's nothing anyone can say or do to magically make things easy. I'm not an academic expert. I can't offer you graphs and charts and double-blind studies. But what I can offer you is my experience, my truth, my mistakes, my regrets and my lessons.

You can read this book cover to cover, or dip into sections as you need. In its entirety it follows the journey of Mum's illness chronologically from diagnosis to death, followed by my journey towards healing. However, in each chapter, I share standalone stories from different points in that timeline, ones that taught me vital lessons and gave me valuable understanding. Not everything will mirror *your* story, but I hope that you will be able to see yourself reflected in these pages.

The years have continued to slip by since my mum passed away and I am still learning about how my role as her carer – and the experience of losing her and Dad – has shaped me and my life's path. My journey hasn't been easy and I can't pretend yours will be either, but I hope this book will help you steer yourself to safe shores a little more quickly and a little more smoothly than I was able to. Most importantly, I hope it serves as a reminder that if I survived, you will too.

# 1.

## Diagnosis

## THE KNOWING

The fridge was fully stocked, *Home Alone* was on TV and I'd shamelessly eaten half a Terry's Chocolate Orange for breakfast. That could only mean one thing. It was Christmas Eve.

I loved being at home with the family, a mountain of food, Mariah Carey on repeat, no reason to leave the house and every reason to stay in my PJs. Annoyingly though, the fun couldn't start until a bit later than usual, because Mum had a Stroke Clinic appointment, following her diagnosis with a TIA a month earlier.

Forcing myself to get dressed and head out to our local hospital wasn't exactly a festive treat, but it was necessary. As luck would have it, we didn't have to hang around in the waiting room for long before Mum's name was called.

'Shirley Bugg?' called the nurse, before pointing to the consultation room where our designated doctor was waiting.

'Here we go,' I said, linking arms with Mum as she stood up, and we walked together into his office. Her steps were slow and deliberate as she'd become more unsteady on her feet the past few weeks. Which was strange because things were meant to be improving.

Mum barely had a chance to sit on the bed before the doctor launched into the usual rigmarole, checking if she could follow his finger with her eyes and push and pull his hand with her 'bad' side. And after a few minutes, he gave a little nod.

'You can take a seat now, Shirley, thank you,' he said.

I leapt to my feet to help her off the bed and back over to the creaky plastic chairs. As we were still making our way across the room, the doctor started running through some exercises for Mum to do at home to strengthen her weak side. And by the time we sat down, he was reaching across to hand her some leaflets.

'I'm very happy with your progress Shirley,' he said. 'There's no need for any more follow-up appointments.'

My eyes darted towards the clock on the wall.

*That was quick!* I thought.

We'd only been in his office five minutes and he was ready to send us on our way. I hadn't even had chance to ask the list of questions I'd been storing up since Mum's last appointment.

I went to speak but froze momentarily.

Would I annoy him if I started asking more questions now? Maybe he was as eager to get home for Christmas with his family as I was.

*Come on, Rochelle. Be brave,* I told myself.

The doctor had finished typing and was now hovering, somewhere between seated and standing, as he prepared for us to leave the office. But before he could usher us out, I took a deep breath.

'Um, I know you just said that Mum's making good progress

but it's just that I've been reading up online...' I blurted out. I could tell he was trying not to roll his eyes at the mere mention of Google, but I continued regardless.

'It seems that the damage done by a mini-stroke stops once you start treatment,' I said. 'It's been about a month now and I feel like Mum's symptoms are getting worse instead of better. It doesn't really seem to fit with everything I've read.'

The doctor was now parked back in his chair, eyebrow raised as he waited for me to finish. My cheeks started to redden, increasingly aware of his thinly veiled annoyance.

'And I know it's probably nothing but she's getting really tired, she's finding it harder to walk and, it might sound really random, but she's started hiccupping quite a lot,' I finished.

The doctor took a long deep breath in. I couldn't tell if it was because I'd thrown so much information at him or because I was getting between him and a stack of mince pies.

'I hear what you're saying,' he responded finally. 'But like I've explained, your mum is doing just fine. There's a bit of weakness still in her right side compared to her left but she's really not that bad.'

'So why aren't the improvements happening as quickly as they should?' I quickly queried, before I had chance to chicken out.

'If you don't feel like she's making progress, then I would suggest it's most likely due to depression. It's quite common when relatively young people have a stroke,' he said, eyes not moving from his computer screen. 'It's hard for them to get their head around not being able to do as much as they usually would.'

Before he'd finished his sentence, the printer in the corner of the office whirred into life.

'Make sure your mum takes these,' he said, handing me the paper the printer had just spat out.

I looked down and frowned. It was a prescription for antidepressants.

I knew Mum had seen it too. I winced at the awkwardness of the whole situation. I'd been such an idiot making my little speech. I had a degree in Marketing, not Medicine. Who did I think I was? Why did I feel the need to question his diagnosis? And poor Mum. I hadn't even thought about how it would sound to her. Everything I said must've come across as if I didn't think she was putting enough effort into getting better, like this was all her fault. That couldn't have been further from the truth.

I was just worried. Something didn't seem right and I wanted to get the doctor's opinion on Mum's strange symptoms. But by asking, all I'd done was hurt her feelings. Her silence said it all as she sat staring down at her left hand, twiddling the wedding ring on her finger.

Guilt washed over me. I needed to get out of there – *and fast.*

As we made our way back to the car park, I tried to pack away my questions and accept the doctor's response. But alarm bells were ringing so loudly in my head that I wondered if everyone around me could hear them.

*This isn't right!* they warned.

With so many subtle shifts in Mum's behaviour over the past few months, there had to be something more to it, I *knew* it, I could *feel* it. I just couldn't quite put my finger on it. Trying to silence the alarms ringing in my head, I turned to Mum.

'Well, that's you signed off! Best we go and get on with Christmas then, hey?' I said.

'Yessss! Let's go, my baby,' she replied, squeezing out a half-hearted grin.

On the way home we stopped at Waitrose, because I had my eye on an overpriced Heston Blumenthal Christmas pudding.

Something about Mum being ill made me want to put even more effort than usual into Christmas this year. I'd already gone totally overboard with presents for her and now I was getting sucked into spending a small fortune on fancy-pants food. Yet despite all my feigned festive cheer and fraudulent joy at Mum's discharge from the Stroke Clinic, I couldn't shake the feeling that something wasn't right.

It was just like with my dad.

Long before the word 'cancer' was ever uttered in our house, I could sense something was wrong. Over a year before he died, when his symptoms had been diagnosed as IBS, we were driving in the car when 'Everybody's Free (To Wear Sunscreen)' by Baz Luhrmann, came on the radio.

*It was our song.*

We quoted the lines back and forth to one another until I heard a particular lyric.

'Get to know your parents, you never know when they'll be gone for good.'

The words went into my ears and straight to my heart, causing me to burst into sobs so fierce that Dad pulled over to stop the car.

'What's wrong, my girl?' he asked, concern shadowing his face. 'You know you can tell me anything. I'm not just your dad, I'm your friend, OK?'

'I know,' I replied.

My body convulsing with tears, I scrambled for what to tell him. Something. Anything. Just not the truth – that I was terrified he was going to die and leave me.

'I'm just worried I'm not going to pass my exams,' I managed to lie eventually.

But something in my brain clicked and the line from the song

23

played over and over in my head: *'Get to know your parents, you never know when they'll be gone for good.'*

In that moment, even though there was no way to know, I *knew* he was going to die. Despite everything the doctors were saying, I *knew* he didn't have IBS. I *knew* it was something more serious. Those lyrics were advice for me, a warning that time was running out. And if my gut turned out to be right back then, how could I ignore the twinge I felt about Mum now?

That Christmas Eve at the Stroke Clinic was just one of multiple medical appointments where I didn't feel Mum and I were being listened to. It was the latest in a long line of meetings with underfunded and overstretched doctors who were under pressure to tick us off their waiting list, redirect us on to a new NHS care pathway and make us someone else's problem.

In many ways, I could see why they thought Mum was fine. When they'd ask her what caused her to first go to the doctor she'd reply: 'Well, I'd made myself a cup of tea and was carrying it back upstairs in my right hand but I just kept spilling it. It's like I couldn't hold it steady.'

It seemed silly. Small. Hardly life-threatening.

And when they tested her motor skills by asking her to write a simple sentence, she could hold the pen and spell words. Yet the doctors were oblivious to how her writing had lost the recognisable shape I'd seen in so many birthday cards over the years. I'd tell them, of course, but they dismissed my fears, as if swatting a fly from their face.

I began to doubt myself as much as they doubted me and started questioning what I knew to be true. I convinced myself that I couldn't see Mum's recovery because I was spending too much time with her, and expecting too much too soon.

So instead of trusting my intuition, I buried myself in distractions and bought Mum extra Christmas presents to try and block out my concerns: A printer so she could type instead of hand-writing anything and a Teasmade so she didn't have to carry her morning cup of tea upstairs – not forgetting Heston's £13.99 Christmas pudding with lunch.

*Problem solved*, I'd thought, but it soon became clear that wasn't the case.

In the end, it turned out that I was right to question the doctors and I was right to stay looking after Mum instead of going back to work. Not because I have psychic powers, but because I knew my mum. I was right, not because I could see into the future, but because I could tell that something was off with the person I loved. And that was my first lesson as a carer...

## Always trust your gut instinct

Never underestimate the value of giving yourself the time, space and quiet to stop and listen to that voice inside. Work out what *feels* right – not what someone has told you, what makes sense on paper, or what seems to be the easiest option.

It took me a while to understand that doctors, as well as lawyers, pilots and professionals of any kind, are still *human*. It sounds obvious, but the implications aren't.

Doctors are just people. Highly trained, yes, but underneath it all, they are no different to the rest of us. They might be tired because there was a car alarm keeping them awake all last night. They might be distracted because they're going through a divorce and can't stop thinking about how much they hate their cheating soon-to-be ex. They might be hurrying to leave work on time so that they can get across town and pick their daughter up from school. That's not even taking into account the pressure they're under at work, the targets they have to meet and the fact that they don't know the person sat in front of them.

It was this understanding that brought me to carer lesson number two. Trusting your gut is only half the battle. When you can instinctively tell something isn't right, you've got to…

## Fight for what you know to be true

Over the course of Mum's illness, I gradually got better at not feeling embarrassed or awkward for speaking up if I didn't agree with a diagnosis, treatment or care decision. But it was a slow and awkward process. At first, I lacked the confidence to make myself heard. I would back down after being told 'no' like the polite young woman I was brought up to be – just as I had done at that Christmas Eve appointment – and I'd scold myself for daring to disagree with doctors, consultants and, later on, solicitors too. All too often I accepted their explanations and dismissals, even when they didn't sit right with me.

If I could rewind time, I'd approach things very differently. I would trust my gut instinct from the get-go and refuse to let it be silenced. I would fight for what I *knew* to be true, not stopping until I found a doctor who was able to see what I already could.

## DON'T GIVE UP THE DAY JOB… OR DO?

Struggling with the sense that *something* wasn't right, I was faced with a decision. Should I go back to London, back to my new job and new flat? Or should I quit to stay home with Mum?

Usually, I would have talked through a big choice like this

with Mum or Dad, just as I had when deciding what GCSEs to take, where to go to uni and if it was too soon to move in with my boyfriend. But now, for the first time in my life, I was at a crossroads that I had to navigate alone.

The question rattled around my mind for days until I finally made up my mind.

*I am going to quit.*

Mum needed me and that was all that mattered right now. I could get another job, but I couldn't get another her.

As I sneaked to my bedroom to make the calls, my stomach churned with nerves. I was hardly going to win any prizes for being employee of the month, given they'd barely seen me in the two weeks since I'd started. But still, I was worried about how my manager would respond.

Trying to calm myself down, I took a deep breath and mentally rehearsed – again – what I was going to say. I felt so shaky, I wasn't sure I could make the call, so I put down my phone and picked up my laptop.

*I'll email him instead*, I thought.

Instantly, I felt more comfortable, taking time to pick and choose my words, rather than run the risk of rambling on a call. After drafting and deleting several times over, I finally had something I felt happy sending, albeit littered with apologies, letting him know I was *SO sorry* and felt *really* bad. It sounded like I was begging for forgiveness about my decision. *Not that it's entirely my choice*, I thought, quickly pressing 'send' before I had any more time to obsess.

With one awkward conversation out of the way, I moved on to the next – calling Rob, the letting agent, to tell him Hannah and I could no longer take the flat. As his mobile rang, I remembered thinking he was hot when we did the viewing. Tall, tanned and just the right amount of confidence without being too cocky. Which made it all the more awkward as I blurted out: 'I'm sorry but we can't take the flat any more, Rob. My mum's had a stroke.'

As the last word left my lips, my composure crumbled, and I burst into tears. I was mortified.

*You're such a loser, Rochelle.*

'Don't worry,' he said, my tears obviously catching him off guard. 'Give me five. Let me speak to my manager.'

'OK,' I sniffed. I wasn't holding out much hope, given the reputation of London estate agents, but to my surprise, Rob agreed to refund our deposit.

'Thank you, thank you, thank you,' I chanted through my tears.

'Listen, I really hope that your mum gets better soon,' Rob said, once I'd managed to compose myself. 'Make sure you look after her – and yourself.'

'Thank you. Honestly, I really appreciate it. Thanks. Bye,' I said, then… *CLICK.* I hung up before I could embarrass myself any more.

Aside from the tears, I was quite proud of myself. I'd anticipated more stress, more resistance, but all I'd been met with was understanding.

*Maybe it's Dad, up there looking out for us,* I thought.

The decision had weighed on me for days, but now it had been made, all at once I felt more relaxed. Knowing I was able to stick around made things feel *right* again.

Now I just had to tell Mum…

Quitting my job to stay at home was probably the first major decision I'd ever made without asking my mum or dad what they thought. Emailing my manager that day marked the scary, irreversible moment where the tables turned and I – the child – became the parent, taking the lead and (quite literally) making the tough calls. I'd always known it would happen at some point, as it does to us all, but for me it happened about thirty years sooner than I was expecting.

Caring for Mum was a change I had to get used to very quickly.

And what I found made the decision-making even harder is that, as a carer, there are no clear-cut, right or wrong answers as to what you should do. There were no hard and fast rules about whether I should look after Mum myself or get professional help. There were no laws on whether I should move into her house or maintain some independence by getting my own place somewhere close by. There were no guidelines on whether I should go back to my job in London, or buy a one-way ticket to a tropical island where I could pretend none of it was happening.

That day saw the first of many tricky judgement calls that I would have to make over the coming years, all of them essentially boiling down to one mind-bending riddle:

How do I juggle normal life with being there for the person I love?

Well, when there's no official guidance, the only thing you can turn to is your *inner* guidance.

I might not have moved home straight away if Dad had still been alive, or if Olivia was older. But with the situation as it was, I did what I *felt* was the best thing to do. And that's all any of us can do, as well as understand that even that is likely to change. As long as you can look yourself in the mirror and know that you're doing your best and going by what *feels* right, then it doesn't matter how many times you change your mind or how many people tell you they would do things differently.

What you're going through is not a textbook situation. There are no answers in the back to turn to, so you must trust you have them inside of you.

## TEARS IN THE TOILET

A couple of weeks after the Stroke Clinic appointment, when the Christmas festivities were over and only a handful of Bounty bars and a stray Milky Way were left in the tin of Celebrations, Hannah, Olivia and I were all in agreement. Not just about our dislike of certain chocolates, but about Mum too.

Something definitely wasn't right.

She seemed different in herself – more anxious, distracted, clumsy and tired with each passing week. But we didn't know why. Was the mini-stroke more serious than doctors thought? Did she need different antidepressants? Whatever the cause, we needed to get to the bottom of it.

As soon as the world returned to normality after the Christmas haze of annual leave and holiday opening hours, I made a decision: I was going to get a second opinion. Picking up the phone, I called a private hospital near to where we lived and made an appointment.

'That will be £250 for 30 minutes with the consultant,' the receptionist informed me.

I nearly had a stroke myself as I balked at the cost, but we'd learned our lesson from the merry-go-round of missed signs and misdiagnoses that Dad went through. Whatever it cost, we were going to get a second opinion. The sooner we knew what was wrong, the sooner we could get her well again, so I didn't hesitate in giving Mum's details to the receptionist.

'You're all booked in,' she confirmed. 'Monday, 13th January at 5pm.'

'Thank you,' I said, scribbling the appointment on the kitchen calendar.

I hung up, then wrote a long list of all the things I wanted to mention to the consultant. If we were paying that much, I wanted to get our money's worth. Before long I had a list snaking its way down the page of my phone's Notes app.

- Choking on nothing
- Snorting sometimes when she breathes
- Yawning
- Hiccups
- Tiredness
- Forgetting words
- Right arm and leg are weak
- Loses her balance sometimes
- Lung problems – as if she forgets to breathe sometimes
- Right eye and right-hand side of her mouth are drooping
- Vision going funny – she keeps rubbing her right eye

I sighed away a sliver of my stress, feeling something verging on excitement about the appointment. I had every faith the consultant would give us the answers we needed.

From the moment we stepped into the consultant's office, everything felt different. Like a fresh breeze blowing through a stuffy room, suddenly there was some relief. He had a kind face and a soft yet confident tone with a warm Irish lilt. Patiently he waited until Mum was ready before starting the appointment.

'OK then, now that we're all settled, what is it that I can do for you ladies today?' he asked.

Immediately feeling at ease, I blabbed away at a million miles an hour, my train of thought darting here, there and everywhere as I was finally able to unload everything I had been storing in my mind.

He really *listened*. As he looked at us intently and nodded thoughtfully, I was filled with confidence that he would get to the bottom of things. Scribbling away on his notepad, he looked every inch the TV crime drama detective, piecing together the evidence.

I decided to help him out with my own clues.

Reaching down to the floor I grabbed my phone out of my bag and opened up the Notes app.

'I've been keeping a log of all the strange symptoms Mum's been having. Would it help if I read them out to you?' I asked.

He nodded gratefully as I started to recite the list on my screen, elaborating on each bullet point I'd made. But as I went through them one by one, the consultant's jovial demeanour gave way to a more concerned expression. He started drawing out his mmm-hmms and I sees and keeping his eyes focused firmly downwards as he absorbed all the information.

Suddenly, he snapped up his head, caught Mum's gaze and offered her an unwelcome invitation.

'OK, Mrs Bugg, what we're going to do is get you into hospital overnight, do a few tests and get some answers for you,' he said.

'No, thank you. I'd rather just wait for an appointment,' Mum piped up. 'You let me know when to come back and I can pop in and have whatever tests I need and then go home to my own bed.'

He may have been prepared for a lot of things, but Mum's stubbornness wasn't one of them.

'Mrs Bugg, it really is important that you go in tonight,' he said, in a tone that made it clear his proposition was less of an offer and more of an order. The way he was talking, I knew we should listen to him.

'Yeah, Mum,' I chipped in. 'Let's find out what's wrong as quickly as we can.'

Twenty minutes of back and forth later, Mum finally relented.

'OK,' she said. 'But I'm not going in an ambulance.'

Mum insisted on stopping off at home first to pack a few things in an overnight bag. As we sat silently on the fifteen-minute cab ride, I thought she was going to persuade me the consultant had got it wrong. Truth be told, I was kind of hoping she would. I wanted her to present a watertight case as to why the doctor was wrong, to prove there was no need for any tests, and come up with evidence that she was, in fact, absolutely, undeniably 100 per cent fine.

*Come on, Mum*, I thought to myself. *Prove him – and me – wrong. Show me that I'm just being a Cautious Carol who's over-reacting and there's actually nothing to worry about.*

But she couldn't.

Within the hour, Mum's bag was packed, and I had dropped her three miles away at the hospital. After settling her in for the night and kissing her goodbye, I made my way home, went straight to my room and perched on the end of my bed. Defrosting from the bitter January weather outside, I'd never felt more alone. How was it possible to feel homesick in my own bedroom?

The minutes and hours dragged by, my frustration growing with every time-check on my phone: 01:13, 01:46, 03:52, 05:02…

*Arrrghhh! I give up!*

There was no way I could sleep.

I remembered the consultant had said he would have Mum's test results first thing. So, since I was up, I decided to make sure I was there when he brought them. Fuelled by the kind of early-morning enthusiasm usually only reserved for getting festival tickets online, I rolled out of bed and showered.

*I'll be there in plenty of time,* I thought.

But the universe had other plans.

First, I was held up with a problem on the buses. Then once I'd finally made it to the hospital, I got lost in the looping labyrinth of indistinguishable corridors. Staring helplessly at the signs on the wall, my anxiety amped up a notch.

I panicked. *Is there any logical process to finding your way around this place?*

But then I saw it. Capel Ward, Bay D2.

Finally!

Skidding around the corner, I arrived just in time to see Mum's consultant pulling back the curtain that had been drawn around her bed, the long blue paper pleats still bunched in his hand.

*Typical! I got up at the crack of dawn, and still managed to miss it,* I thought.

'OK, Mrs Bugg, you just rest and I'll be back to speak to you shortly,' I heard him say. 'In the meantime, if you've got any questions, just let me know.'

As I stood in the doorway, the consultant and his team swiftly brushed past me and on to their next patient. I was annoyed, but oddly comforted too. Mum hadn't even been in twenty-four hours and they'd obviously already found out what was wrong.

'Now, let's get her better and back to normal,' I said to myself, as I walked towards Mum.

But it only took one look at her to derail my train of thought.

Dressed in a faded hospital gown, Mum was sitting in the green plastic armchair next to the bed. I noticed her eyes were locked, trancelike, staring straight ahead.

I didn't even make it across the room to give her a kiss before she spoke.

'Brain tumour. Probably cancer,' she mumbled.

Four words that instantly changed our lives.

For a brief moment the world stopped. Life was temporarily held, motionless, in time and space. I waited for myself to freak out or break down, but I didn't. Instead, to my surprise, I launched into a hyperactive monologue filled with upbeat words.

'Well, it's good that we know what it is now so we can get it treated.'

'This is probably just a sign from Dad to get you to slow down.'

'There's nothing to worry about – we will sort this.'

As my mind slid out of my body, Robotic Rochelle took over, pre-programmed positivity pouring from her lips in an attempt to reassure myself as much as Mum. I felt like a Zen master, chanting affirmations. *This must be because I downloaded the Headspace app last week*, I told myself.

But my response was far from enlightened.

My insistence on this being a blessing in disguise was, in fact, nothing more than a numbing blend of naivety, denial and outright gullibility, cooked up from watching too many Hollywood films and overdosing on quotes from Pinterest.

The sound of a text message on my phone eventually brought me back into myself. Mum's friend Helen had arrived at the hospital to visit, but she couldn't find the ward. She was stuck in the same hospital maze I'd been in earlier.

'I'm just going to find her,' I told Mum, kissing her head.

'Mmm,' she murmured, still staring into space.

My trainers squeaked on the lino flooring as I navigated the beige-coloured corridors, which were plastered in posters. Heading towards the main entrance, Mum's words were still swirling in my head.'

*Brain tumour. Probably cancer.*

Suddenly Robotic Rochelle was gone and I realised that I may well be great in a moment of crisis. But that was it. A moment. Singular. I could handle the specific short space of time in which an emergency incident was unfolding, but beyond that, beyond the initial shock, I was a complete and utter disaster zone.

By the time I spotted Helen hovering outside the coffee shop, I could hardly form a coherent sentence. I launched myself at her with military precision, trying to swallow down the waves of sickness surging up from deep in my belly. I couldn't make eye contact with her; it felt too much, too real, too intense. So instead, as the tears bubbled up, I looked vacantly at my hands, picking at the skin around my nails and mumbled directions to her.

'Go through the double doors, then take a left, a right and go to the third ward down,' I instructed.

She squeezed my hand knowingly as I'd already texted her the bad news while walking to find her, then set off towards Mum's ward.

From the outside, nothing much had changed in the half hour since I'd arrived at the hospital, yet beneath the surface, the landscape of my life had been irreparably altered. Suddenly, I was unable to do anything but focus on two words.

TUMOUR.

CANCER.

The news pulsed through me, those four syllables pounding as constantly as the blood in my head. They echoed in my ears. They flashed before my eyes. They caught in my throat. They just wouldn't stop.

I didn't know what to do with myself as I tried to process the life-altering enormity of it all. I wanted to do everything, and yet I wanted to do nothing. In the end, all I could think to do was head to the toilets and lock myself away from the world for a little bit.

After queuing behind one lady for what felt like an eternity, a loud flush came from the far cubicle and she went in. Then came another, followed by the *clonk* of a lock. I watched as an old woman did a slow-motion forward-moonwalk out of the middle cubicle and towards the sink, hooking the handle of her walking stick over the basin while she washed her hands.

I fought the urge to run into the toilet, instead making three large, purposeful steps, then gently shutting the door behind me. Reaching down to the big round wheel of toilet paper, I tore off a long strip of tissue and lifted it to my face to blow my nose. But before I could, *it* happened.

Contained by those four small walls, I crumbled, frothing and fizzing like a bath bomb from Poundland. The floodgates opened, and an entire ocean of waves came crashing against me all at once. Hell was unleashing its fury and that fury found its way into my eyes, my heart, my throat, my stomach. My tears weren't just trickling, they were streaming hard and heavy, like a tropical rainstorm from which it was impossible to shelter. There were thunderous cries, soul-aching wails of grief, and guttural sobs so hard and deep that it wasn't until I was struggling to breathe that I realised those sounds were coming from me!

It felt as if my heart was being dragged out of my chest through my stomach.

I was overcome by the need to get these feelings out, to purge myself of every last thing inside of me. I wanted to be sick, or for my head to explode. Something... *anything*... physically had to happen because it was impossible for so much panic and fear to stay contained in a human body.

I flipped down the toilet lid and perched on it, my shaking body flopping forward, head hanging between my knees like a tipsy teenager drinking for the first time. But adrenaline was still rushing through my body. I couldn't sit. I couldn't stay still. I needed to scream, or run, or punch something.

I stood up and slammed myself hard against the side of the cubicle, before slowly sliding all the way down until my bum hit the cold hard floor. Knees bent into my chest, hands clenched into fists, I angrily hit my thighs over and over again, my long fingernails digging into my palms where my hands were screwed so tightly together. My brain registered that I was hurting myself, but I was numb to the pain.

It was impossible for anything to hurt more than what I had just been told.

Time melted in the furnace of my pain so I wasn't sure if it was thirty seconds or thirty minutes later, when there was a gentle knock at the door followed by a question delivered in the most wonderfully British way.

'Are you OK, dear?' the voice asked.

To be fair, what else could you ask a wailing banshee thrashing around inside a third of the available toilet facilities, much to the irritation of the growing queue of middle-aged women with weak bladders?

The question snapped me back into reality.

'Yes, I'll be fine. I'm fine really. Thank you. Oh, I'm so sorry, I'm taking up one of the loos. Sorry, I'll get out of your way now,' I replied in an equally British manner as I pulled myself up, grabbed some loo roll and darted out of the cubicle.

Making my way from the toilets to the main entrance, I wiped my eyes with the sandpaper-like tissue, tracing the path of my pain-filled tears. Standing shivering outside, I scrolled through the contacts on my phone, desperate to find a magic someone hiding between A and Z who could fix everything and make me feel a little less alone.

Mum and Dad always told me that I could talk to them about anything, that they'd always be there for me. But who could I turn to now? Who would tell me that there had been a terrible mistake? Or that they knew how to fix this? Who could share some pearl of wisdom that would make everything OK?

No one, I realised.

My head was pounding as I made my way back to the ward. As much as I'd been telling everyone that something more was going on with Mum and that the stroke diagnosis didn't explain her symptoms, the mention of cancer sent me spiralling.

*This couldn't be true, Dad would never let it happen.*

His death was meant to be all our bad luck in one go. After that heartbreak life was supposed to be plain sailing for me, Mum and the girls. This *had* to be a mistake.

Despite 'knowing' something was wrong with Mum for months, finding out for certain shook me to my core. Now that the consultant had confirmed my concerns, there was no going back. No amount of wise words from friends, meditation apps or bawling in a hospital loo could change anything. I had to accept the diagnosis.

My dad had cancer then died. Now my mum had cancer, too.

## DOING INSTEAD OF FEELING

Remember that playground chant – 'first comes love, then comes marriage, then comes a girl pushing a baby carriage'? Well, when a loved one is diagnosed with a serious illness, things go a little differently. It's more like 'first comes disbelief, then comes denial, then comes do-do-doing with a manic smile' (in my case, at least).

After Mum's initial diagnosis, you'd have thought I was doing research for a PhD, the way I googled everything and anything to do with strokes. I subscribed to stroke charity mailing lists, emailed a nearby stroke rehab group enquiring about their sessions and bookmarked websites with diet recommendations to aid recovery.

I can still remember Mum's face when I told her my plan to start Mackerel Monday and Fishy Friday dinners, after reading about the benefits of oily fish. I could have sworn she was ready to kick me out, the way she was scowling at me across the kitchen table. I knew what her expression meant.

*'If you dare add Salmon Saturday, that's it, you're gone, Rochelle.'*

Clearly, she did *not* share my love of omega-3 and food-based alliteration.

I soon realised that I'd been doing Mum's head in with my suggestions for how she could get better. I never wanted to annoy her, but I felt so helpless that it was unbearable to sit around and just wait for things to get better.

Usually in life, when there's a problem, there's also a practical solution.

Car breaks down? Call the AA.

Hate your job? Update your CV and find a new one.

Phone won't charge? Buy a replacement.

So, it was only natural to see Mum's symptoms as something else I needed to sort. I was sure there must be something I could do to make her better; it was just a case of tracking it down. And so I was always looking for something, always trying something, always *doing* something.

My determination to find the 'fix' only deepened as time went on. By the point we were told Mum had been misdiagnosed and in fact had cancer, I had gone into activity overdrive. If I'd annoyed her with Mackerel Mondays, I dread to think how irritating I became with my attempts to find a cure for the tumour.

Spurred on by my suffocating feelings of helplessness, I embarked on a one-woman mission to rationalise, understand and out-trick the cancer. I kept telling myself, if I could figure out *why* it had happened, we could get her the help she needed to make her better. The logical part of my brain knew her best bet was rest and radiotherapy, but that didn't stop me from setting out to find another solution. To find something I could *do*.

*Maybe if I cook her some food her headache will go.*

*Maybe if we make popcorn and watch* Dirty Dancing *she will get her energy back.*

*Maybe if I book a holiday, she will be so relaxed her cancer will disappear altogether.*

I was full of a never-ending supply of aura-cleansing affirmations to repeat, vitamin combinations to swallow and self-help meditations to listen to, and honestly, if the tumour hadn't been so quick to take the use of Mum's right side, I'm sure she would have roundhouse-kicked me out of home.

But she didn't. *She couldn't.*

Not only had the tumour affected her physically, it soon started to take away her personality, the sparkle in her eyes, the things that made her Mum. And that was the saddest thing of all.

I may not have been able to see it back then, but I was *doing* in an attempt to avoid *feeling*. Powered by sickly sweet cans of Starbucks double espresso, I kept busy, buzzing around the house, making lists and ticking off jobs, in the hope that my brain wouldn't have time to focus on the one true task that came with the life-changing diagnosis: processing the fact my mum would soon be gone and dealing with the jumble of emotions that brought.

It wasn't until years later when COVID-19 started spreading its way around the globe, forcing country after country into lockdown, that I finally understood what I was doing when Mum was ill.

Remember those frantic first weeks when coronavirus hit? Everyone coped with their new, crazy reality by enthusiastically joining Houseparty, jumping onto Zoom for quarantini brunches with the girls and signing up for more virtual pub quizzes than any one human should ever subject themselves to. We rushed in with the speed of a sprinter, not realising we were running a marathon and after a month of baking banana bread, Marie Kondo-ing our wardrobes and binge-watching *Tiger King*, things got, well … boring.

The sheen of novelty soon wore off, revealing a chipped and stained reality: monotony. We ran out of things to talk about on video calls, we'd already seen every meme we were sent, the usual thrill of an afternoon nap became redundant and we realised we should have been stockpiling conversation topics, not toilet roll. It's much the same when someone you love is diagnosed with a serious condition.

Just as with lockdown, life as a carer means accepting there's nothing you can actively do to fix the situation. Instead, you have to find a way to live with things while they're broken.

## OUT OF CONTROL

As they wheeled Mum into the ambulance on a stretcher, I saw her head poke up to check *again* that I had her bag. I waved it in the air.

'Yessss, Mum, look it's *still* in my hand,' I called over, giving her a sideways grin before adding sarcastically. 'I bet this isn't what you had in mind when you said you wanted to get out of Ipswich Hospital.'

Even though the tumour had been making her right eye droop, I could tell she was raising her eyebrow at me.

'Very funny,' she muttered, as Hannah followed her into the back of the ambulance, ready to make the fifty-mile journey to Addenbrooke's Hospital in Cambridge where doctors from the specialist neuro-oncology unit would take a sample from the tumour so they could work out what kind it was. Olivia and I followed behind in the car and around ninety minutes later, we were there, getting Mum settled.

It took a few days to complete Mum's pre-op checks, but then it was time for her biopsy. The three of us watched them wheel her to theatre, then stayed sitting on the plastic chairs around the empty space where her bed had been. Somehow it was comforting, being surrounded by all her things and half-sipped glass of water.

While it was completely unspoken, I knew that none of us dared move the seats even a millimetre in case rearranging them was a bad omen. It was as if we'd made a silent pact with the universe that if we left everything as it was, then Mum would magically reappear in no time. The ward sister, however, had other ideas.

'I'm afraid you can't sit here while your mum is in theatre,' she explained.

Like three lost puppies, we obediently got up and walked away, aimlessly wandering the hospital corridors before ending up in the canteen. After each ordering a hot chocolate, we sat at a table too close to the door. A bitter January draught swept past as I mindlessly ate the cream off the top of my drink, leaving the rest to go cold. As the hours dragged along, we took it in turns to go and buy food, simply because queuing gave us something to do, but we didn't manage much more than a mouthful of anything we ordered.

In the end, I couldn't wait any longer.

'Right, that's it,' I said emphatically. 'Let's go back up. I reckon Mum will be out soon. I'm ready to risk the wrath of the ward sister to make sure we're waiting as soon as she's back.'

Our bravery was rewarded. Not long after we sneaked back in, we saw her surgical-stockinged feet coming around the corner. The hospital porters barely had time to get her bed into position before we were tripping over one another to give her a kiss and a hug.

The rest of the afternoon slipped by as we sat chatting and laughing with Mum. We were all upbeat. After all, she had just survived someone rooting around in her head. If she could survive that, surely she could survive anything? We fed her dinner and by the time we left that evening, we weren't just feeling better – we were feeling happy!

But we all knew what would happen next was out of our control.

The moment Mum told me she had a brain tumour, normal life ceased to exist and was replaced by a monotonous haze of disbelief, hospitals and tears. Straightaway, I stepped into a new existence filled with medical appointments and daytime TV, increasingly oblivious to the outside world.

Being a carer was relentless. Mum's cancer dominated each day, dictating my diary from dusk till dawn. I was at the mercy of appointment times and waiting lists, with month after month moulded around medication and meetings. My new, unrequested responsibilities overshadowed every other aspect of my life. I missed hair appointments when radiotherapy sessions overran. I cut short shopping trips after a call to say the shower chair we'd been waiting on for weeks would arrive 'in the next hour or two'. And I cancelled visits to see friends because of scan date mix-ups.

Without weekends to count down towards or after-work drinks to look forward to, I was living in limbo. Seconds stretched and months melted until there was little distinction between the days and it became more difficult to orientate myself. I felt perpetually stuck in *that week between Christmas and New Year* feeling – just with worse TV and less exciting food.

I never appreciated how much choice I used to have over each inconsequential element of my old life – until I was forced into my new one as a carer.

I was used to having a say in every granular detail. Take the simple act of buying a coffee, for example, and the near-infinite options available. Full fat or skinny? Double shot or single? Normal milk or oat milk? Stay in or take away? But from the moment of Mum's diagnosis, my control dissolved like the sugar in my flat white. Choice became a luxury when I'd always considered it a basic staple – and adjusting to that was a lot more difficult than I'd imagined.

The power I'd once wielded over my future tapered off with each tick of the clock. An increasing roster of agencies took away the agency I once had over my own life, and dominion over my day was replaced by dependence upon others. As a family, we became reliant on near-strangers to set the parameters of our life, waiting on them for the guidelines within which we would have to live. Will the oncologist say Mum can travel? Is the technician able to fix the broken radiotherapy machine before they send us home? Will the occupational therapist approve the equipment Mum needs?

The march of time and my loss of control were directly proportional. Where I'd once charted my own course, I now bobbed along like flotsam on a wave, drifting with one current until the tide turned, and I was strewn in another direction entirely. It got to the point where even my own bedtime depended on a number of other people's variables:

How Mum was feeling.

If the carers came on time.

If family called asking for an update.

I could no longer choose when to leave the house, because I had to work around appointments, medication schedules, phone calls and whether one of my sisters was around to sit with Mum. Even the choice of what to eat disappeared. With Mum changing her mind quickly, I'd end up eating what was left over or having the same as whatever she was craving.

With no sway over the big things, I found myself obsessing over minutiae. I became fanatical about *immediately* making my bed each morning with crisp corners and plumped pillows, my small way of creating order in the chaos and distinguishing the end of one day from the start of the next. And I'd dutifully divide and arrange the cushions between the sofa and two armchairs, positioning them *just so* whenever I saw them out of place. These small adjustments were the only control I had left, they were how I proved to myself that my actions still had some impact in the world, that my efforts still counted and that what I did *could* be seen.

Yet what was always undoubtedly visible, even on the darkest days, was Mum's cancer and the effect it was having – on her and on all of us.

Nothing was definite in our situation, except for the fact Mum was going to die. Sooner rather than later. While there was a prognosis and doctors could give averages, statistics and likelihoods, nobody could say for certain just how much longer she would be with us. Although the thought of knowing the exact day my mum would die was too horrifying to contemplate, the not knowing also brought its own challenges. Was I running a sprint or a marathon? Should I charge ahead as fast as I could, temporarily ignoring responsibilities, or did I need to pace myself?

What I didn't fully appreciate back then was that you can't prepare for a race when you don't know how far you'll be running – but that's exactly what's required of you when caring for a loved one who is ill. That part you can't change. You have no control over it. What you *can* change are your expectations of yourself, and what you *can* control is how you approach the journey.

You wouldn't set out on a road trip assuming there will be enough fuel to keep going until you're told to stop at random. No, you'd stop for regular refuels so that you could stay the course. And that's what you need to do for yourself as a carer. That is what gives you your control back. To know you're fuelling yourself so that you're capable of making it to the finish line.

# Treatment

## ARE YOU HER CARER?

'Hi, I need to make an appointment to see the district nurse – it's about my mum, Shirley Bugg,' I said to the GP receptionist.

'Are you her carer?' she enquired.

I stared blankly for a moment.

Head tilted and glasses perched perilously close to the end of her nose, she looked up.

'Are you her carer?' she repeated.

'I'm... erm... her daughter,' I replied, making it sound like more of a question than a statement.

'Yesssssss. But are you also her carer?' she said once more, her words slow and deliberate.

I wasn't entirely sure what she meant, but from the way she was asking I could sense that my answer would make a difference to what happened next.

Glued to the spot, I mulled the question over. I certainly cared for my mum in every possible sense of the word. I'm not sure there were many other people on the face of the Earth who cared for her as much as I did. But 'carer' – wasn't that a term for people who worked in care homes? I was just trying to be a good daughter and look after my mum.

'Do you claim Carer's Allowance?' she barked at me, starting to get irritated.

Her harsh tone jolted me from my train of thought. I could tell from the way she stretched out the word *claimmm* and over-enunciated *Allo-Wance* that she was completely exasperated – with me and perhaps her job in general.

Clearly now was not the time for me to ponder the riddle of whether or not I was a carer.

'Ummmm,' I replied, screwing up my face in confusion. 'Nobody has mentioned anything. Am I supposed to? I... like... I help her out at home and stuff. Would that be the same kind of thing?'

I stuttered as I spoke. It felt like a trick question. I wasn't sure what I was signing myself up for if I agreed, but at the same time it felt ridiculous to say that I *wasn't* her carer. It would be like proclaiming to the whole of the waiting room that I wasn't bothered about my mum.

'The nurse has got an appointment on Thursday at 11am,' the receptionist offered, with a defeated sigh.

I'd read about people having an identity crisis. I knew it happened. I just never expected it would happen to me, aged twenty-five, in a GP surgery in Ipswich. I thought the term was reserved for far more profound issues – your gender, your sexuality, your role in the world after becoming a mother. But it turned out that my identity crisis involved far less soul-searching, but just as much confusion.

Making my way out of the surgery, I asked myself the question over and over again on the short walk home.

Am I her carer?

What was I? What was my role? I was a daughter, undoubtedly, but I was also a parent. I definitely cared for Mum, but I had no health or social-care training, like care workers do. Where did I fit in all of this? Pulling out my phone, I went on the NHS website to look for their definition, hoping for some answers.

> A carer is anyone, including children and adults who look after a family member, partner or friend who needs help because of their illness, frailty, disability, a mental health problem or an addiction, and cannot cope without their support. The care they give is unpaid.

Well, I certainly fitted that description – but I didn't see myself as one.

I didn't feel like a carer, but at the same time I felt like so much more than a carer. The label might have fitted, but it didn't sit right. It was too narrow. Too ambiguous. Too pressured. Too expectant. Too detached. Too inadequate.

But it was the only label that there was.

From that day forward I managed to get into the swing of calling myself Mum's carer. I never liked it; in fact I winced each time the words left my mouth. But it seemed to mean something to other people, certainly a lot more than it did to me. 'Oh you're her carer, right …' they'd say, as if I'd just unlocked a secret level in a videogame.

I was unsure what they envisaged when I told them I was Mum's carer. Giving a name to my role seemed to suggest this was a job with clearly defined duties. That's why I felt so out of my depth whenever I said it. I developed a low-level panic that people would expect me to know more, to do more or simply *be* more given my self-claimed title, as if it was my first day in a new job where I'd exaggerated my experience on my CV.

With time, I realised that 'being a carer' was an over-simplified term bestowed by an inadequate system to make sure you fit neatly into NHS spreadsheets and HMRC calculations. In reality, the true nature of what it is to be a carer is too broad, too varied and too complex to be captured with just one word. It means so much more than the meaning it is given and is worth so much more than the value it is ascribed.

As Mum's carer, my 'role' was more varied, involved and dynamic than the CEO of a Silicon Valley start-up. I charmed and joked my way out of any offence Mum caused as the tumour progressed, eating away at her ability to filter her thoughts before speaking. I smoothed over tensions when a fellow radiotherapy regular with a growth on his face said hello to Mum in the waiting room and she turned to me and said very loudly, 'Woohoo, I've scored with apple head.'

I toughed out the embarrassment of a line of five cars honking their horns at me because I'd had to reverse out of the car-parking space to be able to open the door wide enough for Mum to get in. I pretended I didn't care while one of the drivers was swearing at me as I stood in the pouring rain trying to fold down Mum's wheelchair and pack it into the boot as quickly as I could, before sticking my finger up at him, when all I really wanted to do was run and hide. I chased the council department for the disabled parking badge that could have prevented the situation, calling, emailing and getting passed from person to person nine times over the course of two months.

I dashed in darkness to supermarkets to satisfy Mum's very

specific food cravings – apparently she could tell the difference between a Sainsbury's mini trifle and a Tesco mini trifle. And I fed her those mini trifles with a teaspoon, tiny bird-size bites at a time, pleased that at last she was able to eat something after not being able to stomach food for days.

The NHS definition mentions none of these things. It doesn't prepare you for half the stuff you find yourself doing or the multiple 'hats' you end up wearing as you become a chef, cleaner and call-screener, a flower arranger, family updater and appointment coordinator, as well as taking on 101 other roles. It would have been a lot easier for me to answer the receptionist's question that day if there had been a job description I could check myself against. But there wasn't. Instead, I carried on for months, feeling worthless when, in reality, my efforts were invaluable.

Looking back, I can see there was another crucial role I had as a carer – but one that was always overlooked. *Being Rochelle*. I was still me, a whole separate person, the entire time that I looked after my mum – but it rarely felt that way. My identity as a carer overrode everything else. People addressed me not by name, but as 'Mrs Bugg's carer' or 'Mrs Bugg's daughter'. I was a moon waxing and waning, but never appearing fully in the night sky of my own life. People only saw a small sliver of my entirety. Perhaps that is why it took me so long after Mum had gone, to remember who I was, and that I was still complete without her around.

## A YEAR TO LIVE, OR A YEAR TO DIE?

I finished the last of the ironing just in time to get Mum ready for her latest scan. This one would tell us if the radiotherapy had done its job and got rid of the tumour. As I wandered into her room, she was already drifting awake, as if she knew it was nearly time to leave.

I was glad she'd had the extra sleep: she was going to need it because we'd planned a surprise party later that evening to celebrate the – *hopefully* – good news. As we made our way to the hospital to see the consultant, everything was being organised behind the scenes. Friends and family were driving from all over the country to surprise her and I was in equal measures nervous and excited.

Finding a spot in the waiting room, I glanced at the clock, mentally mapping out the next few hours to make sure I'd get Mum to the restaurant we'd booked on time. But fifteen minutes after we were due to be called, we were still sitting there. Thirty minutes went by, then sixty, then ninety. I'd been up and down to the receptionist like a jack-in-the-box, asking about the delay, but each time her response was the same.

'It shouldn't be too much longer,' she'd say with a dismissive smile.

'It's just that we've been waiting an hour and a half now and we've got somewhere we need to be after this so…' I tailed off, but my attempts at conveying my urgency fell on deaf ears.

'Like I said, it shouldn't be too much longer,' she repeated, a little more sternly than before.

I'd never been more aware of time. Until now, it had been nothing more than an informative fact, the method we used to orientate ourselves and order our lives. But since Mum's diagnosis, each tick of a hand on a clock sounded like loss. Another grain of time with her gone for ever, the hope and potential it once carried slipping through life's egg timer at an alarming pace.

People spend so much time moaning there aren't enough hours in the day, but back then Mum didn't have enough days left in her life and nobody seemed to care. The rest of the world seemed immune to the urgency that haunted me, with people continuing to move at their own too-slow pace. As Mum's illness progressed, I became increasingly impatient, infuriated by every delayed radiotherapy session, wrong appointment time, confused scan date and test result hold-up. I wanted to grab the receptionist who was late back from his lunch break, shout at every porter who stopped to check the latest Wimbledon result on the TV screen, and scream at the nurses chatting about the chocolate brownies Diane had brought in that morning.

I wanted to stand up and scream at the top of my lungs: 'MY MUM IS DYING. SHE DOESN'T HAVE LONG LEFT. CAN YOU FOCUS ON HER PLEASE?'

It was maddening. I never expected life with a terminal illness to be like Disneyland, but I thought there might at least have been a fast-track pass to help us make the most of the days we had left.

At 5.10pm – two hours and twenty minutes after the original appointment time and with no explanation for the delay – we were finally called. I hurriedly pushed Mum into the consultant's office, hoping it wouldn't take too long, so that we had time to get ready before the festivities. The consultant was still tapping away on his computer as I put the brakes on Mum's wheelchair.

'Oh,' he said with a frown, just as my bottom hit the plastic seat.

'What is it?' I asked.

'I don't seem to have any recent scan results on my computer for you, Mrs Bugg,' he remarked, addressing Mum.

'What?' I questioned. 'But that's what we're here for today, isn't it?'

'What do you mean?' he said, shaking his head slightly in confusion.

'We're here to have the scan and for you to talk us through it?' I insisted, brow furrowed.

'No, today is to talk about the *last* scan you had,' he countered. 'I presumed you had one last week.'

I rolled my eyes, unable to conceal my exasperation.

'No,' I explained, annoyed. 'At the last appointment we were told to come again today to have a follow-up scan and talk through the results.'

Suddenly the penny dropped.

'Oh! No, that's not how it works,' he said. 'They should have done the scan already. I am sorry. That's a bit of a pain for you, isn't it?'

*Yes. It is,* I thought.

'That's fine,' I lied, smiling through gritted teeth.

'Well, is there anything else you want to talk about now that you've come all this way?' he offered.

'No, I don't think there's much point,' I snapped, angrily.

We were two and a half hours behind schedule for Mum's surprise party and all for nothing. I wanted to slap him, even though it wasn't his fault.

Spending so long in that soulless, stuffy waiting room might have been nothing more than a minor inconvenience to most, but to me it was time I could have spent painting Mum's nails or helping her decide what to wear to her party. It was time I'd set aside for the simple joy of being with my mum while she was still alive. Instead, our wasted waiting time for a pointless appointment meant we were late for the party before we even got home.

I didn't have time to shower Mum; instead all I could do was quickly change her top and drop her off at the restaurant, before heading back home to get ready myself.

That completely avoidable delay meant I missed the first hour of the last party my mum would ever have.

At the very core of my fear around Mum's terminal diagnosis lay one stark realisation.

*All we have is time. All we don't have is time.*

Knowing she was going to die placed an invisible, yet very loud, ticking clock above her head, never letting us forget that we were on an unwelcome countdown to the inevitable. And life quickly took on a constant underlying franticness because knowing that time is running out immediately makes you want more of it.

Each tick of that clock made every photo, every conversation, every everything take on a greater meaning. Knowing time was running out made me think about what I *really* wanted to say and how I *really* felt. Scribbling a quick *love Rochelle x* at the bottom of Mum's birthday card was no longer enough when I realised it might be the last one I ever wrote to her.

Yet as much as this scared me, it also soothed me. Realising that something would never exist again helped me to find its beauty, however ugly the situation appeared at first sight.

Knowing that one day I wouldn't be able to hear Mum's angry mutterings about late-running consultants somehow made her bitter words sound sweeter. Knowing that one day there wouldn't be a wheelchair to lift in and out of the car somehow made me welcome my bruised shins, evidence she was still around to be pushed. Knowing that one day she wouldn't need me to help her to the toilet somehow made it easier to get out of bed in the middle of the night when she called. Even the saddest, most annoying, most frustrating moments seemed special after realising that they would never, ever, in all the years that the Earth continues to exist, happen again.

Understanding that everything ends isn't something to be feared, hidden from or ignored. The fact that we're all going to die doesn't stop what we do from having meaning; it makes it matter *even more*. Death gives us all the more reason to go after life and puts into perspective what truly matters.

The impatience I felt during Mum's illness has never left me – and I doubt it ever will. If anything, it grows as the years go by. But now, rather than the impatience to be served or for my call to be transferred, it's impatience at being told to sit and wait for life's magic to come to me. I won't wait until I've got less time than a *Countdown* contestant before doing the things I dream of.

I've seen what death is like when it visits – and it rarely turns up at a time when you have the freedom, finances and fitness to do the things you always said you would. I've learned that if I want to do something, I need to get out there and find a way to make it happen. Visiting that country, going on that course, learning that language or moving to that city. These are the memories that will help me pass the time with a smile on my face, if one day I find that it's me sat in the hospital waiting room waiting for *my* appointment.

## MOMENTS MAKE MEMORIES

Leaving the shopping at the checkout, I shimmied Mum's wheelchair to reverse out of the aisle and walked all the way to the supermarket entrance, then back down the length of the store to get to the packing area, cursing the entire shop as I went.

When we made it back to our aisle, the cashier sat staring at our shopping, all piled up.

'£78.46 to pay,' she snapped impatiently as she watched me pack. 'Next time make sure you use the disabled aisle so you don't get stuck again. This one's too narrow to fit a wheelchair down.'

*No kidding,* I thought angrily.

I knew Mum could sense the tension, but the counter was too high for her to reach from her chair to help. I felt humiliated, stupid, pathetic, nothing more than an annoyance. Tears threatened to fall but I refused to let the checkout woman see me cry. That was until Mum spoke up.

'You should come without me in future, Ro,' she suggested, as if somehow she was to blame for the whole scenario.

I was glad she couldn't see the tears that had started rolling down my cheek.

'Don't be silly, Mum,' I said. 'Who'd make sure we got the right wine?'

Mum was a pro at hunting down that week's wine deals. No matter how insignificant it seemed, it was a tiny highlight in our week. I didn't want the supermarket to become yet another place where she felt like she was hassle or inconvenience. It made me sad and frustrated when she dismissed herself from yet another activity.

*Oh no, it's fine, you go without me.*

*I'll just watch.*

I didn't want her to feel like that, like she couldn't join in with things we were doing. It wasn't fair, but as her illness progressed it *was* getting harder to plan things that she could do in a wheelchair.

As we drove home, my mind slipped back to childhood

memories with Dad. It wasn't the big things I remembered most, but the random little things. Him grabbing a banana from the bowl of fake fruit my mum thought was the peak of chic in the 90s, and singing along to *Top Of The Pops*. Or the knack he had for making the school run fun, driving along the unexotic A12, doing stupid impressions and making up silly songs.

I wanted to do the same for Mum. To make the mundane things exciting, to make everything an adventure while she was still here. So, by the time we arrived home from the supermarket fiasco, I made a pledge to myself: I was going to make a conscious effort, wherever I could, to make moments into memories – ones we could treasure for ever.

I once saw a quote etched on a gaudy plaque in a seaside giftshop, its words lodging in my brain as soon as I read them.

*We didn't realise we were making memories, we just knew we were having fun.*

That sugar-sweet saying always took me back to Christmas Day 1999, the last we had as a family of five. Ever since what seemed like forever, Mum and Dad had run businesses together. The last one they had was a bowling alley, open twelve hours a day, seven days a week. Boxing Day was one of the busiest days of the year, when overfed, feuding families were desperate to get out of the house and *do something*.

So on Christmas Day, Mum and Dad coaxed the three of us girls away from the Quality Street and into the car, still in our matching festive pyjamas, because they needed to clean up the excesses of the Christmas Eve parties and make sure the bar was fully stocked for the next day's rush. It should have felt like a chore, but they turned it into an adventure.

With the whole bowling alley to ourselves for a few hours,

we sang stupid songs over the Tannoy system and set up bowling games for imaginary customers called Poo Head and Fart Face. We stole chocolate bars from the diner, poured our own drinks behind the bar and ran riot in the soft play area. It was magical, because Mum and Dad knew how to turn a moment into a memory.

During Mum's illness, that became my motto. I eventually absolved myself of the pressure to orchestrate flawlessly stage-managed moments for Instagram because the idea of a picture-perfect life in the midst of a terminal illness is as fake as a Facetune.

In the end, I realised that it was fun, not finesse, that turns a trivial moment into a treasured memory. Us girls still joke about the phenomenal biscuit-dunking skills that Mum perfected during her morning Triple T routine of tablets, tea and toast. And we still laugh about the Pancake Day when Mum was in hospital and insisted I smuggle in some lemon and sugar crêpes so that she didn't miss out.

Having lost Dad, we understood how memories like these would nourish us once we were starved of Mum's life. Which is why my sisters and I booked a last-minute weekend at Center Parcs to celebrate the end of Mum's radiotherapy. It was the perfect place for accessible memory-making. There was none of the dreaded 'It's fine I'll just sit and watch', because Center Parcs was one step ahead of us with facilities for people with reduced mobility. From the electric hoist that lifted Mum in and out of the pool at the spa so she could enjoy a massage under the water jets, to the Duet, a bike-wheelchair hybrid that meant one of us could pedal while Mum sat in the front. It was lovely to all be able to cycle, navigating the bumpy forest tracks together, rather than having one person 'left on Mum duty'.

And it was our dedication to memory-making that meant,

when Mum told us she wished she could go to the US but was too sick to travel, we brought America to her. We decorated the kitchen with posters of the New York skyline, got a cardboard cut-out of the Statue of Liberty and ordered some miniature Star-Spangled Banners. We filled the table with mac & cheese, cornbread, ribs, peach cobbler and anything else American-looking we could find at the supermarket. Then, we all dressed in shorts and T-shirts, spoke in (very bad) American accents and looked through photos, laughing about holidays we'd had in the past.

We understood from bitter experience that looking back on the small stuff was often just as special as the big stuff – and that gave me hope during Mum's illness. It meant I didn't need to wait for a perfect time within this imperfect world before I could find something for us to enjoy. Even as I trudged through the murky bog of being a carer, I could find moments of happiness – something I never would have thought possible during such sadness.

No matter how long you do – or don't – have left, you should always make time for the timeless moments that will never dull, fade or be outgrown.

# HOS-PICE OFF

Getting Mum to try the day-care service at St Elizabeth Hospice had become a regular tug-of-war at her weekly meeting with the neuro-oncologist. Every appointment, between talk of tablets and treatment, he would try – and fail – to persuade her to go along for a change of scenery and to give us three girls a break. She found endless ways to shut the poor guy down. On our last visit, she'd really excelled herself. Broaching the subject, the consultant opted for the 'your daughters need some downtime' argument. But Mum's comeback arrived as quick as a flash.

'Why do you think I've got THREE daughters? If one of them gets tired and needs a rest I've got another one. Then when that one gets tired, I've got the next one,' she barked.

God love the man for trying.

As much as it amused me, the truth was that I was struggling. We all were.

Earlier on in Mum's treatment it had seemed too big, too scary and too premature to get a hospice involved. The three of us needed the extra support but Mum had made her thoughts about the hospice very clear.

She wasn't interested in day care or respite care, where she could stay at the hospice for a few nights. She didn't say, 'I want to stay at home', she said, 'I *am* staying at home.' Her opposition was so vehement that we hardly dared mention the subject.

But as time ticked by, deep down I knew it was something we'd soon have to face.

One week, after a particularly frustrating string of appointment mix-ups, sleepless nights, and arguments with my sisters, I decided enough was enough. We desperately needed a break and Mum was going to have to stay in the hospice, even if only for a day or two.

Determined to be brave and bring it up, I walked towards her. She was sat in her maroon electric Rise and Recline chair, eye patch on and watching TV out of her one good eye while sipping lemon squash through a straw. I felt nauseous with guilt.

'I was thinking about arranging a stay in the hospice for you in a couple of weeks,' I said, hurriedly, treating the words like a plaster.

*Pull it off quickly and it will hurt much less.*

'Are you sending me there because you don't want to look after me any more?' she asked.

'Of course not,' I said. 'It's just...'

'Do you still love me?' she questioned, looking at me aghast with her piercing blue eyes.

Her words were like a dagger to my heart and I struggled to catch my breath. This wasn't the way it was meant to go. I had to change tack.

Suddenly it came to me.

'Mum! Don't be silly. It's not that at all. I just thought we could swap things around a bit – move the lounge upstairs so you can have a bedroom downstairs,' I explained.

'Oh right,' she replied.

'It just might take a day or two to get everything straight,' I continued. 'What do you think?'

'OK then,' she said, reluctantly.

I think it helped me more than Mum to have the justification. It eased my guilty conscience at what seemed like a betrayal, asking her to do the one thing she'd specifically said she did not want to do under any circumstances.

When the day came, I dropped Mum at the hospice and got her settled before returning home. At first, it didn't feel so bad. I almost convinced myself she was just having a nap in the other room, but as the hours ticked past her absence became omnipresent. I found myself absent-mindedly wandering between rooms, upstairs then downstairs, looking to see where she was, then I remembered.

*She's at the hospice.*

It was a flashing neon reminder that one day soon, Mum would leave the house and never come back, ever.

I knew it had been the right thing to do on so many levels, but that didn't make it any easier. We'd reached a point in her illness where the balance had tipped and the tumour now outweighed normal life. It affected her more with each passing day, working through her senses and taking them one by one. Blurring her vision, eating away at her taste and dissolving her ability to smell.

Each day meant mourning the loss of more minuscule independences, like being able to use both hands to cut her own food and feed herself – *gone*. Being able to articulate what was in her head and express it, whether that was asking for a snack or telling us that she loved us – *gone*. Being able to sip some water and automatically remembering to swallow it without being prompted – *gone*.

As draining as that was for Mum, it was hard on me, Hannah and Olivia, too. We needed a break from the relentless treadmill of caring. But that didn't mean the rest was relaxing when we got it. It was unnerving to be at home without Mum there, but at least this time I knew that she'd be home in three days.

What about when *it* happened?

I shuddered. Tonight was a preview for a film I never wanted to watch, let alone live. A trailer for the horror movie *Life After She's Gone*. And I wasn't ready for it.

*I'm not old enough to cope without any parents.*

*I'm not old enough to be in charge.*

*I'm not old enough to survive a heartbreak this heavy.*

Terrifying thought after terrifying thought tormented me as I sat slumped on the couch. Copious amounts of rosé and reality TV were doing nothing to drown them out so, desperate for reassurance, I texted my friend:

> Being home without her is reminding me that she's gonna be gone for good soon. I know we've had time

to say goodbye, but I still don't think I'm ready.

She replied: I'm not surprised my lovely. You're in your mid-20s. That's too young for anyone to be dealing with all of this.

While I knew that was true, I was confident I'd be thinking the same thing if I was in my mid-thirties, mid-forties, mid-fifties or mid-whatevers.

*You're never 'old enough' to lose your mum.*

As far as I was concerned, you never reached an age where you didn't need your loved ones. You didn't outgrow unconditional love. You were never going to be ready to say goodbye to someone who held a place in your heart, however old you were.

The next day, I got up early and headed to the hospice to check how Mum was doing after her first night there. The whole idea of respite care was for us girls to have some time out from being on call 24/7. But Mum was not a willing patient.

She'd agreed to stay at the hospice but made us promise that one of us would be there with her most of the time, so me, Hannah and Olivia had arranged to do shifts. This morning was my turn. It had only been a day since I'd first dropped her off, but I still couldn't wait to see her.

As soon as I opened the double doors that led from the main entrance to the wards, my ears were assaulted by the sound of *Homes Under the Hammer* at full blast coming from a TV somewhere in the building. Making my way down the long, cornflower-blue corridor, I read the names of the patients written on the small whiteboards outside each room.

*Deborah Huggins, Fazarna Jannat, Giorgio Ricci, Gary Long.*

My heart sank further with each one. Imagine being at death's door and having to listen to a rundown two-bed terrace house in Rochdale being auctioned off.

*Mum must be going mad,* I thought, anxiously, but as I turned into her ward, I rolled my eyes.

*I should have guessed!*

Where there was a property programme, Mum was never far away. It was *her* who was responsible for everyone in a two-mile radius needing ear protectors to block out the offending drivel. As I walked towards her bed, she gave me the biggest smile I'd seen from her in months.

'All right there, Mother? Or have you deafened yourself?' I asked, picking up the remote and turning the TV volume down without waiting for an answer. 'How was your first night?'

Her smile disappeared.

'Oh Ro, it's so boring. Nobody speaks. I tried to talk to her over there,' she said, making a jabbing motion with her index finger at the woman in the bed diagonal to her. 'But she just went to sleep on me.'

'Well everyone here *is* ill, Mum,' I reminded her. 'They're probably not up for a party...'

But before I could finish my sentence, Mum suddenly crumpled. Like a tower block detonated by dynamite, she went from sitting upright and talking to suddenly slumping to one side, head turned to the wall, motionless and silent. A knot tightened in my stomach.

'Mum! Mum! What's wrong?' I said, rushing towards her.

Scanning her body, I searched for signs of the life that had been there just a few seconds earlier, but I couldn't even detect the rise and fall of her chest.

*Was she even breathing?*

'Mum! Mum! Talk to me!' I repeated, starting to shake her gently.

*Try not to panic, Rochelle,* I thought, my body tensing.

But as my eyes darted round trying to find the emergency cord, I heard something.

'Is he coming for me?' Mum whispered.

I turned my head back to look at her. She was speaking from the side of her mouth, eyes still firmly clamped shut.

*What the...?*

Had she finally cracked up? Had the tumour taken over and sent her crazy?

'Is who coming, Mum?' I asked, shaking as I put my hand on hers, praying she wasn't going to say God, or The Grim Reaper.

'That bloody doctor,' she hissed.

A tiny sigh of relief escaped my lips. She hadn't lost it after all.

'He came to speak to me last night,' Mum continued. 'He wants me to stay in for a week. A bloody week! But I told him. I said, "I'm only in here for a couple of days while you get my bedroom sorted at home. I'm not having that." So now if I see him, I just pretend to be asleep.'

'Motherrrrrr!' I shrieked. 'You nearly gave me a heart attack.'

'Well, if I'm asleep he can't talk to me and tell me to stay any longer,' she said, shrugging.

I didn't know whether to be horrified by her scheming or impressed by her cunning plan to get home as soon as possible.

'Mummm, stop being so dramatic!' I said, rolling my eyes. 'You're only here for a few days while we sort stuff at home. Think of it like a holiday. You haven't got to listen to us three girls arguing all the time, and you can have a break from my bad cooking,' I quipped, hoping she would tell me that she understood my reasoning, if only to ease my guilt.

'Hmph,' she snorted, before taking the TV remote and turning the volume back up.

It was clear that Mum wanted to come home quickly, but it was just as clear that it had nothing to do with the hospice and everything to do with her being her. As much as respite care was in my best interests, Mum was adamant that it wasn't in hers. The truth is, there's no one size fits all approach when it comes to dying.

Before Mum got ill, the word 'hospice' came with all kinds of scary connotations for me. The mere mention of the H word had me imagining wards full of dying people crying out in pain and waiting rooms filled with mourning relatives wiping away their tears.

I used to think hospices were places where people were dumped until death came to collect them, horrific hotels for the hopeless and the heartbroken. That's partly why I took so long to involve them in Mum's care. I saw them as the enemy and thought that walking through their doors meant I was giving up hope and surrendering to death. But the reality was nothing like my morbid mind made out.

It turned out that the hospice wasn't just 'not bad', it was absolutely brilliant. Rather than the depressing place I expected it to be, throughout Mum's illness the hospice lifted me up when I fell to my knees, saving so many days in so many ways. Like their 24-hour helpline, which I used for questions big and small. They always had Mum's notes to hand and they knew our situation, so I didn't have to talk someone through it from the beginning like I did if I called 111 or 999.

While so many others focused on Mum's physical illness, the hospice took a broader view. They asked what *we* wanted, rather than coming in, taking over and telling us the best way to do things. More importantly, they could see what other agencies, processes and pathways often overlooked – that a key component of making sure Mum got the best care was making sure I could care for her as best as I could.

They supported me so that I could support her.

As well as helping me manage the symptoms of Mum's cancer, they helped me manage the symptoms of being a carer. I began to think of them in the way I did the endless cups of coffee I downed as my dissertation deadline was fast approaching. I wished I didn't have to rely on them, but I knew I needed the short-term fix to help me stay focused for long enough to get the job done.

The hospice wasn't just a building with blankets, cushions, a meditation garden and smiling nurses. It wasn't just a place where death was less painful and frightening as it otherwise would be. It was a rich and complex community of support and comfort that extended far beyond its brick walls. Its role was not to make *death* 'not so bad', but to make *life* 'not so bad'. The hospice allowed us as a family to live as well as we could, even while death loomed like a storm on the horizon.

I've often heard people say, 'What a terrible way to die', referring to a freak accident or long, torturous illness. But perhaps more heartbreaking than a tragic end is for someone to remark *what a terrible way to live*. The hospice stopped either of those things happening with Mum. It took me so long to let them into our lives, but after I did, I wondered how we'd ever managed without them.

# IT WILL PASS

I rushed up the stairs, darted into the office and shut the door, swiping to answer my phone before it went to voicemail. It was Mum's consultant oncologist calling with the results from her latest scan.

'Morning. Is that Mrs Bugg's daughter?' he asked.

'Yes, speaking,' I replied.

His tone was flat and serious. I knew that meant bad news.

Not that I was surprised. I didn't need a scan to tell me Mum wasn't doing well. I could see it for myself every time I looked at her.

'I'm afraid it's not what we were hoping for,' he said, solemnly.

In an instant, my world became hazy and muffled. Only the odd word from the consultant's spiel managed to break through the thick fog that had descended around me. By the end of the call, as I put down the phone and looked at the notebook in front of me, I realised that despite speaking for fifteen minutes, I'd only scrawled down five words.

*Worse.*

*Some changes.*

*Try chemo?*

The consultant hadn't been explicit, choosing his words carefully as I'd come to expect. But after the latest scan, there was an implicit understanding between us. We could dance around things as much as we liked, but I knew what he was saying.

We were coming to the end of the line.

*So why was he suggesting we try chemo now?*

It all felt so hopeless. I wondered if we should just accept the situation in all its horrific, nightmarish glory and let the brain tumour chart its own wild course without any attempts to stop it, slow it or shrink it. But to not even consider chemotherapy felt like telling Mum I wasn't bothered about her being around, as if I'd given up on her.

That was the last thing in the world I wanted.

It had to be worth a try, at least.

Two days after the consultant's call, we were back at the hospital and ready to discuss the possibility of chemo. It was an option that Dr Michaels had previously called 'the very last resort' because the side effects were so bad, they would likely outweigh any advantages the treatment could offer.

We listened as he made it abundantly clear that there was no chance the chemo would cure the tumour; it would just stop it from growing for a while and buy Mum more time. As Dr Michaels talked us through treatment timelines, I began storing up questions in my head, ready to ask at the end.

The first cycle would last five days, followed by a five-week rest period to allow Mum's immune system to recover, then a second round for five more days, with a scan another five weeks after that to see if it had worked. After explaining the treatment, he moved on to the side effects.

Extreme fatigue.

Severe nausea and vomiting.

Increased risk of infection from lowered white blood cell count.

As he continued, an unexpected thought floated into my head.

*Don't do it, Mum. Don't put yourself through this.*

There was nothing I wanted more than time with Mum, but I also wanted her to be able to enjoy it. She deserved to have some quality of life, not to spend our last few months together dragging herself through the hell the consultant was describing.

But as quickly as the thought popped into my mind, I shooed it away, horrified.

*What is wrong with me?*

Why would I question something that was going to give Mum more time with us? Was I a horrible person to even think it?

Suddenly I became aware of the silence in his office. The consultant had stopped talking and I forced myself out of my ruminations and back into the room. He clasped his hands on his knees and looked at Mum.

'I know it's a lot to take in, Mrs Bugg,' he started. 'But from what I've said today, do you think you would like to go ahead and try the chemotherapy?'

*Hang on a minute!* I thought.

There was so much information to process. I had my doubts and about 143 questions whirring around my head, so I could only imagine how Mum—

'Yes, of course I want it!' she piped up before I could even finish my train of thought.

'Wait, Mum—' I started.

'I'm gonna try everything you've got,' she added, swatting me away. 'When do I start?'

In the blink of an eye, it was decided. Mum was going to start her first cycle of chemotherapy the following Monday.

Over the next few days, I tried to push my doubts about the chemo to the back of my mind. But what had happened in that appointment felt so heavy, so significant. I couldn't put my finger on which part exactly, but there was a distinct sense of unease bubbling deep in my belly.

*What is wrong with me?* I cursed myself, appalled by my own thoughts.

Why was I not happy? I should have been elated that the wonder of modern medicine had given us another treatment to try, another chance to grab some more time. Instead I felt downcast and deflated. But most of all, I felt guilty.

I couldn't possibly tell anyone what I was really thinking about the chemo, how I wasn't sure it was worth it. They'd think I was crazy, or evil. Or both. But I worried that Mum felt obliged to put herself through chemotherapy for the sake of us girls.

*Is she just doing this for us?*

The knot of unease in my stomach tightened instantly as I realised my reluctance around the chemo was inextricably connected to Dad. After watching him fade away in his final weeks I knew that after a certain point, life with cancer isn't living.

The last time I ever saw him, he didn't even recognise me.

I've forgotten so many things over the years – my PIN number, friends' birthdays, the speech I learned by heart for my French GCSE – yet my brain has never been able to erase the memory of walking into Dad's hospital room that final time.

'Look who's come to visit you,' said Mum, already there with him.

The pain it caused Dad to move his head even a fraction was clearly visible, so I moved closer, lining myself up with where his eyes were already focused.

'Who is it?' he murmured.

The words cut like a knife and, all at once, I felt abandoned, betrayed, scared and alone.

That was my dad, the man who had promised he would always be there for me.

Now he didn't even know who I was.

Cancer had left him with no option but to break his promise to me. He wasn't always going to be there. And as much as that hurt me, I knew it would have devastated him even more to know he wasn't able to recognise his own daughter.

Now, eleven years on, as I walked into the kitchen and saw Mum watching TV, I wondered. *Was it selfish of me not to want the same to thing happen to her?*

I thought about how adamant she was to go ahead with the chemo. How the hell could I argue with her when she was quite literally fighting for her life?

Who was I to think I knew what was best for her? It was my job to support her choices, not make decisions for her. I may have been her carer, but this was still her life.

In the weeks that followed Mum's decision, I watched helplessly as the chemotherapy's poisons seeped into her bloodstream. They were meant to destroy the tumour, but it felt like they were wiping *her* out faster than they were the cancer.

A few days into her second cycle, she developed a severe infection and I found myself sitting by her bedside in the ICU with a plastic apron over my clothes, hands sweating inside disposable gloves. Things were so serious that we prepared to say our goodbyes. Thankfully, she made it through, but I knew from that moment she'd never recover.

Like a piece of elastic that has been over-stretched time and time again, she could no longer spring back into shape.

I kept thinking how quickly Dad deteriorated once he'd started on that downward trajectory. The day he married Mum he was really ill, but he was still laughing, still making jokes. He was still *being Dad,* but in his final three weeks, even that slipped away. As Mum struggled through the chemo, my brain was constantly trying to match up where she was at in her journey with where Dad was back then.

A fortnight or so after Mum was discharged from ICU, the consultant told us the chemotherapy hadn't had the effect we'd hoped. That it hadn't stopped the tumour's growth and was unable to stop the cancer spreading to other parts of Mum's brain. That wasn't a surprise, but some of the feelings that came with it were.

Watching Mum slowly die triggered my brain to unbox all my long-forgotten memories from Dad's death. Fourteen-year-old me must have found it so painful to watch her father suddenly slip away that she filed those last few weeks deep in the dark recesses of her mind. Until the final frames of Mum's life, I presumed that I had accidentally recorded over the memories of watching him fragile and in pain, replacing them with more 'useful' things for a teenager in the early 2000s – like Destiny's Child lyrics and my new mobile telephone number.

But my blissful ignorance was not to last. Throughout Mum's chemo, every single memory came back to me in HD, 3D and with surround sound. My brain had two tabs open, playing both videos at full blast, at the same time. What was happening with Mum and what had happened with Dad were blended together like a club DJ mixing two tracks I hated.

It was too much.

*Too much for my ears. Too much for my eyes. Too much for my heart.*

The only way I could keep going was to stop about 100 times a day and remind myself of one universal truth: However long it may take, everything passes eventually.

Even now, when I'm in my darkest moments, I remember that *it will pass* and wait for the light. When I feel there's no point in carrying on, I remember that *it will pass*, and continue forward. When I feel I can never possibly be happy again, I remember that *it will pass* and trust I will smile and laugh one day soon.

Even the most unimaginable, heartbreaking pain passes.

You may never heal completely, you may never be whole

again, but you will make it through. Time will continue to tick by and you will cope. You will trudge through, however tough the terrain and make it to a place where you still have painful memories, but you no longer have a painful reality.

Nothing is permanent.

This bittersweet law of life means you'll always end up losing what you love, but it also means you can be sure that each and every scar from your all-consuming hurt will eventually fade. Things may never be the same again, but they will be OK again. Someday, someway, somehow, things will be OK again.

# 3.

## Feelings

### FEEL IT TO HEAL IT

It was the day of Mum's first counselling session. As I wheeled her into the hospital's Cancer Information Centre, I congratulated myself on finally getting her to agree to talk to someone about what she was going through.

The place was an oasis of calm – all plump cushions, neutral furnishings, and diffusers wafting the scent of a sea breeze – a world away from the plastic chairs and smell of disinfectant that filled the main hospital corridors and wards. As the therapist collected Mum, I dared to relax, sitting back in the comfy waiting-room chair and picking up a trashy magazine.

But I'd barely finished the article about some D-list celebrity's botched Botox when Mum's counsellor poked her head around her door and started scanning the waiting room. As soon as her eyes landed on me, she scurried over.

'Umm, I think you may have brought your mum here under false pretences,' she said in a hushed yet firm tone, standing right in front of my chair.

'Sorry… um… w-what do you mean?' I stuttered, head slightly tilted in confusion.

'I think it's probably best if you come with me,' she said, beckoning to follow her.

As I walked in, my eyes popped out of my head in a way I thought only happened to cartoon characters. Mum was in her wheelchair, using her one good foot to scoot herself towards the door, picking up quite a pace. I rushed towards her, grabbed the handles of the wheelchair and flicked on the brakes before she managed to squeeze past me and escape.

'Mum, what are you doing?' I shrieked.

She gave me a look I hadn't seen since I was seven years old, the time she told her friend we couldn't stay for dinner because I had a swimming class but I blurted out that she was lying, blowing her cover.

*I was in trouble.*

'This woman asked what I want to talk about,' she replied, equal parts flustered and frustrated. 'I haven't got anything to talk about. I've got cancer. The end. How's she gonna fix that with talking?' she added, pointing to the counsellor accusingly.

'Well… I thought…' I started, desperately racking my brain for an answer. But I had nothing. I turned to the therapist.

'I'm so, sooooo sorry.' I apologised whilst doubled over, wrangling to get Mum's shoes back onto the footplates of the wheelchair so I could get us both out of there as quickly as possible. 'At least she's freed up some space on the waiting list for everyone else,' I offered with a tense smile, desperately attempting to mask my embarrassment with humour.

During the drive home Mum was completely silent, leaving my mind to wander. At first, I was annoyed with her for not even giving it a try, but then I imagined how she must be feeling.

A whirlpool of terror, guilt and panic swirling inside her belly every moment of every day of every week. Painful physical flare-ups as her body fought against her. And the way the cancer was corroding her treasured independence. But worse than that, there was the knowing. The understanding of what she was doing to me, Hannah and Olivia. Soon, she would have no choice but to drift away and leave her babies to mend their broken hearts alone. The hearts she knew *she* was going to break when the time came for her to go. This beautiful, strong, capable woman was facing her impending death and she was helpless to stop it.

I cursed myself.

*No wonder she didn't want to talk about it.*

I'd booked the counselling because I thought she might want a safe haven, an hour each week when she could be honest about her pain without fear of upsetting the person she was talking to. But instead what I'd done was pull loose one of the last remaining frayed strands of independence and agency she had left and discarded it, carelessly, on the floor. I'd forced her to look directly at the harsh reality of her situation when she'd been quite happy to turn the other way.

I just wanted to do everything right. I couldn't face the thought of looking back and feeling guilty for not having given her everything she needed to be at peace when she said goodbye. I thought getting professional would help her without it being *me* helping her, because I worried that she was holding her tongue in an attempt to protect me. It had never crossed my mind that she might be doing it to protect herself.

*Who the hell was I to tell a dying woman that she was doing dying wrong?*

As the realisation struck me, so too did the pressure it brought with it. If she didn't want to speak to a professional, did it fall to me to fulfil that role as well as all the others I was juggling? Was I supposed to be a psychologist now as well as a physio and a pharmacist?

The suffocating combination of guilt and duty that had been stalking me all day, followed me into the night. I couldn't even find relief in sleep. At 2am, after hours of tossing and turning, I kicked off the duvet, feeling so claustrophobic that I was unable to bear even the weight of its feathers on me. However deeply I tried to breathe, I couldn't get enough air into my lungs.

The fragile balance of my life had irreversibly tipped. The relentless regime of Mum's radiotherapy had worn me out and I doubted I had the strength to keep going. I always expected treatment to be a tough slog for Mum, but I didn't bank on it being hard for me too. During the last few weeks of her daily radiotherapy, everything was intensified. The schedule of her treatment sessions reigned relentlessly over our days – a constant metaphorical reminder of the way Mum's cancer now controlled family life. Each and every element of our world organised around it.

For whatever reason, Mum turning down counselling was the final ingredient in the toxic soup of shame, embarrassment, irritation and confusion that had been bubbling inside of me for weeks.

I was trying to do what I thought was best for Mum.

Trying to do what I thought was best for the girls.

Trying to do what I thought was best for myself.

But all three couldn't calmly coexist. Like oil pooling atop water. Each one was so separate, so opposing, that they were impossible to mix.

I felt my chest tighten and my breath shorten.

*Can you choke on your own feelings?* I panicked, clutching at my throat, which felt as if it was closing. *I can't do this any more.*

I'd had enough. Enough of being brave, resilient and responsible. Enough of holding back the tears, the anger and the hate I had for what the universe/God/whoever was doing to my family.

Coaxed from my bed by desperation and adrenaline, I silently drifted downstairs. Still in pyjamas, I chucked on a coat hanging by the front door and slid on a stray pair of Converse I'd kicked off earlier that day. With tears welling in my eyes, threatening to fall at any moment, I snuck out as quietly as I could.

Aimlessly strolling the residential roads, I stifled my sobs in case someone saw me, thought I was a lunatic and reported me to the police. I mean, here I was wandering around in the middle of the night and I didn't even know what I was crying about. I took a long, deep inhale, drinking up the chilled night air, then watched my breath fog up in front of me as I let it out.

*At least out here I can breathe,* I thought.

Slowly lumbering, Zombie-like, I eventually made it to a nearby park. I couldn't remember exactly how I got there, but I'd cried the whole way. I was almost hyperventilating, my snot bubbles, lip trembles and puffy eyes giving that infamous Kim Kardashian 'ugly cry' meme a run for its money.

Through my tears, I could just about make out the blurry outline of one of those bizarre-shaped wobbly things that seemed to be in every new playground that popped up. Feeling unsteady on my feet, I perched on it. Thinking about the last few weeks, I twisted myself into a pretzel of emotion crowned with salty tears. I couldn't tell if it was my body shaking uncontrollably, or whether the thing was still jiggling from me plonking my bum on it, but as I sat there, a thought drifted into my head.

Perhaps the reason I'd been so annoyed with Mum's reaction to counselling earlier wasn't because I was mad she wouldn't try it. Maybe it wasn't about her at all. Maybe it was about *me*.

Tears streaming down my face, I realised I was no different to Mum. I'd been trying to escape dealing with my emotions just as she had done when she scooted herself out of that therapist's office. It seemed that Mum's 'coping mechanism' – totally ignoring everything that was going on and pretending she was fine – had rubbed off on me.

I'd been talking the talk – letting everyone know I understood the importance of speaking about my feelings. But what about *feeling* my feelings? Could I honestly say I was doing that? Or had I just been paying lip service to my emotions, never quite getting around to swallowing the bitter pill of truly facing up to them?

I knew the answer instantly.

*You can't do this any more, Rochelle,* I told myself. *You can't keep ignoring your emotions.*

For the first time since Mum's diagnosis, I was honest about the gritty truth of my feelings and stopped brainwashing myself with the sanitised version of events I was peddling to everyone else, day in, day out. As the acknowledgement settled in, slowly seeping beneath my skin, I felt a strange sensation wash over me.

*Comfort.*

To my surprise, allowing myself to feel my feelings didn't make me more desperate, angry or hopeless. Instead, it soothed me.

All at once I was snapped out of the spell which had been cast over me. My tears swiftly subsided to a few stray whimpers. I lifted my head, stood up from my wibbly-wobbly seat and wiped my eyes with my sleeve. Turning towards home I lovingly pulled my coat around me, as if wrapping a newborn in a blanket, and made myself a promise.

I wasn't going to hide from myself *or* my feelings any more.

As I yanked my coat sleeves down over my cold hands and started walking home, I vowed that, from that moment on, I would *feel* my feelings, because it was the only way to be free from their control. Until that point, I'd been making the mistake of running from them, stupidly believing that freedom came from making sure they never caught up with me.

But I was wrong.

All the time I was trying to escape them, they still had control over me because they were dictating my path. That night, my body let me know in no uncertain terms that it was time to rid my system of the emotional build-up I'd been denying even existed.

There's no 'new starter induction' when you become a carer. No manual explaining how the ground beneath you will become an emotional minefield. No guide to navigating the explosive feelings you will come to experience and no welcome talk with tips on how to handle it all.

So as Mum struggled, I thought I was supposed to be upbeat and supportive. The one who kept her going when it was all too much. After all, it wasn't me who was ill. I was just her carer.

Yes, I would nonchalantly tell friends that it was hard, confessing to having a down day every now and then. But I never dared admit to myself, let alone anyone else, that I sometimes resented Mum. Instead I pretended not to begrudge the way I was forced to contort my life to fit hers.

Time and time again I would daydream about escaping, but still never let myself feel just *how much* I wanted to give up and walk away. Instead, I shut the thoughts down immediately, knowing it was impossible to do so without hurting someone, or leaving somebody else to pick up all of the pieces.

I spent hours journaling about how I wished I could pause the world and not be part of it for a while. But rather than explore those feelings, I dismissed them, labelling them as the over-dramatic ramblings of a drama queen.

I never allowed myself to admit just how much I was haunted by the hopelessness of not having even a remote chance of a happily ever after.

I doubt I'm alone. I think it's something a lot of carers go through.

I was actively avoiding my emotions because I was worried they would be too much, too strong, too overwhelming. I was convinced that, once unleashed, they would surge through me, a wild torrent, flooding my system until I drowned in my own sadness.

*What good would I be to Mum and the girls then?*

But, to my amazement, that never happened.

In fact, I found the opposite to be true and soon learned: You've got to feel it to heal it.

Now when those big feelings bubble to the surface, I let them flood through me, giving myself permission to cry and scream. Because I know they always stop. Without fail. At some point, the switch flips back, I wipe my tears and carry on with life.

Not because I have to but because I'm *ready* to.

I've come to think of my mini meltdowns as temporary timeouts which are part of a bigger dance routine to which it's impossible to mess up the steps. Like Beyoncé's backing dancers in a Super Bowl production, you need to trust that you'll know when it's your turn to start moving again. Take a moment, catch your breath, and when it's time to blend back into the perfectly choreographed routine of life – you'll know.

## ENERGY IN MOTION

When it comes to 'feeling your feelings', identifying them is only the first step. The next is working out what to do with them.

About four months after Mum died, I took a spur-of-the-moment trip to Italy. Getting home from the airport, I opened the front door and was greeted by a smell so pungent I was certain I was going to puke.

Following my nose into the kitchen, it was clear there had been some kind of stand-off between Hannah and Olivia over who should empty the kitchen bin while I was away. The lid was open and there was the most elaborate jumble of rubbish on top, stacked with such precision that it could have passed as a modern art installation. One box even appeared to be moving.

I inched closer to investigate, holding my breath, then retched. It wasn't the box that was moving. It was hundreds of tiny white bodies wriggling and writhing among the mish-mash of rotting food.

It was crawling with maggots.

A bucketful of bleach, several cans of air freshener and one vile clean-up job later, I managed to get the full story out of the girls. It wasn't so much a stand-off, more that they were both busy making the most of the bank holiday, taking trips to London, going out with friends and enjoying the sunshine. Neither of them wanted the hassle of taking out the rubbish and putting in a new bin liner, so they just left things piling up – a gross game of junk Jenga over four days.

'It was all balancing on top, so we thought it would be OK...'

Not in twenty-six-degree August heat it wasn't. The mess they left for me to clean up was far worse than if they'd just taken the rubbish out when they first noticed the bin starting to get full. But as annoyed as I was with them both, their attitude was not entirely unfamiliar.

I'm not saying I've ever followed their lead when it comes to household chores – I'm too much of a germaphobe for that – but my approach to dealing with my emotional rubbish was an entirely different matter. After Mum died, it was tempting to keep brushing difficult feelings under the carpet. It seemed like the most sensible approach.

*Make it look like there's nothing wrong for long enough and hopefully I'll start to feel that way.*

So that's what I did. Every day I swallowed down my emotions, force-feeding myself pain, sadness and anger like a foie-gras goose. But the more I stuffed things down, gorging on grief, the more my feelings threatened to explode. I feared that showing even the slightest hint of a 'weak spot' would unleash an army of emotions so strong and powerful that I couldn't go on.

You see, what I didn't factor in to my pessimistic prediction was what emotions actually are. And that's because I didn't know. It wasn't until years later, at a meditation workshop, that I finally got it.

Emotions are energy in motion.

The word itself is spelled E-motion. Think of that 'E' as energy, just as in Einstein's famous theory. Emotions aren't static, they're made of energy which needs to be constantly flowing. That's why you can't swallow feelings away, push them down, or bury them deep. You have to let them move through you.

Trying to stop yourself from feeling is like blocking the natural flow of a river – sooner or later the pressure of the rising water will force any barriers to burst. What you resist persists. The more you keep pushing away your sadness, anger or fear, the more that energy builds and the stronger your feelings will come back fighting.

Thinking about emotions as 'energy in motion' shone a whole new light on losing Dad. About six months after he died, I began telling myself I should be over it. I cried and got upset every now and then, but I tried my best to carry on with life as 'normal'. I thought I was coping just fine and so did everyone else around me. But about two years later, I realised I was falling into a deep depression and I wasn't sure I knew how to climb out of it.

With hindsight, I see it was inevitable. According to the Oxford Dictionary, the word 'depressed' means 'in a lower position, having been pushed down', and that's exactly what I'd been doing to the feelings inside me. Pushing them down and down, like the rubbish in that bin, piling things on top and letting it all fester.

It wasn't until I finally allowed myself to look at *everything* I was feeling that I took my first steps towards finding my way out of that dark maze called depression. Nobody had told me just how far-reaching grief runs – let alone advised me how to work through it. I thought mourning only brought sadness with it, but it often comes with anger, frustration, insecurity, a sense of abandonment and a whole host of other complex emotions.

In time, I learned to stop telling myself that I couldn't be angry with Dad for leaving me – *because I was*. To stop telling myself I couldn't be annoyed with Mum for not trying counselling – *because I was*. To stop telling myself I couldn't be jealous of other people and their perfect families that they took for granted – *because I was*.

Burying, ignoring, or simply not dealing with your feelings is no different to the way Hannah and Olivia left that bin. Technically, all the rubbish was where it should be, so surely it was fine to leave it? No harm done. But that's not how it works – not with rubbish and not with your emotions.

Six months or a year after losing someone, you may think you should be 'over it', so ignore the fact you're not. But no matter how much you blank out your feelings, they'll keep building up inside, festering until the energy they contain manifests into something you can't ignore. Just as with the bin, the longer you leave things, the worse the mess when you finally get around to taking out your (mental) trash.

Logic and timelines are futile when it comes to the illogical and timeless process of grief. I had to learn to face my emotions head-on, however painful that was, and however often they showed up.

Now, instead of telling myself that I should be over it, that I should be grateful for all the good times we shared, or that I should be happy because Mum and Dad are back together again, I allow myself to feel angry that someone else I love has been taken. I allow myself to feel sad that I'll never see her again and give myself permission to scream, hit pillows, write angry letters I'll never send, and sob for hours. When all I want to do is stay in bed for an entire weekend not doing anything but crying and sleeping – that's exactly what I do.

I no longer panic that my emotions are too much to handle because I've learned that when you let emotions do their thing, they flow and then they go.

## GRIEF: ROUND ONE

You lose someone (or something). Then you grieve the loss.

Cause and effect.

Simple.

Or at least that's what I used to think before Mum was diagnosed with cancer. Because when you're *in it* – when you're living it – grief is far more complex and nuanced than we tend to acknowledge, especially when your loved one has a terminal illness.

In my experience, grief is not linear. It doesn't always wait for the loss to occur before making itself known. No, often, it starts far earlier than that, turning up to greet you long before it's time to say goodbye.

One day, about seven months after moving home to become a carer, I was heading upstairs to give Mum her trusted Triple T of tablets, tea and toast. The carpet fibres gently bristled against the door as I slowly pushed it open, not wanting to wake her in case she was still asleep. As I peered into her bedroom, I could see that she was already up, but immediately I sensed that something wasn't right.

As the worry set in, our usual morning pleasantries went out the window.

'Are you OK, Mum?' I asked, more intently than usual.

'It's my head, Ro, I don't know what's happening,' she said, voice wobbling with terror. 'It's never been this bad. This headache.'

'OK…' I began, but Mum continued.

'It's too much. And my eyes. I can't see anything. Just a few blurs. That's it. I can't see anything, Ro,' she said, the fear from her words lingering in the air.

Her panic and urgency was palpable.

'It's OK, Mum, I'm here,' I said. 'We'll sort it. We'll get them to fix it.'

As I heard the words come out of my mouth, I knew I didn't have the faintest idea how to fix it. My chest tightened as I tried to force my brain into formulating a practical plan, but I couldn't focus. Sombre thoughts spiralled through my mind, knocking down any hope of a logical response.

*How lonely it must feel to be trapped inside a body that's slowly giving up on you.*

*How it must feel to just wake up one morning and suddenly be blind.*

*How unfair that she had to go through this on top of everything else.*

My poor mum. I wanted to hug her so tight that I could take the pain from her, to hold her so close that every last bad cell could drift from her body into mine. I tried to swallow down the ball of heartbreak lodged in my throat, but I couldn't. My breath became shallower as I put down the tray and climbed into bed next to her.

'We can't have you feeling like this, can we, my mummy?' I said, stroking her arm the way she used to when I was off school ill, praying that my quavering voice didn't betray my air of reassurance.

Outwardly, I was trying to show her that I was in control. That it was all going to be sorted.

Inside I was repeating a frantic mantra: *Please let her be OK. Please let her be OK. Whoever is up there listening, please let my mum be OK.*

I called the GP surgery, explained what had happened and they promised to send someone as quickly as they could. To Mum, I may have appeared collected, but beneath my calm exterior, my chest felt as if it was cracking open, revealing a vast empty space with nothing left to protect my heart. Breastbone shattered by the sheer force of just one emotion. Grief.

*My grief.*

I fought to stop my body from shaking, to swallow down the tears and push away the pain, because this moment wasn't allowed to be about me and my feelings. Mum didn't get to walk away when things were scary, so neither did I.

It was a couple of hours before the doorbell chimed and the duty doctor arrived.

'As the tumour advances it starts to cause more swelling in the brain,' he explained after examining her. 'Let's try upping her steroid dosage.'

By the end of the day Mum's vision started to return and I said a silent prayer of gratitude to whoever it was looking over us. The panic was over, but the upset lingered.

I was angry – at myself.

In the midst of everything, I'd been almost overwhelmed by grief – but why?

*'Your mum's still alive so what are you actually upset about?'* a bullying voice in my head jibed. *'Make the most of the fact you can still talk to her, hug her and hear her say she loves you.'*

Conflict and confusion stirred inside me.

Was the voice right? Was I being self-obsessed? Was it melodramatic to mourn Mum's impending death before she had actually died?

*'You'll have the rest of your life for grief once she's gone,'* it pushed.

But the more my brain absorbed the self-criticism, the further my already-fragile heart began to crack. Yes, Mum was still here. But I knew that one day soon, she wouldn't be. We were hurtling towards an unwelcome future and there was absolutely nothing any of us could do but buckle up for the ride and brace for impact.

And *that's* what I was struggling to deal with.

Although Mum was still physically with me at that point, I'd already lost so much. I was already grieving.

Grieving for the fact that I was still Mum's daughter, but I was no longer her child.

For the hopes, plans and dreams Mum would never get to live out.

For all the years to come when Mum wouldn't be here with me.

For the man I would one day marry who would never meet the people who made me.

For my future children who would never get to be hugged by their grandparents.

For all the darkness that, from the bitter experience of losing Dad, I knew I still had to face.

Yet no one else seemed to be registering these things. They'd tell me to be grateful for the now. To make the most of the situation, despite the sadness looming on the horizon. It made me feel foolish to grieve what hadn't happened yet, even when I knew it was inevitable. And so I took on board every word that bullying voice said to me, plastered on a fake smile and packed away my feelings, rejecting them until each anticipated heartbreak became reality.

From the moment of that fateful first phone call telling me Mum had had a mini-stroke, I felt like I was never more than a few seconds away from losing it. On the whole I managed to keep it together by focusing on the positives. But some days forced me to face reality, engulfing me in a noxious cloud of choking grief.

I didn't understand it fully at the time. After all, Mum was still with us. How can you grieve someone who's still alive?

'*If you think you're sad now, just wait until she's gone.*' I'd taunt myself like a playground bully.

I naively thought that just because Mum was still alive, I couldn't be sad about knowing she was dying. I hadn't yet registered that looking after someone who is dying is its own distinct experience, separate to the one you go through after their death.

You don't just grieve once when caring for a loved one with a terminal diagnosis. You grieve constantly – for what *has been*, what *is right now*, and what *is still to come*.

Years after we lost Mum, I discovered there was a technical term for what I'd been feeling as I watched on, helpless, while the cancer slowly turned her body against her: anticipatory grief.

Anticipatory grief is different from the type we all know about, the sort that follows a loss. As its name suggests, it comes while the person you love is still with you, referring to the horrible hurricane of emotions you go through simply by knowing that someone you love is going to die imminently. It's not a replacement for mourning their loss once they're gone, rather an additional stage in the struggle to make it through.

What's more, the grief you feel as a carer is not just about loss but about deprivation too. It's a fruitless quest to get back all the things you are beginning to lose with your special someone. There's a deep sense of sadness, loneliness and helplessness that comes when you realise they can no longer fill all the roles they once did – whether as a gym buddy, a confidante or a financial support.

Grieving for someone who's terminally ill starts long before they die. From the moment of that diagnosis, you begin to mourn a lost future, the plans and ambitions that will never come to light and the possibilities that can never be. You face two losses – the person you love and the tomorrows you'll now never have together. How do you reconcile the layers of sadness this knowledge brings with it?

To this day, I haven't found anything that can ever take away that pain, but what I have found is a change in perspective. Knowing that everything could all be over tomorrow is a reminder not to wait for a 'good' time, a 'right' time or a 'better' time to do something you want to do. It's no use planning on getting around to doing all the fun stuff 'after', 'when', or 'as soon as'. Excuses will always be there – time won't.

We've all got that list of things to do, people to see and places to go that we say we will get around to doing 'one day'. But if losing both of my parents so young has taught me anything, it's that you need to start making today that 'one day'.

# TOXIC POSITIVITY

As a carer, you're often told to 'think positive'. It comes from friends and family, from medical professionals and care workers, from strangers – and even from yourself. We're taught to believe that 'positive mental attitude', PMA, can cure all ills. For the most part, the idea of 'staying positive' is borne of good intentions, but that doesn't mean the impact is always as great.

Take my friend Nina, for example. While Mum was sick, she sent me a surprise care package. It was filled with a packet of chocolate Hobnobs (my favourites), an arty postcard telling me how proud she was of me (made me cry), a mini bottle of wine (insert praise emoji hands), a gel pen (she knows about my stationery obsession) and a notebook.

*She's so cute,* I thought, examining my new goodies, feeling like a YouTube star doing an unboxing.

The spine of the notebook creaked as I bent it open and leafed through the eighty lined lilac-coloured pages with my thumb. In the bottom right-hand corner of each, an italic font declared *An Attitude of Gratitude.* Immediately, I flipped the book shut, looked at the cover and rolled my eyes. There it was, embossed in gold lettering.

Gratitude Journal.

I rolled my eyes.

Everyone seems to be #grateful these days and it had really started to wind me up. It's easy to fill out a gratitude journal each night when you've got things in your life to be grateful for. But back then, what was I going to write in mine?

> *I'm grateful my dad's dead.*
> *I'm grateful my mum's got cancer.*
> *I'm grateful things are over with me and my boyfriend.*
> *I'm grateful I've had to abandon my career and live off £55.55*
> *Carer's Allowance each week.*
> *I'm grateful to be living 200 miles away from all my friends.*

I'm not sure my depressive content was quite what Paperchase had in mind when they printed their pastel pages! I'm sure a gratitude journal would have been great at helping me stay positive if I was living a normal life, but back then, it felt like rubbing salt in the wound.

I texted Nina to say thank you for the parcel, feeling like an ungrateful cow for tossing the book in a drawer as I pressed 'send'. The thing is, unwrapping that notebook felt symbolic of how the world was expecting me to cope with Mum's illness. You know, the 'Hollywood' way – ticking off her bucket list, running sponsored marathons, learning life lessons and making sure I *grow through what I go through*.

To come out of it all a better person.

Most of the time I wasn't sure I'd come out of the experience a person, let alone a better one. Yet I still kept scolding myself for trying and failing to cope the 'Hollywood' way. One Saturday evening, I sobbed my way through the movie *Stepmom*, telling myself I had to do better. As the credits rolled, I vowed to make a patchwork quilt of photos like Susan Sarandon's character and felt jealous of the tender moments she shared with her children. Then promised myself I'd make Mum's last Christmas as picture-perfect as Julia Roberts made theirs.

Every Sunday evening, I'd psych myself up, telling myself that as from Monday morning, things were going to be different. I was going to make losing my mum as picture-perfect as possible. Out would come the Sharpie, I'd scrawl 'THIS WEEK'S GOALS' on the top of a piece of white A4 paper and proceed to write a list of all the things I needed to do to be the perfect carer. Most weeks, it looked a bit like this:

1. **Batch cook meals and freeze** – preferably organic, lots of veg.
2. **Total spring clean of house** – get through whole ironing pile.
3. **Take more photos** – capture candid moments. Videos too where poss.
4. **Go through Mum's Facebook** – message any old friends she wants me to contact.

5. **Waitrose** – buy posh bits for visitors (nice biscuits, herbal teas, cafetière and coffee beans – no more instant).

6. **Better emotional support for Mum** – google how to talk to terminally ill people about their condition.

7. **Quicker replies to messages from friends and family** – stop letting them build up. Be more cheerful with people – it's not their fault you have to repeat the same news ten times over.

8. **Memory boxes** – Look up ideas on Pinterest. Buy craft supplies from eBay.

I'd stick the list to the back of my bedroom door and think *no excuses*, but as soon as the Blu-Tack squidged beneath my fingers, I already felt like a failure.

It's little wonder those to-dos never got *done*. Batteries need a positive and a negative to work – and so do our brains. To only talk about the good things was a self-betrayal, doing a disservice to just how hard it was for me to keep going back then.

*Good vibes only* might be a great slogan for a T-shirt, but for life? Not so much. Such a maniacal focus on only ever being positive can, ironically, have a very negative impact. It's a form of denying reality, gaslighting yourself about the truth of a situation. Each time I wrote another list, I was unintentionally poisoning myself with Toxic Positivity. But back then, I didn't even know that was a term, let alone realise I was subjecting myself to it.

Why would anyone (myself included) think I'd be able to be persistently positive with everything that was going on? I wouldn't expect someone to stand in the middle of a rainstorm and be grateful that their left armpit was dry while the rest of them was drenched. No, I'd think it was perfectly acceptable for them to moan about being soaking wet while running for shelter. So why did people expect so much of me? Why did I expect so much of myself?

One day, quite unexpectedly, I got my answer.

I was on the train home after seeing friends in Leeds, head against the window, using my scrunched-up scarf as a makeshift pillow. I was trying to sleep but a rowdy hen do in my carriage was making sure there was no chance of that. Unable to snooze as the Prosecco-fuelled party played a game of Never Have I Ever, I stared out of the window at the grey rainy cityscape. The view was about as miserable as I felt.

Suddenly, the group of girls shrieked in unison as the Mother Of The Bride admitted to something I don't want to repeat – and I spun my head to see them all cackling away. But as I turned, I was distracted. Out of the window on their side of the carriage, the sun was peeking out from behind a cloud in an increasingly blue sky.

I looked back through my window. Still grey.

I turned my head a few more times in disbelief at how different the weather was on each side of the train. That's when the penny dropped. I could either keep looking at the grey rainy landscape through one window, or at the sunny scene through the other. It's the same in life. At any given point I can choose to focus on the good or focus on the bad.

This isn't about telling you to 'always look on the bright side' or to 'cheer up, coz it might never happen'. No, it's about realising that there's always going to be bad *and* good, just as there was bad and good weather on the train that day. The two co-exist. They are not mutually exclusive.

Just because you're looking at one, it doesn't mean that the other stops existing.

I used to think that being positive during a difficult time was a fancy form of denial. That you'd chosen to gloss over the bad stuff and pretend life is all sunshine and smiles. I still think it's a choice, but now I realise it's one that involves both options. You can still look at the sunshine, even if you're standing in the rain.

Gratitude doesn't mean forgetting the bad things that are happening, but equally it doesn't mean forgetting the good things that are happening at the same time.

That evening, I got home and dug out the gratitude journal Nina sent me from the back of the drawer. Despite my revelation on the train, it still felt like too much of a stretch to be grateful. So instead, I changed the focus and repurposed the notebook to create a different kind of positivity tracker, my 'That's crap but it could have been worse journal'.

Instead of logging gratitude daily, each time a dark cloud appeared on the horizon, I would try to find the silver lining and began to fill the notebook with entries like:

Took Mum for radiotherapy today but the machine broke just before she was due to go in. Had to wait four hours until it was fixed.

*That's crap but it could have been worse, at least you had the money to get coffee and cake in the hospital canteen while you were waiting.*

I absolutely hate everything today. I've had enough. I can't go on. I can't do it any more.

*That's crap but it could have been worse, at least Mum is still alive so you can go and give her a hug and forget for a millisecond that she's dying.*

Mum was rushed into A&E with a suspected infection from the chemo.

*That's crap but it could have been worse, at least the junior doctor who saw her was really hot and seemed friendly.*

Took Mum to the seaside today to get fish and chips. She was so tired by the time we were leaving to come home, she didn't have the strength left to stand so I had a nightmare trying to get her back into the car. Think I've pulled a muscle in my back trying to lift her.

*That's crap but it could have been worse, at least the fish and chips were nice and it wasn't raining. Imagine doing all that while it was tipping it down.*

The lists didn't minimise my experiences. Writing each day didn't mean I couldn't still feel sorry for myself or wish these things had never happened. Instead, it served as a gentle reminder that the entire world wasn't against me, even though it often felt that way.

It's an approach that I still use today. Thanking heaven for small mercies, as the saying goes, is my way of remembering that I *am* being looked after and that luck *is* on my side, albeit in micro-doses. My daily lists are about remembering the light *and* shade in each day.

## WOULD YOU SAY THAT TO A FRIEND?

'I'm sorry, I don't mean to go on. There are people *far* worse off than me so I shouldn't complain really,' I said to my friend Negin, embarrassed as I rounded up my woe-is-me monologue. Eleven months into caring for Mum and the slog of daily living was dragging me down.

I'd almost composed myself when another round of tears suddenly sprung from nowhere.

'Sorry, I don't know why I'm crying again. I don't even know why I'm upset,' I spluttered down the phone.

It was a familiar scene. All too often I'd find myself censoring, apologising or justifying my emotions. My conversations with friends, family and professionals were littered with disclaimers and dismissals as I downplayed what I was going through.

But, as you'd expect from a friend, Negin reassured me that it was fine.

'Nah, don't be silly. Anyone would feel how you do, given the circumstances,' she said softly.

I knew that if the roles were reversed, I would have been saying something similar. And I would mean it. I would tell her, hand-on-heart, that every single one of her emotions were valid and I would give her my full support through what I considered an awful situation.

I would not for a second think she didn't have the right to complain because someone, somewhere out there in the world was in a worse situation – perhaps caring for their dying mum while they were pregnant, in debt and without a car. No, in that scenario, I would feel empathy and compassion both for my friend and also for the other person.

Why couldn't I show myself the same understanding that I had for others?

Instead I picked at my every move, criticising and condemning. I'd tell myself I wasn't coping properly, that I was over-sleeping and under-exercising. That I was drinking too much wine and eating too little veg. But slowly, in time, I realised there was no need to hold myself to a higher standard than the other seven billion people on the planet. Rather, I should treat myself just as I would treat my very best friend.

Watching someone you love live with an illness is, by its very nature, painful. I think of it like a spin class – the ache you feel is proof you're doing it right. So, whether you're making your way through a life cycle or SoulCycle – don't forget it's designed to hurt the whole lesson through.

I now realise that the heartbreak I felt watching my mum die was not something to judge myself on, but rather confirmation that I was living and loving just the way I was meant to.

*If you're finding being a carer really difficult, that's because it is.*

*If you're finding coping with your feelings really hard, that's because it is.*

We're so used to products and services stepping in to soothe even the slightest pain point, we've forgotten some processes are too human to be mechanised. Dealing with dying, death and all the difficult emotions that come with them is most definitely one of those processes.

When you wonder why you aren't coping 'right' or why you can't 'fix' it, remember you're reacting in exactly the way a human is supposed to respond to a human experience. Stop expecting yourself to behave like a soulless robot – then berating yourself when you don't.

When those fearful feelings flood out and you catch yourself apologising, worrying that you're being selfish, feeling guilty for taking up someone else's time, or accusing yourself of making a big deal out of nothing, stop for a second, take a breath and ask yourself: *'Would I say that to a friend?'*

Remember that our feelings are what give us the power to care and the strength to carry on. Your pain is as valid as the next person's and you deserve the same compassion and understanding that you give so freely to others.

# PROGRESS OVER PERFECTION

After a morning spent ploughing through a mountainous ironing pile, I finally had five minutes to eat, so I dashed into the kitchen, popped two slices of bread into the toaster and grabbed a plate out of the cupboard. As I did, I noticed something red and sticky on its surface. It was covered in tomato sauce.

*Mum...*

It had been happening more and more. Mum doing things like putting dirty plates back in the cupboard, coat hangers in the washing machine and laundry powder in the dishwasher. I knew she was trying to help, that she wanted to feel useful and keep some semblance of independence. I could see that she was desperate to still feel like a mum who was able to look after her daughters – but the tumour was shifting everything. It was making her confused and muddled, causing her to change her mind constantly and demand that everyone instantly fall into line with her random plans.

I kept reminding myself it was the tumour – not her – doing all these things, but it didn't make it any easier. Coping with caring seemed to have stepped up a level and I found myself getting increasingly frustrated and annoyed with everything. But the anger was always followed by guilt, because I knew I should count myself lucky that Mum was still here for me to look after and that I was in a position to do so.

As the relentlessness of being a carer sunk in, light tasks became heavy iron weights, dragging me down while I desperately tried to tread water.

It was getting harder and harder to stay afloat.

Despite the clock ticking over Mum's head, I didn't have a 'get out of jail free' card to sidestep financial responsibilities, ignore mundane tasks or even just get an easy ride. Bills still needed paying, washing still needed doing and food still needed cooking, regardless of how I was feeling or what I was going through.

I never thought I'd be told my mum had a brain tumour and then come home to spend an hour trying to find her online password to pay the overdue British Gas bill. I'd never have believed that I'd be told my mum's cancer was terminal and two hours later have to pop to Tesco to buy some milk, then hang up the washing I put in that morning. But that's exactly how things panned out.

As well as the household chores, now that I was a carer I had more admin than a high-flying PA. There were Power of Attorney forms, meetings for wheelchair assessments, GP appointments, flu jabs from the district nurse, rearranging carers' visit times, applications for a disabled parking badge and paperwork to register a disabled vehicle. All that before I could even think about doing something for myself.

Life quickly began to feel like one long false start.

Each time I knocked something off my to-do list, five more tasks appeared. It was impossible to get a handle on everything I needed to do. Sometimes I didn't even know where to start and I was beginning to wonder if I should even bother.

I was a failure and I was letting Mum down, so why even try?

One night, I lay in bed, mentally running through everything that needed to be done the next day. It had become my new routine. Examining what I'd failed to do and what needed to be added to tomorrow's list. But that night, I thought of Dad.

As a business owner, husband and father to three girls, he'd had a long to-do list as well. There must have been things that he never ticked off, in fact I *knew* there were, but the fact they never got done? It didn't matter. Not in the long run.

Not once did I look back on the time he took us camping in North Norfolk, when we pitched a tent together and toasted marshmallows over a fire, and think, *But I really wish he'd got around to painting the front door like he always said he would.* I never got lost in memories of Dad two-stepping to music, glass of beer in one hand and tongs in the other, as he tended to burgers sizzling on the BBQ, then stop to remember, *But the kitchen cupboards were in a right state, not organised at all, tins at the back at least two years out of date.* At no point had I ever longed to be five years old again, sat in the passenger seat with Dad driving us down winding country roads after a walk on the beach, singing along to the radio, windows down and wind blowing through our hair, but then paused to comment, *It's a shame I had a neon orange stain down my dress from the Calippo I'd just eaten.*

In the end, none of that mattered.

Until I became a carer, every situation I'd been in, whether it was a school exam or a work presentation, came with clear guidelines. Someone would set me a task they knew I was capable of completing, tell me what was required from me, and by when. So I guess it was natural that I approached caring for Mum with the same mindset, viewing it as a test to be passed and looking for the marking scheme to compare myself against.

*For 10 points, please care for your mum, ensure the household is running smoothly and be there for your sisters as best you can until you're told otherwise.*

Ever the diligent school girl, I pushed myself to ace the test on time and with a decent grade but – and this is a BBL-sized but – what I hadn't realised was there *are* no benchmarks, no KPIs, no minimum requirements or grade boundaries for being a carer. I was the one setting the standards and it took me a while to see that I was a harsh examiner.

I expected myself to keep everything ticking along exactly as it was before, but with the added responsibility, emotions and jobs involved with looking after Mum. For every good thing I achieved in a day, I would list at least ten that I hadn't done well enough, if at all. And if someone congratulated me on doing a good job at looking after Mum, my brain would reject the compliment.

*You wouldn't say that if you knew I haven't changed the bed sheets this week, or washed my hair, and that I had Maltesers and wine for dinner last night.*

I had to learn to shift my focus from what I hadn't done and what was still left to do, to what I had done and what was already crossed off my list. I needed to congratulate myself for managing to do *anything* while my world was crumbling around me, even if some days that was nothing more than breathing calmly amidst the chaos.

My dad always used to say to me, 'As long as you're doing your best, my girl, that's all anybody can ask of you.'

Sometimes life is so complicated, so tough and so draining that the mere ability to survive means you've aced the test. Just because you're not doing everything, doesn't mean you're not doing everything you can.

I may not have realised it back then, but now I see that *I was doing my best and that's all anybody could ask of me.*

# 4.

# *Practicalities*

## BREAKING NEWS

Hannah, Olivia and I were squashed together in the back seat of the car, while Mum was sat up front with her friend Susie who was driving. The silence in the car was deafening as we pulled away from the hospital. After all, what is there to say when you've just found out your mum has an incurable brain tumour, with a 25 per cent chance of survival past two years?

*Anaplastic astrocytoma.*

I'd never heard the words before, but now they were all I could hear. Sadness engulfed me as I turned my head to stare out of the window, watching the rush hour traffic that had started to build.

*Buzz.*

As the rain fell on the window, the sea of red and white lights was magnified and distorted into a ruby and diamond blur.

*Buzz.*

Instinctively I reached my hand across to find Hannah and

Olivia's, seeking reassurance that they were still there, checking whether I was in a bad dream, about to wake up.

*Buzz.*

A wave of tears began to rise inside of me as I replayed everything the consultant had just told us. Somehow, I managed to swallow them back down in a painful, heavy gulp.

*Buzz. Buzz.*

But before I knew it, they rose up again, another wave of heartbreak that I couldn't hold back, tears silently falling from my eyes and rolling down my cheeks.

*Buzz. Buzz.*

*Buzz. Buzz. Buzz.*

That bloody thing better stop buzzing soon, I thought as I quickly brushed my tears away, not wanting to set everyone off crying again. The only thing as consistent as my sadness was the vibration of my mobile in my bag. It had been going non-stop since my signal returned outside the hospital.

My phone was usually my lifeline, helping me to Google Map my way to job interviews, Uber taxis home and use emojis to communicate when I was too hungover to form a sentence.

But now it felt like a deathline.

Handbag on my lap, I could feel my phone vibrating with eager messages asking how the appointment had gone. Begrudgingly I pulled out my mobile, but the more my screen filled with missed calls, voicemails and texts, the more I filled with rage.

Rage that it would fall on me to ruin their day.

Rage that replying meant repeating the consultant's words, making them even more real.

Rage that I'd have to deal with their emotions when I'd barely begun to process my own.

I looked at their upbeat, hopeful messages and started seething.

**I just know it will be fine, your mum's a fighter.**

An hour earlier a text like that would have reassured me, but now I just wanted to scream. *Oh, you just know, do you? Well, guess what? You don't know! She's not fine! What have you got to say now?*

I put my phone on Do Not Disturb and shoved it into my bag for the rest of the hour and a half journey home, which seemed to be taking an eternity. But even silenced, I knew the little green notifications were still piling up on my screen. I appreciated that people were asking because they cared, but as we sat cramped in that car, choking on our devastation, it felt as if they were making it all about them.

At that moment, I never wanted to speak to anyone else again, other than my mum and sisters. I didn't want to give anyone else my attention. I thought about doing a 'send all' voice note of me screaming: 'GO AWAY – YOU DON'T WANT TO HEAR WHAT I'VE GOT TO SAY. STOP ASKING ME THINGS. I'VE GOT ENOUGH TO DEAL WITH AND YOU CAN'T HELP US ANYWAY.'

But I knew I couldn't.

And nor could I avoid telling people for ever.

Arriving back home, I got Mum settled, then decided to face my phone. More messages had popped up on the screen, all with increasing levels of urgency. I couldn't ignore it any longer; I was going to have to share what happened today, even though I hadn't had time to process it myself.

Slinking off to my room, I sat on my bed and tried to formulate a sympathetically worded message that would clearly but gently break the devastating news. I made five attempts and deleted them all, none of them feeling quite right, but as my thumb hovered ready to start a sixth draft, something inside me snapped.

*No. Why should I protect you all?* I thought.

The consultant certainly hadn't softened the blow for us, with his stark delivery. Why should anyone else get anything different? An argument raged in my head as I pictured all the people hounding me for news.

*Why should I dress it up and make it sound not so bad? It is bad. In fact, it's awful. It's the most heart-destroying news I can ever imagine. And it's not even your mum. It's not going to hurt you like it's hurting me, so why should I protect you with a nicely worded message?*

My fingers erupted into action, angrily hitting the keypad as I typed a group text message.

*Rare brain tumour. No cure. Radiotherapy can contain it but not cure it. 25% chance of surviving up to 2 years.*

'Send'.

I winced as I heard the whoosh of the message leaving my phone and heading into the ether before it scattered out to friends and relatives. I knew that everyone would think I was being insensitive.

*It's cool, I probably am,* I thought.

But from the moment Mum had her 'stroke', it had been so exhausting taking on the role of messenger on top of everything else. Mum was one of nine brothers and sisters. Keeping them updated felt like a full-time job, without even taking into account people on my dad's side of the family, as well as friends. It was hard enough to listen to bad news from a doctor and see Mum deteriorating in front of my eyes without repeating and explaining things over and over to everyone else, dealing with their emotions as well as mine.

I flopped, face-first, onto my bed, as if the whoosh of that message had taken all the energy from my body with it. For the first time, I truly understood what it meant to be emotionally drained.

I read back my message and felt instant regret. I wasn't purposely trying to be careless or hurtful. I just had so much on my plate that I couldn't stomach taking on the role of Media Spokesperson as well. I hoped that people would be able to read past the short, sharp message and see the girl behind it, crushed by the most devastating news possible for the second time in her life.

But it was time to face facts – the stress of keeping everyone up to date was getting too much, and with Mum's terminal diagnosis I knew it was only going to get worse. I needed to get a handle on this *now*. I suddenly remembered an old work colleague setting up a private Facebook group when her sister was ill. She added close friends and family so they could coordinate hospital visits and share visiting hours and ward numbers. It sparked an idea in my head.

*I'm going to start a blog.*

That way I'd only have to explain things once and everyone could keep themselves up to date.

Sliding my chair under the cheap IKEA desk, I opened my laptop and set to work. Within an hour, the blog was set up and, through tears and with the help of a large glass of wine, I started writing my first-ever post. Twenty minutes later, I typed the last sentence.

> *This blog is the story of three sisters trying to make sense of what seems to be a bit of a mean world and hoping so desperately that one day we Buggs will live 'Happily Ever After'…*

I took a deep breath and hit 'publish'. Exhaling slowly, I realised that tapping away on the keyboard seemed to have had a bizarrely therapeutic effect. I felt lighter, as if I'd freed some of the pain I'd felt since Mum first fell ill, pouring it out of my heart and onto the page.

When I made that first post, I didn't have the slightest idea that blogging would morph from a metaphorical sanctuary into a literal lifeline for me. Writing quickly became the worn and jagged thread by which I stayed tethered to my sanity. I was fully aware that posting paragraphs about hospital visits and treatment plans was far from Charlotte Brontë levels of literary genius, but that didn't matter.

Being a carer feels like slowly being sucked into a swamp. A murky sludge of emotions silently yet relentlessly building up inside you, dragging you down deeper with each passing day. It's so important to find a way to dislodge those emotions and get them out from inside of you. For some people they emerge as colours on a canvas, for others musical notes on the breeze or steps on the dance floor. For me it just happened to be words on a page.

## WHO CARES FOR THE CARERS?

Mum and I were sitting side by side on the cold toilet floor, her body weight leant against me so it was little easier for her to stay upright, as she reminded me that she'd fallen *before* she'd gone to the loo.

'I'm *bursting*, Ro,' she said, panicked.

'I know, Mum, the paramedics will be here soon,' I soothed.

It had been about an hour since she took a topple while the two visiting carers were helping her to the small downstairs toilet. She tried to break her fall by grabbing the metal towel rail, but had ripped it out of the wall and hurt her shoulder and ankle.

The carers had been useless when it happened. I even had to prompt them to call an ambulance before they rushed off to make their next visit. Thankfully, the paramedics worked with much more urgency when they arrived, getting started straightaway. But as they prepped an inflatable cushion to help lift her up, Mum started repeating over and over, 'I'm so stupid! Why do I do it?'

She was shaken and annoyed with herself, so I teased her gently, hoping to lighten the mood.

'You're just an attention seeker,' I joked, smiling.

'We're going to have to mark you down as a troublemaker, Shirley,' said one paramedic, playing along. It seemed to work. A smile flickered across her lips momentarily. But after being rescued from the bathroom floor and finally going to the loo, Mum's mood dipped again.

'I want to go to bed,' she demanded.

'But it's only one o'clock,' I protested.

'Oh, just put me somewhere I can't make any more trouble,' she said, insistent.

Her request was tinged with a little too much self-loathing for my liking, but I did as she asked. I tucked her into bed and lay next to her so we could watch TV together. After a while, I sensed a pair of eyes on me. Turning my face towards Mum, I caught her staring intently at me, two tears dribbling down her face. I immediately wrapped her into a hug.

'Come here, you wally,' I said, stroking her head.

It was my way of telling her it was OK for her to have a little cry. To be fair, given the situation she was in, she was allowed to drown the entire planet with her tears if she wanted to.

But I knew she never gave herself that permission. After a few moments, she looked at me again.

'Will everything be OK, Ro?' she asked.

My heart wasn't ready to hear Mum say those words. In fact, I don't think in a million years it would *ever* be ready to hear them. But there they were. My mum, asking me for reassurance.

'Of course it will, my mummy, don't you worry,' I told her.

Giving a satisfied nod, Mum brushed the tears away with her good hand.

'That's all I need sometimes,' she said. 'I just need someone to tell me everything will be OK.'

In that moment, my soul started silently sobbing for my mum and, to this day, it has never stopped. It's straightforward enough to explain why the practical side of being a carer is hard, but it's moments like that which nobody prepares you for, let alone gives you the recognition you deserve for them.

Whenever I spoke to people about how difficult and over-whelming I found it looking after Mum, well-meaning friends and family would chip in with endless 'Why don't you just...' suggestions:

*'Why don't you just get professional carers in?'*

*'Why don't you just call this helpline?'*

*'Why don't you just send your mum to a hospice?'*

Yet, more often than not, rather than being valuable, their 'two-pence worth' ended up being costly. Costly to my mental health because it was jarring to think of people looking in and presuming I could easily get the help I needed if only I made the effort to put in a couple of calls or send a few emails. And costly to my self-esteem because I felt those suggestions underestimated how much strength it took for me to get through each day.

After a while, I started to think that they must be right, telling myself that I was only finding it so tough because I wasn't asking for enough help. It was a big thing for me to admit that I couldn't cope but, eventually, I did.

*Job done*, I thought. *I'll ask for help. They'll give it to me. This is what we pay taxes for.*

How wrong I was.

It quickly became apparent that the friends and family who made these suggestions had never used the services they so freely recommended. If they had, I am certain they would have been astounded by how much money, how many phone calls, how much paperwork and how many reference numbers it took to carry out even the most seemingly simple of things.

I'd already tried much of their advice, but, regardless, I forced myself to give some of their ideas a go. My first stop was trying to secure some help for me – an increasingly frazzled carer. I booked a GP appointment to ask for a referral to social services so we could get some professional support in place and give the three of us girls some time to ourselves. Sounds simple, right?

The reality was far from it. I spent a week on hold, leaving voicemails and explaining the situation in endless phone calls, then another week filling out and posting off forms and arranging meetings with various people from different organisations. I spoke to and met with social services, care agencies, carers' charities, Customer First (the first point of contact for social services in Suffolk), the GP surgery, the hospice, Macmillan, the district nurse, occupational therapists, and the oncology consultant. In the end we had some positive news though: we qualified for professional carers to help lighten the load.

But it wasn't quite that simple.

I met with Karen, the care-company manager, to talk through

Mum's reluctance to accept help. I explained that I wanted her to build a bond with someone she could talk to and come to think of as a friend, as well as helping to wash and dress her. Karen assured me that her team had lots of experience dealing with people who were hesitant about receiving outside support, so they knew how to build trust. I breathed a sigh of relief as she left, thinking everything was about to get easier.

Until the letter confirming Mum's care entitlement arrived.

Mum was only allowed half an hour in the morning and half an hour in the evening each day, with different carers sent for each slot. No consistency, no relationship building, just whoever was on shift.

On the first day a young boy turned up in a dirty uniform with holes in his shoes. Was Mum meant to feel comfortable with him washing and dressing her when it looked like he couldn't even do it for himself? A week later another carer asked Mum for her mobile to get her girls' numbers. 'You've got three very pretty daughters, you know, Mrs Bugg,' he said, creepily. Then came the carer whose motto was 'I'd like to see what your mum can do by herself.' I told her that she needed to pick up Mum's bad foot and lift it up each stair, but she stubbornly refused.

'No, I think your mum can do that herself,' she insisted ignorantly, while watching Mum struggle.

Next I tried a local charity I'd been told provided respite care. Sending off for the application form, I was hopeful at the promise of experienced volunteers with medical backgrounds who could take Mum out or simply sit and chat with her. When the letter with their stamp dropped onto the doormat, I ripped it open excitedly, only to be crushed by the first line.

*Our funding has been cut so unfortunately we are unable to offer these services free of charge as previously. Please find enclosed our price list.*

My heart sank as I glanced at the prices – £17 per hour or £95 for an overnight stay from 11pm to 7am. At the time, I received £55.55 per week Carer's Allowance, which meant I'd have to save up for two weeks to afford cover for a night out – and another week if I wanted to do anything on while I was out.

I'm not moaning. Drunkenly dancing the night away certainly wasn't my top priority. I'd chosen to give up my career, move home and care for Mum and I still stand by that decision 100 per cent. At any point during Mum's illness I could have walked away and made it a problem for social services, then caught up on sleep, regained my sanity and worked my way out of my overdraft.

I'm not claiming to be a victim, but I still think carers are owed an explanation for the system they inadvertently find themselves a part of. It's a system that is woefully inadequate at supporting the very people who mean it even exists at all. The more forms I was asked to complete, the more chaser emails I sent, the more reference numbers I regurgitated down the phone, the more questions I had.

*Why are carers so unrecognised and undervalued?*
*Why is Carer's Allowance so little? In particular, why is it less than Job Seeker's Allowance?*
*Why doesn't the level of payment and support for carers reflect the massive amount of money the country saves from the work they do?*
*Why can only one person claim Carer's Allowance when looking after a person who requires two people to help them?*

What's more, even in the midst of the nightmare I went through with Mum, I knew that I had things better than some. I can't imagine how much worse it would have all been if I'd been struggling to pay rent, worrying about eviction, or was a single mother trying to look after a child as well as Mum.

I'm well educated with English as my first language, yet even I sometimes found it difficult to take in all the medical jargon and understand the phrasing on forms. So how must it be for others? In many senses I was privileged in this situation, but in my daily life I felt far from it.

I slowly found peace with the fact that fate dictated I would lose my dad to cancer aged fourteen and then have to go through the same heartbreaking journey with Mum. However angry I got, however many tears I cried, however many nights I spent awake asking, 'Why?' I knew there would be no answers, no logic, and no rationale to my situation. I had no option but to play the hand I'd been dealt. But there were elements of my journey that *could* have been changed, and which I believe *should* be changed for current and future carers. Those are the things that, even now, years after I stopped being a carer myself, still concern me.

In total I spent nearly seventeen months at home caring for Mum, during which time things got progressively more difficult and challenging. We went from having to cook for Mum, to having to feed her, to dripping water into her mouth when she couldn't even sip. When it came to getting about we had to hire a wheelchair for £5 a week from the British Red Cross, because even though Mum could barely walk from the house to the car, at first the hospital said she wasn't ill enough to qualify for one of theirs. We eventually got one, along with a Zimmer frame, but it wasn't long before Mum even struggled to get around with those. We had to keep Mum looking and feeling pretty too, washing, dressing, shaving, brushing her teeth and getting her to the loo, all of which became progressively more difficult.

As Mum's brain tumour grew, so too did the level of care that she needed. There were pills of every shape and size to be taken at specific times in specific combinations. And because cancer didn't care what time it was, there were frequent calls for help at all times of the day and night. We couldn't listen to music through headphones in case Mum shouted for us, we cut phone conversations short if she needed help with something, and we took turns sleeping with a baby monitor in our rooms in case she needed us during the night.

Yet despite all of that, I wouldn't have had it any other way. Well, aside from making her well again. It was a privilege to go some way towards repaying the woman who dedicated her life to making sure my sisters and I were OK. I chose to be her carer because my mum needed help. As her daughter, I wanted to be the one to give her that help, just as she did for my dad when he was dying.

But I found the system that was set up to take care of us carers often seemed to work against me as I tried my best to fulfil the role I'd taken on. It still does for other carers today.

Nowhere is this clearer than when it comes to financial support.

I shot myself in the foot the second I quit my job to look after Mum. I admit I'm no Carol Vorderman, but even I can tell there's something about the mathematics of the benefits and resources available to carers in this country that doesn't add up. It only takes a few simple sums.

I received Carer's Allowance of £55.55 per week, however,

at the time of writing, this has increased to £67.25, so we'll use that figure.

Between Hannah and I, we spent around fifteen hours per day, seven days a week either directly caring for Mum or undertaking care-related tasks. That adds up to 105 hours per week. But for fairness' sake, let's round it down to 90 hours per week, discounting some time for Olivia stepping in when she wasn't busy with college and to account for the 'easy' weeks where Mum didn't wake up much during the night for help.

Despite two of us caring for Mum, only one person was entitled to claim Carer's Allowance, so that payment of £67.25 had to be shared between Hannah and I, ending up with us being paid about £33.62 per week each, or 75p per hour. At the time of writing, Job Seeker's Allowance is £74.35, meaning I would have been paid *more* to look for a job, than do the job of looking after my mum.

If, like me, you're wondering why, if Mum required two people to care for her, only one of us was being paid, it's a good question and one that I still don't have the answer to. All I know is that the government believes if you're caring for a family member, one person should be able to do it alone, despite the fact that in any professional setting, such as carers provided by social services and nurses in hospital, *two* members of staff are allocated for Health and Safety reasons. Similarly, if you care for more than one person, you can still only claim one lot of Carer's Allowance.

That £67.25 is taxable and dwindles further when you discover that you can't claim Carer's Allowance if the person you're caring for goes into hospital. Don't be fooled into thinking this is a holiday from being a carer. You couldn't be more wrong. When Mum was in hospital, we often spent the majority of the day with her because the staff were so overstretched that they left Mum with food that she couldn't eat because it hadn't been cut up; they didn't have time to regularly check if she needed the toilet and they left her to take her medication unsupervised, which meant she dropped or lost pills.

*And don't even get me started on the cost of hospital parking.*

We'd regularly pay £8 for six hours each day, on top of travel and accommodation when Mum was transferred to hospitals further away for specialist care. The bitter icing on an already rancid cake came a week or two after Mum had died when a letter came through the post. It explained that they would be deducting money from my final Carer's Allowance payment because Mum had died on a Saturday, and I therefore hadn't cared for her for the whole week.

I'll be the first to admit that I don't understand the whole welfare system in great detail, but I often wonder if the MPs in charge of it do either. It's obvious to me that they don't realise what it's actually like to be a carer, but I think it's about time they did. Will those working at the House of Commons ever stop, take stock, and realise it's time to take a sabbatical at the House of Common Sense?

Luckily there are services and charities out there trying to help. But at the time it felt too frustrating, too exhausting to search them out and access the help we so desperately needed. It's such an uphill battle and there's still so much to be done, but there are some organisations that are making great strides in *caring for the carers* (see Resources, page 335).

## CHARITY BEGINS AT HOME

It took a while to find out about the support services available to us, so it wasn't until around ten months into Mum's illness that I asked for a Macmillan nurse to come to the house and see if she could help with anything. Mum was quietly watching TV when she arrived. As I handed the nurse a cup of tea, she introduced herself cheerily.

'Hello Shirley, I'm Sue,' she chirped.

'Hello,' replied Mum, barely moving her eyes from the screen.

I gave Sue a half-smile by way of apology for Mum's lukewarm response and tried to draw her attention back to me.

'It's so lovely to meet you,' I said overenthusiastically.

Like Mum, I'd largely ignored Macmillan's offers of help because I knew that speaking to them meant I was acknowledging the reality of the situation. But as the days became steadily and consistently tougher, I had no choice but to give in and book the appointment.

Sue beamed back at me. Then she put her tea on the side, dumped her bag, which was brimming with folders, on the carpet by her feet, and waited for me to speak.

'I've got everything under control really, it's just that sometimes it feels like a lot to juggle, and I was wondering if there's any help available. Because it just seems non-stop. There's so much to remember and I want Mum to have the best care possible, but I don't always know if I'm doing things right, or if I could be doing them better...' I twittered on, trying to get my point across without saying anything in front of Mum that might upset her, or make her feel like a burden. Sue sat and listened intently, absorbing my every word. Only when she was certain I'd finished did she speak.

'Well, the good news is that you and your mum don't have to cope with this alone,' she said, putting a hand on my knee. 'And it's certainly not unreasonable to want a bit of time to yourself each week. We can help you with that too.'

Without missing a beat, Sue started to reel off one helpful suggestion after another. I quickly opened the Notes app on my phone so I could write down her advice before I forgot anything. Typing away, I felt tears welling in my eyes. Sue was offering solutions to things I hadn't even registered as issues that could be solved – things like buying a pill cutter so Mum could swallow her large tablets more easily. I'd been so consumed with just putting one foot in front of the other that I'd accepted so much as 'just the way it is'.

I felt a weight being lifted as she listed some of the help available for carers, in particular from the local hospice. I had no idea they offered everything from relaxation sessions to house-sitting services that would allow me to do things without having to plan a military-style operation to take Mum with me.

I was as engrossed in Sue's information as I *thought* Mum was in the episode of *A Place in the Sun* she'd been watching. But then she suddenly piped up. 'We're coping fine,' she snapped. 'Maybe if things get bad later on, we can give you a call.'

*She'd been listening all along.*

'I understand,' said Sue, gently. 'But it might be good for you to have a change of scenery at the hospice *and* allow the girls to get some rest...'

'No, I'm quite happy at home and the girls can go to their rooms while I watch TV so they can have a rest if they need to,' Mum insisted.

She may have spoken quietly, but her words were loud. Immediately, I felt the weight of responsibility drop back onto my shoulders.

'Well, thank you for your time, Sue,' I said. 'It's been really useful.'

'You know where I am if you need anything else,' she added, with a knowing nod.

The understated yet understood pressure I faced was something she must have seen a thousand times before. Just because *I* had reached the stage where I knew I needed help, it didn't mean everyone else was ready. Mum's response may have been brief, but it told me everything I needed to know.

*She* wasn't there yet.

They say charity begins at home, but I wish I'd been more open to letting it begin in *my* home. As a carer navigating state-provided support and its reels of endless red tape, I soon became jaded. Government-sanctioned help rarely seemed worth the hoops you had to jump through to get it, plus I didn't want to feel like a charity case. But the case for accepting their help grew stronger as time went on and things became more difficult.

A few months after Sue's visit, I eventually found the courage to put my hand up and ask for support. That was when I finally reached out to St Elizabeth Hospice and convinced Mum to use their day care and respite care services. It's not that I was trying to impress anyone by going it alone; it just didn't dawn on me there was another way to balance my needs with Mum's feelings.

It wasn't until nearly a decade later when I heard a Brené Brown podcast that I realised *just because I can do something all alone, it doesn't mean that I should do it all alone.* I listened to her honey-smooth Texan drawl, as she said:

> *There's no shame in needing someone…*
> *Dependence is a natural part of being human…*
> *Accepting help doesn't make you less than…*

*Our neurobiology is such that we are wired to do life together*
*– not alone...*

Her words struck a chord so deep I felt the reverberations in my soul. I wish I'd known all that when I was a carer. If I could go back and do things again, I wouldn't spend so long searching for a permission slip to accept help – and you shouldn't either.

There's a wealth of support out there that I'd encourage all carers to embrace. If you're looking after someone with cancer, I'd recommend Macmillan and Marie Curie. But there are also more general carers' charities that offer support regardless of your loved one's condition. Not to mention local hospices and targeted charities with specialist knowledge of your family member's illness, which, for us, was The Brain Tumour Charity (see Resources, page 335).

Initially, I expected very little from these services, assuming all I'd get was a handful of generic leaflets. Instead, I found people who were my voice when I was too upset and exhausted to speak up for myself, like Suffolk Family Carers who arranged a disabled parking badge for me in under a week, when I had spent two months trying to get one with no luck. It was Macmillan that demanded the hospital give Mum a wheelchair after I'd been told she wasn't ill enough for one, and it was the 24-hour helpline at St Elizabeth Hospice that sent a specialist nurse to the house quicker than 999 could get an ambulance to us.

# 5.

# Family

## FAMILY RESEMBLANCE

I popped my head around Mum's door to make sure she was still sleeping soundly, then tip-toed back across the hallway and resumed pacing up and down the kitchen, only stopping to call Olivia's mobile.

It rang out and went to voicemail *again*. This was the thirteenth time I'd tried to call her in the last hour. *Where the hell is she?* I wondered, worry working its way through every part of my body. She'd left the house that afternoon, around 2pm. It was now 3.30am!

With each failed call, my mind spiralled further out of control. The fear that something had happened to her was so intense that I was mentally role-playing what I would say to the police when they came to tell me she had been mugged, abducted or – worse – murdered.

Eventually, on the twenty-fourth attempt, she picked up.

'What?' she snapped as she answered the phone.

'Oh my god, Olivia! Where the hell are you? Why aren't you home? And why haven't you been answering your phone? I've been so worried about you. Where are you?' I panicked.

'I'm out. I'm fine,' she replied in a clipped tone which annoyed me even more. It was as if I could hear her rolling her eyes as she said it.

'Olivia! You're seventeen years old. Why are you acting like you know everything? You don't. You're still a child. I'm only asking where you are.'

'Yep, great. Thanks for letting me know how old I am Rochelle. Would have forgotten without your handy reminder,' she replied, with as much contempt as was humanly possible.

'Olivia, I'm serious. I'm at home trying to look after OUR mother. Who's dying by the way, if you hadn't noticed. I can't sleep if I don't know that you're safe. And if Mum finds out you're not home, she won't be able to sleep either. It's four in the bloody morning for God's sake. You've got college tomorrow. And you haven't been at home one night this week so far. Just... just come home... please,' I begged.

'You're not my mum! You can't tell me what to do! Leave me alone,' she barked in the tone of a teenager trying to sound cool in front of her friends.

Before I could reply, she hung up.

My deep rage was tempered only by the relief that she was safe.

It was the last thing I needed. Me and Hannah had already fallen out earlier that day. Over dirty plates, of all things.

'What are you doing in my room?' she'd growled, walking in to find me on all fours looking under her bed.

'It would appear that I'm on a magical mystery hunt for plates, glasses and spoons,' I snapped sarcastically, pointing to the small pile of cutlery and china I had already built up next to me. 'Have you got some kind of phobia about bringing stuff back down to the kitchen and washing it up?' I snarked.

'Oh for God's sake, Rochelle! There's no need to be so bloody dramatic. It's a few plates and what, like, three glasses? It's hardly the end of the world. I told you I'd do it, but I've been out,' replied Hannah, wearily.

'Yeah, but when? I've been asking you to bring them down for days,' I nagged.

'Just get your nose out of my stuff, Roch-Elllllllllle!' she screamed, pronouncing my name in such a way that I knew I had crossed a line.

'Fine! I'll go downstairs and tell Mum to drink water out of a frying pan. That's about all that's bloody left down there,' I shouted back. 'I'll leave this little pile here for you to bring down. But obviously you were going to do that anyway,' I sniped in a sugary-sweet tone that I knew would wind her up.

It might have looked like I enjoyed getting the last word in, but that was far from the truth. The cruel laws of biology meant that, as sisters, we were always destined to lose our mum at the same time. I could see we were all going through a difficult time but it was hard enough to drag myself through life, let alone help the other two. And I knew the age gap was having an impact too – I was twenty-five, while Hannah was twenty and Olivia was seventeen – but even that didn't explain how we were all coping with things *so* differently.

As I made my way downstairs, I sighed.

All three of us were children of the same two parents, brought up in the same way, in the same places. Surely then, we should all think the same, feel the same and react in the same way to Mum's cancer?

But it wasn't happening like that.

I couldn't cope with the way things were between me, Hannah and Olivia. Emotions were running high and there were more misunderstandings and miscommunications than a *Real Housewives* season finale. With Mum's condition deteriorating, I knew it was time for me to have 'the conversation' with them. It was the same one Mum had with me a week or two after Dad died.

'Now Ro,' she'd said, sitting next to me on my bed, both of us side by side. 'I'm going to start needing you to help out a bit more.'

I looked at her confused. I *had* been helping out more. Pausing the film I was watching to hang out the washing as soon as the machine beeped, instead of turning the TV up and ignoring it. Walking home when I had a 'double free' at school to make spaghetti Bolognese, ready for that night's dinner, instead of sitting in the common room. And doing the ironing on Sunday morning while binge-watching the *Hollyoaks* omnibus instead of staying in bed snuggled underneath my duvet.

I wasn't sure how much more she expected me to do.

'But I have been helping, Mum,' I protested.

*Has she not noticed all the extra effort I've been putting in?* I wondered.

'I know,' she soothed, sensing my hurt at the suggestion I wasn't pulling my weight. 'But things are different now there's only four of us.'

Looking at my puzzled expression, Mum sighed.

'Think of it like a pizza,' she said.

Those were the magic words. Fourteen-year-old me immediately had the image of a Domino's Stuffed Crust Meat Feast in her head and my interest was most definitely piqued.

'When your dad was here, the pizza was cut into five slices,' she said, calmly and confidently.

*She's rehearsed this*, I thought.

'But now there's only four of us,' she continued. 'So we need to share that extra slice – your dad's slice – between us.'

'That's gonna be a big slice considering how much Dad loved food,' I laughed, still unsure of where she was going with her clunky metaphor.

'Imagine I'm cutting up your dad's slice into small pieces and we all take some and put it on our own plates,' she went on. 'I'll take the business bit. I need to make sure everything at work keeps running smoothly, so I'll be spending more time there now. Which means I'm going to need you to do a few more bits for me around the house.'

'Yeah. Of course,' I replied nonchalantly, as if this was nothing new to me.

'Ro, because you're the eldest, I'm going to have to start relying on you more to look after the girls,' she announced.

*The girls?*

The two words rolled around my mind like marbles, leaving me unable to focus on the list of chores she'd started reeling off.

*Tidy the house.*

*Do the ironing.*

*Make dinner some nights…*

Until there came those words again…

*Pick the girls up from school.*

The girls.

That day was the first time she'd ever used that phrase without me being a part of it.

She still had three daughters, yet all of a sudden it appeared she only considered two of them to be 'the girls'. I felt proud and wounded at the same time, as if I'd been promoted to the role of chic, cool European au pair. I was going to be let in on 'grown up' secrets and trusted to help with everything. But the excitement quickly faded, as it hit me. Did that mean I no longer had anyone to look after me? After all, au pairs were *like* family, not a *part of* the family.

My stomach lurched.

It wasn't the expectation of doing more that shook me. From the moment Dad started getting ill, there were extra chores. I used to dread going downstairs at weekends because I knew what was waiting for me. A to-do list from Mum, left on the kitchen counter before she went to work. I could spot them a mile off. They always looked the same – '*RO*' written in capitals and underlined twice at the top, so there was no chance of pretending not to know it was meant for me, followed by a numbered list of tasks, all signed off at the end with '*Mummy xxx*'.

As much as I hated those lists, I'd accepted them without complaint. Soaking up all the new demands placed on me like an ever-expanding sponge, I felt denser and heavier with the responsibility that now weighed on me. But that didn't matter. I understood it was down to me to mop up all those tasks, so that nobody else had to.

I got on with things, but I still secretly resented those lists. They were a symbol of the double standards I had been singled out to endure. A physical manifestation of the way I was being treated like a child who needed to be told what to do, yet was still expected to behave like an adult.

But this? This was a step further.

Suddenly, at fourteen years old, I was being wrenched from my place in the family hierarchy. As if everyone thought I no longer needed the same parental care as my sisters. Our family was no longer 'James, Shirley and the girls' – it was 'Shirley, Rochelle and the girls'.

But if I wasn't 'the girls', what was I?

What was my role?

As those feelings of confusion and displacement from my teenage talk with Mum came flooding back, it dawned on me. *So that's why I've been clashing with Hannah and Olivia.* Without realising, I'd already started doing to my sisters what my mum had done to me. Asking them both to become adults before they were ready. An extra chore here, a nag about a pile of unwashed dishes there. And they were pushing back, just as I had wanted to as a teenager.

We were entering a new, uncertain future. And there was no way to make it palatable. It was inevitable we would disagree about who should do what while we were going through yet another fundamental change – not only to the structure of our family but to our lives.

Did I even have the right to ask this of them?

For now, we were still Shirley, Rochelle and the girls. But I knew soon we'd be Rochelle, Hannah and Olivia. A family-size pizza cut into just three huge slices.

Looking back, I can see the problem was not that Hannah and Olivia weren't acting in the same way as me, but simply that I was expecting them to. How could I demand for them to share my views and opinions when even my own changed from day to day? If my own behaviour didn't follow the pattern I predicted, how could my sisters'?

As time went on, I realised that our little family unit was not a twelve-inch deep pan that needed to be divided, but a four-piece band that needed to be united. I learned it was OK for each of us to do or cope with things differently, as long as we came together as one when it was 'showtime'. It didn't matter if we played different notes on different instruments, as long as we were all following the same music and singing the same song. If one of us lost the beat for a while, or went off-key, the rest of the band simply needed to play louder, helping them find their rhythm once more. That way, we knew that whatever happened – the show would always go on.

## PARENTING YOUR PARENT

Having a parent with a terminal illness pulls apart your entire family structure and reassembles it into a completely new shape. For me, it meant swiftly being elevated to 'parent in waiting' to my siblings. That was a challenge in itself to navigate, but, being the eldest, it was one I already had a little experience in. However, what nothing could have prepared me for was my mum, the person who had cared for me my entire life, suddenly having a childlike reliance on *me* – the same way that I once had on her.

I gradually transitioned from daughter to parent through a sequence of scenarios that ranged from the harrowing to the hilarious, like the time I caught Mum about to drink the water from a vase of flowers because she was thirsty. My slow slide along the scale from daughter to parent began right after Mum's diagnosis, but as time went on, it gathered pace. Circumstances smoothly and swiftly steered us into a maze of frustrating wrong turns and dead ends, leaving us lost and disorientated.

Our roles were irrevocably reversed in a matter of months and I realised that so many of the worries I was facing were the same ones that she and Dad must have had for me, Hannah and

Olivia growing up. I found myself swapping her usual wine glass for a plastic one from the picnic set, checking the temperature of her food and ordering a bed guard so she couldn't roll out in the night, just as she had toddler-proofed our home with plug-socket covers and stair gates.

The problem is, when you're caring for your parent, no matter how much it feels like it, you *aren't* parent and child. Rather you are living in a mirror image, your reflected roles blurred beyond recognition. You try to limit their independence where they once encouraged yours. But whose judgement is trusted more? Who has the final say?

I used to feel awkward telling Mum what to do and she didn't listen to me anyway. Let's face it, why should she? Would you take orders from the newly trained manager, when it was you who taught them what to do in the first place? For the last twenty-five years, she'd looked after me, foreseen the hurdles I would have to jump and did her best to equip me to be able to clear them. But then the roles reversed, and Mum had to concede there were some things I did better than she could.

I surreptitiously slid into Mum's shadow and tried to make the moves I imagined she would have done. But like a satnav booming out directions when you already know the way, I irritated her.

Not ready to relinquish her role, Mum fiercely and fearlessly charged into battle each day in the name of defending her independence. Half woman, half machine, she would scoot around the house using her one good leg to propel herself forward in her wheelchair, crushing anything in her path. She ignored my pleas for her to ask me for help before doing certain things, instead insisting on doing them herself as soon as my back was turned.

The end result would usually mean more work for me –

something to clear up, to put right, to correct. I'd get annoyed, knowing that I could have done it quicker and more easily, but Mum just saw my increasing irritation and presumed that it was aimed at her.

In a way she was right. I begrudged being a carer, but only because each task solidified my reality. Showering Mum or cutting her food was like surveying the ruins of a once revered ancient temple. There was an overwhelming sadness in seeing what it had been reduced to.

As much as I felt like a parent with a 'troublesome teen' that I wanted to ship off to a boot camp in rural Arizona, I worried that perhaps I was the problem. I wanted to be a helpful presence but instead I became concerned that I was suffocating Mum in her own home. Was it me, not the tumour, who was turning her into the moody, resentful teenager I'd once been when she'd opened my letters or made me food I didn't fancy?

The truth is, you can't blame anyone in this 'parenting a parent' situation. It's nobody's fault that you're in this evolving yet constantly incompatible limbo. Even the English language lacks a word to describe the role you have taken on. And if it did, would it label you a 'chilent' (a child acting like a parent) or a 'parild' (a parent who's still a child)?

Being a carer for a parent is tough. You have to navigate a no-man's land where you have all of the responsibility but none of the authority, and they have all the authority but none of the responsibility. When looking after your mum or dad, all boundaries are blurred. There is no clear-cut template on what you *should* be doing or thinking or how you *should* be behaving. So, you have to make your own, one that works for you and your family and your situation. No comparisons. No judgement. No guilt.

# SAY GOODBYE TO THE FUTURE

A year or so after Mum's cancer diagnosis, seemingly overnight, doctors, nurses, staff at the hospice – in fact everyone in the know – started using phrases like 'have quality time', 'enjoy being with your mum' and 'make the most of it'. I realised what those phrases meant, I understood the direction in which they were pointing us. But I didn't know how long it was going to be until we arrived at our destination.

For a few weeks, I managed not to dwell on it, shooing away thoughts about how long she had left like I would a wasp at a picnic. But one night the 'not knowing' became unbearable. Our lives were on pause, yet I'd never been more acutely aware of how quickly time was playing out. The opposing push and pull of those two truths became so excruciating that I did the only thing I could. I sat on my bed, pillows propped behind me, opened up my laptop and googled: 'Final stages of a brain tumour'.

0.26 seconds of searching and there they were: All 110,000 results waiting to tell me how long I had left with my mum.

I scrolled down the page and clicked on a link titled 'Symptom Timeline', stomach already churning as the page began to load. Just like holding the envelope with my A-level results inside, I wanted to look, I had to read what it said to know what was coming next in my life, but at the same time I couldn't stomach it. A jumble of thoughts raced through my mind:

*What if it's not what I want to see?*

*What can I do about it if it's bad news anyway?*

*It's too late now to change anything.*

*Maybe it's better not to know.*

But I pushed them to one side, took a deep breath and looked at the timeline on the screen, working my way along the arrow comparing Mum's symptoms to the different stages, trying to find the one that best described where she was.

*This one*, I thought, as I found a description that seemed spot on.

Cross-referencing the stage with its colour-coordinated counterpart in the explanatory table below, I began to read.

*At this stage patients typically have six to twelve weeks.*

SIX TO TWELVE WEEKS?

W.E.E.K.S.

Six weeks' school summer holidays had once felt endless, but I was no longer a child. I knew how quickly that time would pass. I stared at the screen, momentarily paralysed by fear before quickly being jolted into panic mode. Shock rippled through me and my chest filled with physical pain, while simultaneously feeling absolutely empty.

*No*, I told myself. *Mum wouldn't go anywhere before Olivia's eighteenth birthday. No chance.*

Her birthday was 20th April, fifteen weeks away.

*Surely Mum wouldn't go anywhere before then?*

My panic was swiftly followed by denial. Scrolling back to the top of the page, I checked the symptom descriptions again. Did I really think that was the stage that best described Mum's current situation? Was I being pessimistic?

Three more times I went through that timeline.

I don't know why I kept going over it, because the results didn't really come as much of a surprise. Nobody had ever given us hope that things could head in any other direction. Not one person had ever suggested there was a chance the tumour might decide one day to quietly slip away. Yet, somehow I'd always harboured hope that things would work out. But now, there it was in black and white. The bleak future that we'd been looking at all along.

As painful as it was to be given a timeline, I needed it to orientate myself and prepare as best I could. Every other routine and sign of normal life had already disappeared – sleep patterns, hobbies, mealtimes. As a family, our focus had become so microscopic that we aimed for nothing more than to make it from one moment to the next. I'd lost track of where we were on our journey and I'd turned to Google to try and regain some control over the situation. How could I make an informed decision on how best to spend the time we had left, if I didn't know how long we had left?

I was overloaded, mentally, emotionally and physically. New circuits shorted and sparked within me each day. Laughter would turn into uncontrollable sobbing within seconds, and somewhere in between those two emotions I would burn with intense anger as my mind looped back around to the one thought, that was streaming on repeat in my head.

*I NEED MY MUM. DON'T YOU DARE TAKE HER.*

I couldn't bear to think about the decimated disaster zone I imagined would be left when me, Hannah and Olivia had to face life without Mum by our sides. We were still young. We warred over stupid things like boys, clothes and whose turn it was to take the bins out, and Mum was the only person able to wave the white flag of peace amongst us. How were we meant to cope with big, scary real life alone? Friends and family would assure me that I'd cope just fine when the time came, because I was coping just fine now. *How can they not see?* I would think to myself. *How do they not know that I am only coping now because Mum is still here?*

Just as Samson's strength was in his hair, I was convinced mine was in my mum. I was certain I could only be brave because she was still there, keeping us all going, giving us a sense of direction and telling us that it would be all right. I was petrified of the day that I would no longer be able to run to her in moments of joy and moments of crisis.

This sounds an obvious fear for anyone facing the loss of a loved one. It's understandable. You expect to start mourning the future you will no longer share together. But not long after Mum's terminal diagnosis, I was hit by a new, unexpected panic. We weren't just about to lose the future with her, we were going to lose the past with her, too – all the memories, stories and advice that she'd stored up, but hadn't yet got around to sharing with us.

I became overwhelmed by a frantic need to learn everything I could from Mum, mapping out all the situations, problems and dilemmas I could potentially face over the course of my life. I thought about all the big milestones I'd previously presumed she would be around to guide me through – buying a house, getting married, having my first baby – and imagined what I might need to know.

*What should you look for when you're buying a property?*

*How do you know what mortgage to get?*

*How did you know Dad was 'The One'?*

*Did Dad drive you crazy sometimes?*

*How did you get me to sleep as a baby when I wouldn't stop crying?*

Even trivial, inconsequential things became burning questions when I realised that soon she wouldn't be around to answer them.

*How do you make your roast potatoes so crispy?*

*Is it better to get a gas or electric hob for the kitchen?*

*What's the exact time I was born? I need it coz I want to get an astrology reading.*

It wasn't just advice either. I suddenly realised that when Mum went, she would take the puzzle pieces containing snapshots of her life and my own with her. There would be nobody else left on the entire planet who'd remember how long she was in labour with me, if she had any cravings, or if she was in love with anyone before she met Dad. The outlines of my half-remembered memories would be forever left blank because Mum was the only person able to colour them in.

*Didn't something funny happen when you took me horse riding for the first time?*

*Why did you have that operation when I was four or five? Was it something hereditary?*

*What happened when we went to that butterfly garden when I was little? Is that why I hate them flapping close to my face now?*

As the enormity of the realisation weighed down on me, rage and regret boiled up inside. Why had I not thought about this earlier? Why did I not begin asking before the tumour started melting her memories? I knew snippets but I wanted to know it *all*. Every night out, boyfriend, hope, dream and ambition. Her happiest times and her saddest times, because I didn't want her story to end when her life did. I didn't want her to go and take all of her memories with her. I wanted to know everything so that I could tell my future husband, the children we would have, and the whole world all about her.

Contrary to what I believed back then, I *have* learned how to get through life without Mum and Dad, albeit with a few more mistakes than I would have made if I'd had parents around to ask.

Just as with that symptom timeline, Google has helped me find most of the answers I've needed when it comes to the practical stuff. Yet no search engine can find the missing memories and unshared stories that only Mum and Dad knew. That's the bit that doesn't get any easier. While some parts of my grief have softened over time, others are sharpened by each passing year. The older I get, the more milestones I reach, the more I wonder what Mum and Dad would be doing, saying and thinking if they were still here. Their absence from my future has become more painful than losing their presence in the past.

# 6.

# Self-care

## CHECK YOURSELF BEFORE YOU WRECK YOURSELF

I sat in the doctor's surgery waiting for my appointment, staring at a hotchpotch of haphazardly arranged posters about everything from sepsis to smear tests, and doing what I usually did before any appointment about Mum's care – rehearsing.

Not long after her diagnosis, I realised there was a well-worn formula to what healthcare professionals ask in appointments. It was as if they all got the same list of preamble questions when they qualified, a checklist to churn out before delving into the intricacies of their patient's problems.

*Why are you here today?*

*How did this start?*

*How long has your mum been ill?*

*What treatment is she receiving?*

You get the idea. Basic facts they'd already know if they had read her notes, but which they always asked to hear 'in my own words'. By now, more than a hundred appointments in, I was expert in reeling off answers to their stock questions and just as much of a pro at predicting their responses. There was usually lots of nodding, plenty of 'I see' and numerous 'I'll make a note of that', but rarely much more. But today's appointment was different.

It was one I'd been putting off, spending months dodging it and another few dithering over it. But now, finally, I was going to speak to my GP about getting a Carer's Assessment. I'd eventually given in, accepting that I had to make the appointment because it was the key to unlocking more professional help for Mum going forwards. But truth be told, in the weeks since I'd made the appointment, things felt as if they'd calmed down.

As the weather improved that spring, so too did my mood. I'd even found time that morning to sit outside in the sunshine, eating a Solero with Mum before going to the GP surgery. I started to wonder if I even really needed the appointment. No doubt it would be just another thing to follow up on, more red tape to navigate, an extra task added to my to-do list.

But I wanted to find out what support was available for Mum.

Staring at the posters on the wall, their colours and shapes bleeding into one another, my mind drifted and I wondered what might come of the appointment. Would we be able to get an electric wheelchair to help her get around a bit easier? Perhaps they'd arrange for a professional carer to come in a few days a week.

Suddenly, I was snapped out of my thoughts.

*BEEEEEEEEEEP.*

A buzzer pierced the stuffy silence of the waiting room. I looked at the 'next patient' screen and saw my name with the instruction to make my way to room five. I stood up, walked across the surgery and tapped politely on the designated door.

'Come in,' said a friendly voice. As she slowly spun her swivel chair to face the door, I could see the doctor was in her early fifties, wearing her warm auburn curls pinned in a loose twist. Her tortoiseshell hairclip and oversized maroon wool cardigan reminded me of my primary school art teacher.

'Thanks,' I replied, slipping around the door and taking a seat in the plastic chair next to her desk.

Then it began.

'So Rochelle, why are you here today?' she asked.

'Well, my mum has been diagnosed with a brain tumour. I don't know if there's really anything you can do to help, but I was wondering about a Carer's Assessment...' I started, half apologising for even daring to ask for support.

I wasn't hopeful that anything would come of it – after all, I hadn't had much luck up to this point.

'I see,' she said, nodding. 'So how long has your mum been ill?'

*Here we go again. Same old...* I thought.

'Sooo, she's had symptoms for around six months but only been officially diagnosed the last three,' I rattled off quickly, my brain shifting into automatic pilot.

'Right, OK,' she responded, tapping away at her keyboard, noting what I had said. 'And how did this all start?'

A monologue of events started making its way out of my mouth, a smooth flow of words rolling from my lips as I relaxed into my pre-prepared script.

'Well, in November Mum was diagnosed with a TIA but she didn't seem to be improving,' I began, just as I always did. 'So we went back to the hospital, they did some tests and it turns out she never had a mini-stroke. It was a brain tumour all along.

Incurable,' I continued, completely matter-of-fact. 'I moved back home from London to help look after her, as my youngest sister is still at school and my other sister is at uni, so I couldn't really leave her to manage on her own...'

'Do you have any other family at home?' she asked, gently.

'No,' I said. 'It's just the four of us. My dad died of cancer about ten years ago.'

'Oh. I'm so sorry,' she replied, concern flickering across her face. But I barely flinched and instead kept churning out the list of events, one after another.

'It's fine. I'm mostly managing with everything. I just wondered if there's any help available, you know, that might make things a bit easier. It seems like recently every time I phone to organise something for Mum, they say I need a Carer's Assessment first so—'

Suddenly, she cut in.

'This must be really hard for you,' she offered, softly. 'You're having to be a mother to your sisters and your mum. It's a lot of responsibility for someone so young.'

I opened my mouth to reply but nothing came out. I was silent, stunned, struggling to find any words.

*This is off-script*, I thought to myself as I swallowed away the lump in my throat, cast my eyes downwards and tried to ignore the way my heart felt as if it was about to pump straight out of my chest.

I wasn't used to doctors or consultants considering my place in all this. They usually just asked about Mum's care. I looked back up and caught her gentle gaze.

'Err, yeah,' I stuttered. 'I guess, but it's OK, we're doing fine.'

I fought to get back to my familiar spiel, but then she tilted her head a little to the side, and really *looked* into my eyes.

'You say you moved here when your mum got sick?' she delved. 'Did you grow up in Ipswich?'

'Well, no. Mum moved here while I was at uni in Leeds,' I replied. 'I'd actually just moved to London to take a job there, but then everything happened with Mum and...' I tailed off.

'Oh, so all your friends live far away, too?' she queried, already guessing the answer. 'You poor thing. And I bet with your dad not being around, you're trying to be an emotional support to your mum, when really you want her to support you, right?'

The kindness in her voice winded me all over again. I didn't know what to say. I never predicted these questions. I hadn't rehearsed for this. No one had ever asked me about this side of things before. Not once. Before I even had chance to respond, she looked me straight in the eye and gave her head a slight, slow shake.

'I would hate to think of one of my daughters having to go through this,' she added.

As the soothing, sympathetic sentences tumbled out of her mouth, something unexpected happened. I'd been keeping myself inside a protective bubble for months now, making sure I never fully came into contact with reality – but then it popped. Right there and then. It popped.

I suddenly became acutely aware of my surroundings.

My heartbeat was now not only in my chest but my head too. And my hands. And my feet. My whole body was pulsating. As the blood rushed through my veins, I could feel a flush of red rising up, first turning my chest crimson, then my face.

I heard my own voice saying something I'd never admitted before.

'I don't know how much longer I can keep going like this,' I croaked.

Looking after Mum, the house, the girls. Dealing with my emotions, needing support where there was none.

*It was hard. Really hard.*

After months of soldiering on, telling the story and getting on with it, I realised – this wasn't just a script, a list of facts that had happened. This was my life. It was really happening. To me. To *my* family.

*And not for the first time either.*

Speaking to the GP, I finally saw the full picture through someone else's eyes. A sad, sorry story that I knew would break my heart if I heard it told about a friend. What's more, her gentle reassurance and acknowledgement of just how bad things were, was exactly what Mum would have been doing if it was something else causing me all this pain. She was giving me the care and support that I desperately longed for from my mum, but which was impossible to get.

Tears started streaming down my face, wild, uncontrollable, with a life force all of their own. I drifted away into my own little world, forgetting I was in a GP surgery with an allotted ten minutes, and for the first time I let myself feel it all. Three times I tried to pull myself together enough to get my words out. But I couldn't. The grief had temporarily taken over.

Pulling tissues out of the box on her desk, like a magician grabbing an endless chain of fabric from his sleeve, I told her everything.

How scared I was to lose Mum after what happened to Dad.

How I worried I wasn't doing enough to help her.

How I couldn't sleep at night concerned how Mum must feel knowing she was going to die soon.

How I wondered whether me and my sisters would all get cancer and die young now that both our parents had had it.

Each statement prompted another question from her – all of them about *me* and how *I* was feeling. Not the ins and outs of the cancer, nor the logistics of looking after Mum. For the first time since all this started, I felt like someone was listening. Not just to my words, but to the meaning beneath them.

She was listening to *me*.

She had opened the floodgates, holding space for me to pour all my worldly worries onto her desk so that she could then soak them up into her computer screen.

Once I was silent, she spoke. 'I will do my best to make sure we get you the support you need,' she said. 'I'm going to send the referral off today so someone from social services will be in touch with you, probably in the next week to ten days. You'll talk to them about how you help your mum on a day-to-day basis, what you struggle with, that kind of thing. Then they'll let you know what specific support they can offer.'

Her unwavering kindness almost prompted a fresh wave of tears, but I managed to keep them at bay. I took a deep breath, swallowed down hard and blew my nose with yet another tissue. Then I retreated back into my protective bubble, mentally sealing it back around me. Safely cocooned inside my invisible armour, I was ready to once more dissociate from the reality of my situation, fake smile plastered on my face.

'I'm fine, really. Really, I'm fine,' I tried to assure her, unconvincingly. 'I'll wait for social services to get in touch. But really it's fine.'

Out of the corner of my eye, I caught sight of the empty tissue box.

'Oh, and I'm sorry for finishing all your tissues,' I added, trying to lighten the mood as I picked my bag up off the floor and scurried out of the door. I walked out briskly, head down pretending to look at my phone, hoping nobody in the waiting room would see how red my eyes were and that I'd been crying. The practical outcomes of the appointment were minimal. A free gym pass I used once or twice, some leaflets on being a young carer, and advice on filling out the benefits claims forms I had already struggled through alone. But it had a huge emotional impact. I realised that becoming a carer means you are suddenly a voice for someone else. And often when that happens, you lose your own voice in the process, forgetting that you too need care and support.

I didn't realise it at the time, but that appointment was my first true act of self-care after moving home to look after Mum. Yes, I'd gone on a spa day with my then-boyfriend and treated myself to a shopping spree in the January sales – but they fell far short of the help I needed. They were superficial acts. Plasters on a gaping wound. Up until that point I had held off getting a Carer's Assessment – or any kind of help really – because admitting I couldn't do it all alone felt like admitting I was failing in my duty to look after Mum.

It's funny because the final push to book that appointment came out of nowhere really. Somewhere between radiotherapy sessions, household chores and hours spent on hold to some council department or another, I found myself rummaging around the garage, trying to find our long-abandoned toasted sandwich machine (to satisfy Mum's latest random craving). While I never did find the toastie maker, I did stumble across my old Business Studies textbook. Flicking open the familiar yet forgotten black and green cover, I suddenly remembered how case study after case study spoke about the importance of leveraging other people's skills.

In business terms, that means getting someone else to do

the stuff that 'just anyone' can do, so that you've got time to focus on the tasks only you can do. Think of it like this. Karren Brady doesn't spend her time cleaning her offices and ordering paper for the photocopier. No. She gets other people to do that, so that she can focus on making big strategic decisions and attending important meetings. As a young carer, your time and energy are precious resources. Treat them like Karren Brady treats hers and remember this one vital thing:

**You can't do it all yourself. And you don't have to**

Stepping back, I realised that I needed to take the emotion out of asking for help. I shouldn't have seen it as a failure in my responsibilities, but instead as a business decision. Over time I learned to reframe asking for (and accepting) help as a strength. The more I thought about it, the more it made sense to delegate 'boring' tasks like ironing, cooking and chasing appointments to friends, family, or even paying for outside help. That way I had more time to look after Mum, my sisters and – not forgetting – myself.

I still find it hard to ask for help today, but when I slip into old ways and take on too much, I remind myself that if royalty, presidents, CEOs and Beyoncé have a team of people working to support them, there must be something to it. Sharing the heavy load of being a carer with other people frees up time for the most important thing of all: looking after yourself and spending time with the person you are caring for. Asking for help isn't a failure, it's fuel to help you keep going. The ultimate act of self-care.

I wish I could tell you that once you realise you don't *have* to do it all yourself, everything falls into place and self-care becomes easy. But when your 'business decision' to ask for help is inextricably linked to looking after someone you love, it's not quite so simple.

Despite being praised at the appointment for how well I was coping, in the weeks that followed, I drifted into a deep darkness. I kept telling myself it would pass, with the same monotonous mantra I'd spouted as I left the appointment still endlessly looping through my brain: *I'm fine. We're fine.*

But the more I repeated it, the more I knew it wasn't true.

The doctor made me see what was really happening to us, not the story I'd been telling myself. She didn't disclose anything I didn't already know. There were no lies. No untruths. No exaggerations. She simply joined the dots that had been there all along and talked me through the scene she had drawn.

The problem was, I wasn't prepared to see myself in the picture.

When I finally did, reality hit hard.

From the moment I walked out of that appointment, my head felt as though it was clamped between an ever-tightening vice. I had heart palpitations as if a thousand butterflies with concrete wings were trying to escape from my chest and it took all my energy to move from the foetal position on top of my bed to under the covers. And Mum? I could barely even look at her without dissolving into tears.

After finally seeing the truth of my situation, time became one long, fuzzy blur. My internal calendar no longer had neat boxes of distinct days. Life became a continuous smudge across the page, a blur except for a few common themes.

*The routine of medication.*

*The rawness of heartbreak.*

*The relentlessness of my love for my mum.*

# DOES SELF-CARE MAKE YOU A SELFISH CARER?

The hardest thing about making time to look after yourself when you're caring for someone else is that no matter what it is – a holiday, a bath or ten minutes on your phone – self-care and selfishness are easily confused because they look so similar.

While I was looking after Mum a niggly, judgey voice made it its daily duty to barge into my mind and question everything I did. It taunted me with thoughts that, after Mum was gone, I'd hate myself for every moment I had spent writing a blog post or answering a text from a friend. It would torment me with the shame that future-me would feel for not spending my time making her laugh or memorising the sound of her voice so that I'd never forget it, like I had Dad's.

Worst of all. That internal voice? It was me.

Doing anything alone began to feel like wasting precious time we could be together, so I didn't give myself a moment's break. Even trivial tasks like going to the supermarket started to involve some tough emotional wrangling and even tougher judgement calls.

Shopping with Mum when she was ill took at least four times as long as doing it alone. From finding an elusive shopping trolley for wheelchair users, to trying to work out what she meant when she demanded we buy 'brown logs' (wholemeal bread rolls) or 'the dessert that can go up hills' (banoffee pie – *still trying to work that one out*). And as guilty as I feel for admitting it, it was a hassle.

Going by myself was far quicker and easier. But I could never shake the thought that once Mum was gone, I'd have the rest of my life to do Tesco trips alone. Shouldn't I make the most of being able to go with her while I still could?

Already knowing what it was like to lose someone you love meant I was my harshest critic. I understood exactly what it was like to never get any more time with someone. Ever. Not even a fraction of a second.

But did looking after myself make me a selfish carer?

From the moment of Mum's diagnosis, I tried to replicate what I saw her do for Dad when he was ill, seeing it as a blueprint to work from. I told myself I had been trained for this role before anyone knew there would be a vacancy. Yet even if I hadn't, the tacit job description for any carer is clear: *Put your life on hold and focus on the wants and needs of the person who is ill.*

I understand my logic of trying to repeat what I'd seen: If Mum survived looking after Dad by doing XYZ, then I'll survive looking after her by doing XYZ too. But looking back, I realise I was blindly following the instructions to build a bookcase, with a box of flat-pack parts to make a bed. You see, there was a fundamental flaw in my panicked plan to simply copy what fourteen-year-old me saw my mum doing for my dad.

Burnt-out, twenty-five-year-old me was mimicking what my younger self had *perceived* my mum to be doing. What I *thought* I saw. The bits I *chose* to remember. Things like her being with Dad about twenty-two out of twenty-four hours each day and sleeping in a hospital chair at his bedside. Those were the bits I focused on replicating. But the fact my grandparents moved in to look after us three girls so she could be with Dad? The likelihood that she shielded me from some things? The near certainty there was plenty I had completely forgotten? I didn't take *any* of that into account.

I was treating it as a like-for-like situation, when the reality was more a case of 'same, same – but different.'

Yes, they both had cancer. Yes, they both had terminal diagnoses. But that's where the similarities ended. Everything else was different. The timescales. The physical symptoms. The mental effects. The prognosis. The treatment options. The legal and financial implications. The support systems available. What's more, the impact on me of Mum getting sick was very different to that which Dad's illness had on Mum. Losing a husband and losing a parent are two very different things.

But you can't always see that when you're in it.

In fact, there were a lot of things I couldn't see back then. As a carer, I was tasked with always (at least that's how it felt) putting the wellbeing of my loved one before my own. I didn't realise that I was allowed to look after myself – let alone prioritise me. I thought that went against the job description. Selfish. Self-indulgent.

That's why it haunted me whenever I dropped Mum at hospice day-care sessions. I took her on Thursdays for four hours. For those 240 minutes, I'd make it to the surface of the water I'd been drowning in all week and take a long, deep gulp of air to see me through the next seven days. It was vital to my survival, but months into the routine, it still felt like a selfish act, despite people constantly trying to tell me otherwise. People like Sandy, one of the hospice nurses.

Wheeling Mum into the recreation room, I kissed her on the cheek and said, 'Are you *sure* you're OK? It's only for a few hours.'

In typical Mum-style, she didn't utter a word but shot me a look that said, *I'd much rather be at home, Rochelle, but you've dragged me here now.*

On my way out, the same pangs of guilt gnawed away at me as they always did. Only, this week, it must have been showing on my face too, because Sandy took me to one side as I was making my way out.

'How are you, Rochelle?' she asked.

'Yeah, you know. Ups and downs, good days and bad,' I responded with a half-smile, hoping it would satisfy her and she'd let me get on my way.

*Not today.*

'Are you sure? Are you finding the time to look after yourself as well as your mum?' she asked. 'You know it's OK to put yourself and your needs first sometimes. It's like what they say about oxygen masks when you're on a plane...'

I rolled my eyes so far back in my head that I feared I'd swallow them. Honestly, by that point I was so fed up of people telling me how important it was to look after myself, and I was particularly sick of hearing that same analogy over and over again.

But I bit my tongue.

'You know when the safety video tells you to put your oxygen mask on before helping others,' she explained. 'It's the same with you and your mum. You need to make sure you're OK before you can help her.'

Suddenly, I snapped. You see, I *got* it. I wasn't thick. I knew what she was getting at, but I just didn't think the logic applied to me and my situation.

'Yes, but I'm healthy and Mum's not so she needs the oxygen more than me,' I started. 'I can just hold my breath while I put hers on.'

Not content with just making my point, I pushed even further.

'In fact, I've got two hands, so really I should be able to put them on both of us at the same time,' I added. Was it sarcasm? Perhaps, but it also sounded very much like my inner critic having a sly dig that I *couldn't* do both things at once.

After a millisecond of silence, the nurse's kind eyes holding my gaze, she spoke again.

'I understand,' she said. 'Just remember that it's OK to look after number one sometimes.'

With a half-hearted nod and tears welling up in my eyes, I turned and walked away. I still remember the wave of shame that washed over me as I turned the corridor corner. I felt horrible for being short with her, not to mention embarrassed for clearly taking the metaphor too far. But it still didn't change my mind. I just didn't get how nobody seemed to understand that my 'number one' wasn't me. It was my mum. She'd been my 'number one' since the moment of her diagnosis and I knew that she would be until she didn't need me anymore.

For someone who usually picks up things quickly, I was remarkably slow at grasping the concept of self-care. It wasn't until a couple of years later, around eight months after Mum died, that I finally realised what the nurse had been trying to get through to me that day.

On a nondescript Tuesday morning, I got lost down an Instagram scroll-hole and spotted a quote.

*You can't give from an empty cup.*

That was all it took for the penny to drop. This simple statement highlighted what the oxygen mask analogy failed to convey. We all have a finite supply of energy that naturally drains away, even under normal circumstances. Which is why, when you're going through a period of stress, you need to be even more careful because it's like having a cup with a hole in it. The greater your stress, the bigger the hole. Getting through each day zaps your mental and physical energy as quickly as water leaks from that cup. This is true for everyone. But as a carer, it's a double whammy. Not only has your cup got a hole in it, but the person you're looking after is drinking from it as well as you.

Back when the nurse pulled me aside at the hospice, my cup certainly did not runneth over. I barely had a drop left – for me or for Mum.

While I knew at the time I was struggling to cope, I still couldn't see self-care as anything but a selfish act. But after coming across that Instagram quote, I realised that everything I'd heard about the importance of self-care – all the talk of meeting up with friends, getting enough sleep, eating well and taking time out – it wasn't about being selfish or self-indulgent, it was about self-preservation.

Filling your cup, so to speak.

And the motivation for keeping your cup full?

*To make sure you can keep looking after the person you love.*

As a carer, you need to make a conscious and consistent effort to top up your cup whenever you can. Without frequent refills, it won't be long until it's dry.

**How can you give your loved one a drink when they get thirsty, if all you've got is an empty cup?**

## THE 'SHOULD' TRAP

I put the brakes on Mum's wheelchair, took a seat next to her in the hospital waiting room and grabbed a book to pass the time until we were called to see her oncologist.

The electric blue cover of *The Power of Now* in one hand and a lukewarm machine coffee in the other, I wriggled to get comfortable in the right-angled, standard issue hospital chair. As I turned the pages, I began to lose myself in the author's words.

In the book, Eckhart Tolle explains how moments we experience are the direct result of the choices we've made about how to spend them. At any given point, we can take an action which has the power to change the course of our lives for ever.

That's when I realised.

Just like Paddy McGuinness would say to a *Take Me Out* contestant: *the power is in your hands*.

As a carer, I was forever falling into The Should Trap – telling myself that I *should* be learning a new language, *should* be repainting the kitchen, or *should* be taking up yoga – and then getting annoyed with myself for not doing it.

But the *not doing* wasn't actually the problem.

You see, I *had* been taking action. The action to *not* take any action.

When it comes to daily decisions, whatever you're not changing, you're choosing. If something is important to you, you'll find a way. If it's not, you'll find an excuse. Obviously, I'm not talking about the big stuff. There's no action I could have taken to singlehandedly get rid of Mum's cancer. No, I'm talking about the mountain of shoulds I told myself I had to scale each day (and then inevitably failed to do so), the one made of infinite niggly to dos.

As a carer it's overwhelming to cope with all the things you *have* to do, let alone beating yourself up over stuff you feel you *should* be doing. But I didn't know that back then, so as Mum's illness progressed, the physical, mental and emotional strain of caring for her became unbearable. I was exhausted and desperate to find a way to recharge, but I ignored that need and put myself under pressure to carry on pushing.

Becoming a carer made the voice of my inner critic ten times louder. I called her Jessica. And she would take daily delight in delivering judgements like an irritating know-it-all work colleague.

I imagined Jessica – *Jessss-Ick-Arrrr* as I pronounced it in my head – wasn't senior staff but she thought she was because she'd worked there two months longer than me and her dad knew the MD. She loved to play with her hair and had a permanent Insta-influencer smile plastered on her face as she pointed out all my failings.

'*Is that pile of ironing still there?*' she would tut.

'*Why haven't you gone to that HIIT class like you said you would?*' she'd say in a whiny fake American accent. '*That's three weeks in a row you've missed it.*'

'*What's that? A takeaway menu?*' she liked to drone with an eye roll. '*Would it really be that difficult to get yourself organised and batch cook some healthy food to freeze? Surely even you have heard of meal prep, you lazy cow?*'

Every time she piped up, my response would be the same.

'She's right.'

I should have finished the ironing.

I should have gone to the HIIT class.

I should be batch cooking for the family.

Should. Should. Should.

I couldn't see it then, but when I used the word 'should', more times than not, I was putting myself under pressure to do something I didn't really need and/or want to do. When you are caring for someone, chances are you're never going to get it all done (at least not right away). By prefixing everything with *should* I was keeping near-impossible volumes of tasks hanging over me as 'evidence' I was a failure who lets people down and who wasn't being a good carer.

I wish I'd given myself a break.

Left that pile of ironing.

Skipped the HIIT class.

Decided not to cook and have the takeaway instead.

Looking back I can see that, instead of berating me, Jessss-Ick-Arrrr would have been better off telling me to be clear with myself about what I was going to do (or not do) and to then go for it – 100 per cent. Once I committed to my course of action (or inaction) for the day, Jessss-Ick-Arrrr would have reminded me there was no feeling guilty about it. I was free to enjoy my choice.

If she had, life would have looked a bit more like this…

If I woke up one Wednesday and the world felt too much, I'd give myself permission for a full-on slob-out-a-thon. I'm talking a lie-in, followed by *This Morning* and a bit of *Loose Women*. I'm talking an afternoon nap wrapped in my duvet on the sofa, staying in my PJs all day, not even bothering to have a shower. I'm talking a full-on Netflix binge, ordering Domino's and having a glass or two of wine while I wait for it to be delivered. More importantly, I'd have permission to LOVE every lazy moment of the day. Under no circumstances would I be allowed to spend it thinking, *Right one more episode then I'll do the hoovering* or *I'll do the ironing while I'm watching this* or *I really should get up in a minute and wash my hair*.

The key is to make your decision, then delight in it.

Of course, the opposite is also true. Once I'd recharged and had the energy, it would have been better to go all-out and be super-productive, burning through my to-do list. No coming out of the shower, sitting on my bed in a towel then realising I'd spent fifteen minutes scrolling Instagram. No making a new Spotify holiday playlist even though there was no chance of going anywhere for months. No hours spent making a dream wedding board on Pinterest when I didn't even have a boyfriend...

Consider the task. Decide. Then do.

Scrapping 'should' – that ominous grey cloud of the English language which looms, threatening to ruin everything – allows so much guilt to dissipate and so many mental burdens to be shrugged off. Your world becomes filled with 'will' and 'won't'. You *finally* give yourself permission to take a break – and it's that break which allows you to recharge and go further than you could have done before.

## MENTAL HEALTH –vs– MENTAL WELLNESS

Self-care and mental health are inextricably linked. I get that. I understand the direct correlation between the two. Which is why it's so worrying that in our wellbeing-obsessed world, self-care has been transformed into the latest glossy trend. It often feels like we're one more baby-goat yoga class away from forgetting the difference between mental health and mental wellness. For me, the distinction is much the same as the one between physical health and physical wellbeing.

Say it's flu season. You're fit and healthy but take an echinacea supplement, buy some antibacterial hand gel and have a Prêt Vitamin Volcano smoothie for breakfast. You do this to *keep* yourself well and put you in a stronger position if you do catch something. It's a pretty sensible course of action. But what about if you've already got the flu and have chronic asthma? Those suggestions soon become pretty useless. Nobody would expect some blended fruit and germ-killing gel to 'fix' you when you're two days deep into a raging fever, non-stop sneezing and a tickly cough that won't shift. You're more likely to turn to Nurofen and Night Nurse.

With physical illness, we understand the things we do to *avoid* getting sick are different to those we need to *recover* after already getting struck down. Why can't we lend the same understanding to our emotional wellbeing? Self-care is a great way to maintain your mental wellbeing. But, to me, struggling with your mental health is a whole different ballgame.

We all have mental health. It can be good or bad, depending on a whole range of internal and external factors, from being overworked or underpaid to relationship break-ups and family breakdowns.

I absolutely agree that trauma and tragedy are not a competition; after all, it's just as bad to drown in one metre of water as it is to drown in six metres of water. And I'm all for people speaking more openly about their emotions – destigmatising mental health is long overdue. But when people talk about mental health on social media, they often forget it's a sliding scale.

There's a difference between *feeling meh* for a while and needing to focus on self-care, and mental health issues that demand far more than what you see suggested on the socials.

Instagram-brand self-care can be very misleading when you are deep in the darkness of a mental health struggle. This is particularly true when you're a carer because, statistically speaking, you're more likely to be in a worse state of mental health than other people your age who don't have a caring responsibility. When you're looking after a loved one who is seriously ill, you already have three million other things to worry about, so it's easy to brush over the internal struggles you're having, convincing yourself you just need more sleep or a spa day to sort yourself out.

Is it too much to ask that 'mental health' stops being used as the hook to tout monthly subscription boxes with monogrammed scented candles and unique tea blends? Those things might be just what you need for sustained mental *wellness*, but they're barely going to scratch the surface of an ongoing mental *health* issue.

I first picked up on this issue about a year after moving home to care for Mum. Scrolling absent-mindedly through Instagram, I saw a reality TV star posting about her mental health. The caption was peppered with emojis and hashtags explaining how much she struggled to share the photo of herself in her #gifted underwear because 'I don't like the way my arms look in it and I'm not wearing any make-up'.

I would have been better off skipping past it but couldn't resist a peek at the comments. As I looked through the responses, my skin prickled with irritation. There were thousands of comments telling her how 'brave' and 'inspirational' she was for 'finding the courage' to post a photo of herself with 'no make-up'.

*That's if you don't count the fake tan, micro-bladed eyebrows, lash extensions, lip filler and acrylics on her nails,* I scoffed.

At this point, I could best describe the state of my life as 'falling apart like a Cadbury's Flake'. Every single area – friendships, family, career, finances, body image, relationships – was plummeting sharply. I had gone beyond rock bottom, my knees still bleeding from the rocks I hit on the way down, and there was no sign of stopping my dramatic descent, let alone working out how to turn things around. I was shouting into the void, begging for help – from the GP, from friends, from family – but all that came back was the echo of my own voice, making me feel even more alone. Nobody was able to do or say anything to make life any less spectacularly crappy.

The post niggled away at me all day but I couldn't quite work out why.

*Was I jealous? Did I begrudge her the attention?*

In the end, I realised, yes. I did – but not in the way you might think.

I wasn't jealous of the replies where hundreds of people typed 'thinking of you hun' or 'babe you're so strong'. None of that would have made the slightest difference to my situation, let alone pulled me out of my dark hole of despair.

So, I wasn't jealous of *her* as such.

I was jealous that society seemed to 'approve' of and fawn over her mental health struggles, but not my own. I was jealous of her and her fellow influencers gaining clout for their shiny, palatable take on mental health when the reality of my mental health was dull and unappealing.

I was jealous that when she had a tough day, she took the afternoon off work for a vegan lunch in a trendy Notting Hill café before picking up a new Free People dress. But my tough days consisted of a few bites of a tasteless hospital canteen sandwich and a swig of Ribena taken after watching my mum be violently sick from her latest round of chemo.

I was jealous when she managed to get a last-minute appointment with her 'amaaaaazing therapist', because the week before, I'd finally worked up the courage to ask my GP for counselling, only to be told that I'd be on a four- to six-month waiting list because I wasn't suicidal, so I wasn't a priority.

I was jealous that while she wore her #gifted mix and match leisurewear in her carefully curated #ad about a mini at-home spa break, I was sat with my greasy hair scraped back in a ponytail, eyelids red raw from crying and my bathroom cabinet decidedly devoid of any miracle skincare regime to save them, so I had to make do with a slick of Vaseline from an old pot I found in the car.

I was jealous that when it all got too much for her, she could livestream her sobs and monetise her tears. But when I cried myself to sleep for the 293rd night in a row, I was as quiet as possible so that Mum, Hannah and Olivia couldn't hear because I didn't want to add my struggles to their own. All while waiting for my weekly £55.55 carer's allowance to hit my bank account. No #aflinks or #sponcon to get the money rolling in for me.

I was jealous that there was no way for me to put a glossy veneer on the depression my situation brought with it. This 'picture-perfect' poster girl for mental health, and other influencers like her, were getting what I desperately needed, and it felt like there was none left over for me.

While I know it's not a competition, I felt sad that my voice – and the voices of thousands of young carers like me – were drowned out by their shouts. Society seemed to skim over *our* reality of living with mental health struggles, simply expecting us to fix ourselves.

## MAKE MINE A SELF-CARE COCKTAIL

Fed up and feeling rejected by the healthcare system which didn't deem me worthy of counselling, I decided to try some of the self-care advice I'd seen online, naively believing that a green juice and meditation app would somehow make the whole situation bearable. Each time I came across something which sounded useful, I'd note it down on my phone and, after a week or so, decide to give it all a go. My efforts at self-care went a bit like this:

Monday: *Meditate for 15 minutes – FAIL.*

*Left*: Mum and Dad before us kids came along, sneaking a kiss at the first business they owned together – a pub called The Carousel in Lowestoft, Suffolk.

*Right*: An early picture of me and Mum with her very 80s hairstyle. Lowestoft, Suffolk.

*Left:* Celebrating Christmas with the family at Grandma and Granddad's.

*Right:* Me on my dad's shoulders during an evening stroll on holiday in Portugal.

*Above*: Hannah and I on Southwold beach on a seemingly endless summer day.

*Below* Fun in the sun! Learning to write in the sand with Mum on holiday in Praia da Rocha, Portugal.

*Below*: Olivia, just a few months old, being held by mum on her first holiday at Center Parcs in Elveden Forest.

*Above*: Sisterly love! Me, Hannah and Olivia together at our childhood home.

*Below*: Family fun during simpler times. The five of us (and one very big cuddly toy) having loads of laughs together as we always did.

*Above*: Testing out my (very dodgy) face-painting skillsaDad in the garden, with Hannah.

*Above*: Obligatory 'back to school' photoshoot in the garden with my sisters.

*Above*: Love amidst heartbreak- Mum and Dad cutting the cake at their wedding, held in the hospital chapel just over two weeks before Dad died.

*Above*: A day-trip to Norwich for lunch at Grandma and Granddad's.

*Below right*: A Christmas to remember – Me, Mum, Olivia and Hannah visiting Discovery Cove in Orlando, Florida on Christmas Day 2009.

*Above left*: Mum and me at my graduation in July 2007.

*Above*: A bucket-list moment for Mum as she swam with dolphins at Discovery Cove in Florida.

*Left*: Grandma, Hannah, me, Mum and Olivia having dinner at a restaurant on holiday in Side, Turkey.

*Right*: Mum taking a champagne break on a girls' shopping trip to Westfield, London.

*Left*: Breakfast in bed – Celebrating Mother's Day on holiday in Tunisia in 2003.

*Right*: Olivia getting stuck into some cake to celebrate Mum's birthday, just six weeks before her stroke diagnosis.

*Below*: Olivia and Hannah visiting Mum in Ipswich Hospital, the day before we found out she had cancer.

*Above*: Lewis Hamilton watch out! Mum was having trouble steering the mobility scooter on holiday in Spain so Olivia had to sit on her lap and ride it back to our hotel.

*Below* As Mum's tumour progressed she lost the use of her right side so we had to help her with everyday tasks like brushing her teeth.

*Above*: Me by Mum's bedside at Addenbrooke's Hospital just after she had come out of surgery for her biopsy.

*Left:* The three of us have been through so much together, but we still manage to have fun (usually with the help of a Prosecco or two).

*Right:* Olivia, Hannah and Me ready to head out for roast on one of our 'Sister Sundays'.

*Above left:* When life feels too much, I think back to happier times with Mum and for a brief second, I get lost in my memories and forget that she's gone.

Right: Off for a birthday meal, with my sisters by my side, at Sheesh in Chigwell.

Tuesday: *Do a purifying face pack and nourishing hair mask – FAIL.*

Wednesday: *Start the Couch to 5k plan – FAIL (unless you count downloading the app a win).*

The things that were meant to be building me up and making me 'better' just dragged me down further into depression. Not only was I failing at making my mum better, failing at being a girlfriend, failing at holding my friendships together and failing at clearing the ironing pile, I was now also failing at doing self-care 'right'.

And so, on top of everything else, I began to think something must be wrong with me.

That I couldn't even do self-care properly.

*Everyone else is happy after a barre class and some journaling, Rochelle,* I'd tell myself. *You're so lazy. You really need to motivate yourself to do a workout like other people. Stop using looking after Mum and keeping the house clean as an excuse.*

According to Instagram, everyone else found it easy to get rid of any heavy feelings that were dragging them down. The ones I felt too. Yet I couldn't shake them, no matter how many scented candles I burnt or yoga sessions I did.

It took a while for it to click, but the real reason none of the advice I saw online was working was because the tips and tricks I was trying were *preventative*. I was *already* struggling, sliding fast and free down the mental health scale. I was balancing precariously at a point where I needed a remedy or an intervention, something like counselling or consistent daily support with my caring duties.

Social media self-care, with its saccharine-sweet, peppy doses of advice in quotable format are all well and good, but for a young carer, they just don't work. Time and time again I'd come across Insta-advice that people swore had solved all their problems, but which was woefully inadequate for the situation I found myself in. Things like:

**'Just love yourself and those around you'**
Great, thanks. Any advice on what to do when your problems stem from the fact you deeply, deeply love those around you but fate has decided you have to watch them suffer?

**'Just keep positive'**
Okay, just one question. How do you stay positive while watching the woman you love most in the world slowly die in front of you?

**'Ignore the haters'**
Cool, but my 'haters' are experienced oncology consultants telling me to stop searching for alternative treatments and the government writing to say Mum doesn't qualify for a stairlift grant because she wasn't expected to live long enough to pass their eligibility threshold. How do I ignore them?

As well as the self-care soundbites, there are the influencers who swear a face mask and a cheeky kombucha is all you need to *'turn that frown upside down'*. They're the same ones who claim a chilled night in watching Netflix in new pyjamas, is all they need to get themselves *'out of a funk and back on track again'*.

Posts like these used to leave me feeling a whole load of things. None of them helpful. I felt envious, lacking, angry, irritated, unseen, frustrated, lazy, pathetic. But above all, I felt – and still do sometimes – not good enough.

Eventually, I came to the unscientific but nevertheless certain conclusion that self-care was a load of crap. I felt lied to. Every article, blog post and influencer worth their crystals charged under the full moon seemed to talk about these techniques like they were silver bullets that could turn my whole life around.

I wasn't so much annoyed with what people recommended you do during a stressful time. I could see the arguments for the healing benefits of everything from knitting to napping. It's more what they claimed it would do for you. And that's because I still wasn't making the important distinction between mental *health* and mental *wellness*. The things that help when you're feeling 'a bit down' are not, and never will be, the same things that can 'fix' clinical depression or anxiety.

But all of this did trigger one really useful revelation. One evening, while I was still on my self-care binge, working through all the shiny recommendations, I drew the curtains, lit a candle in my room and told myself that tonight I'd actually do a 'goddess hour'. I'd read somewhere about blocking out the hour before bed for some phone-free pamper time where you 'treat yourself like a goddess'. Apparently, it was meant to help you to unwind, sleep better and teach you that you're important.

*Blah, blah, blah.*

I gave it a go, but I only got as far as moisturising one leg before my patience ran out. I blew out the overpriced candle, got straight into bed and picked up my phone.

*Who am I kidding?* I thought. *Goddess hour? I need a decade of pampering before I begin to look or feel anywhere near a goddess. Goblin minute seems more apt.*

Suddenly focused, I decided to temper my expectations, stop

171

wasting my time and get realistic. Opening up the Notes app on my phone, I wrote:

> **READ BEFORE READING/BUYING/TRYING ANYTHING ELSE!!!!!**
> Nothing that you, or anyone else, can say, do, read, burn, drink, eat, or take a class in is going to make the process of losing Mum easy, enjoyable or even OK. Stop trying to be, do, or feel normal in an abnormal situation.

Silently, I read my note back a few times and let out a deep sigh of relief. In those few lines, I'd admitted how awful it all was. But rather than scaring me, acknowledging it gave me an instant sense of freedom.

I'd been feeling down. Really down. More down than I'd ever been. Then just when I thought I couldn't get any more down, I would fall another level. On my self-care mission, I'd been blaming myself for that. I was convinced something I was doing was stopping me from fixing myself, certain there must be something wrong with me.

But there wasn't.

### It was the situation that was wrong

In that moment, something shifted at such a deep level of my psyche that I felt it in my body. Lying in bed, I finally gave myself permission to stop trying to fix the unfixable. My shoulders dropped from where they'd been scrunched up by my ears and my eyelids fell heavy. I relinquished responsibility for having to be perfect at self-care as well as everything else.

That night I slept longer and deeper than I had in months.

In the days that followed, I shunned anything self-care related, re-reading my *note to self* whenever I got tempted by a lightweight folding meditation stool or a deep-sleep pillow mist. But something still niggled away at me: *Why do I keep getting drawn to these products when I know they can't fix anything?*

One evening, I got my answer...

I was making Mum's lemon squash – its sharp acidity the only thing her taste buds could register at the time. I poured the cordial, then ran the tap for a while so the water was ice cold – just how she liked it. As I topped up the long glass, I watched the two liquids hazily merge. And it made me wonder.

*Had I been too black and white with this self-care stuff?*

Maybe I should be treating it more like cocktail-making.

The shock of diagnosis, the disorienting reality of being a caregiver, the ominous spectre of what the future holds – that was a triple shot of the cheapest, nastiest, strongest vodka. Moments of self-care are like adding a splash of your favourite mixer.

2 x glugs of meditation

1 x spritz of FaceTime with a friend

1 x generous dash of a neck massage

They don't make the vodka taste particularly pleasant, of course. None of them stop the burn as it goes down. But they make it a little bit more palatable. *Maybe making my own self-care cocktail might mean I'm able to down this week's vodka, without it taking me down too*, I pondered, as I carried Mum's drink to her.

The thought fresh in my mind, I got out my phone and opened the Notes app once again. This time, I wrote the title 'Rescuing Rochelle'. Underneath it I started listing everything, big and small, that I'd found helped me feel even a little bit better. A perfectly tailored shopping list of self-care resources that I could pick and choose from, according to my mood when I felt I needed a boost.

- A guided meditation on YouTube
- A lie down with my weighted blanket
- Watching old cartoons I loved when I was little
- Smelling Mum's perfume
- When anxious – breathe in for 4 counts, hold for 7 counts and exhale for 8 counts

I knew that what helped one day, might not the next. I also realised that complete improvement wasn't the goal. A 5 per cent lift was what I was aiming for, but even a 2 per cent progression would do. Anything that would mean that when I slumped into bed at the end of the day, I might be on 55 per cent rather than 40.

As the weeks went by, I kept adding to my list. Likewise, if I tried something and it didn't work, I deleted it without any sense of failure.

Self-care isn't selfish. But nor is it a wonder cure. Rather, it's a remedy. A reliever. A dash of sweet mixer in the bitter cocktail that life has served you.

You might be responsible for the care of another, but that doesn't mean you can't care for yourself. You still need – *deserve* – something to make *your* life better while you're making *their* life better.

# 7.

# Friendship

## MY 'RIDE WHILE DIES'

Sitting at the desk in my bedroom, I was listening to Aretha Franklin's cover of 'Let It Be' playing on repeat. Over the last week or so, fourteen-year-old me had needed her mellow tones and reassuring lyrics telling me *there will be an answer*.

I couldn't quite put my finger on it, but something was definitely off with the atmosphere at home. As if everyone was waiting for something bad to happen. Things had been strained for months, with Dad going back and forth to the hospital for tests. But recently something had shifted. Everything felt different and everyone was acting *really* strange.

*Come on, Rochelle,* I coaxed, forcing myself to focus as I searched through the verb tables in the back of my French textbook. Lost, deep in concentration, suddenly I heard:

*CREEEEEEEEEAK!*

My bedroom door squeaked open and I jumped clean out of my seat, smudging ink across my exercise book. Spinning my head round, I saw Mum standing in the doorway.

'Mum,' I gasped, bringing my hand to my chest, as my heart leapt with surprise.

'Sorry, Ro,' she replied, shutting the door behind her. 'I didn't mean to scare you.'

Mum sat on the bed and gestured for me to sit next to her. I got up from my desk as Aretha's tones were still carrying on the cool autumn air coming through my open window, telling me again *'there will be an answer'*. Making my way over, it suddenly struck me that amidst all the uncertainty, I wasn't entirely sure what question it was that I needed the answer to. But there were certainly lots of things playing on my mind.

*Why have Grandma and Granddad more or less moved into our house over the last few weeks?*

*Why hasn't Dad had any treatment? When will they give him chemo so he can get better?*

*Why did Dad break down when I took him that big collage of photos I made? I thought it would cheer him up, but I've never seen him cry like that – ever.*

I snuggled up to Mum silently, resting my head on her chest, as she wrapped a warm arm around me and planted a kiss on my head. It was the permission I needed to relax. All at once, the underlying, unspoken tensions that had been simmering away for weeks finally bubbled to the surface and before I knew it, tears were streaming down my cheeks.

This was usually the part where Mum would soothe me in the way that only mums can.

*It's all going to be OK.*

*There's nothing to worry about.*

*We're going to be fine.*

That's what I was expecting to hear. But this time her silence was deafening.

176

*Why wasn't she saying anything?*

Stomach churning, I willed her to speak, but nothing came. Then, as she cradled my head like she had so many times before, something different happened. There they were, falling slow and steady like raindrops on my hair.

Tears.

*Her tears.*

A wave of panic washed over me and the questions I'd been stuffing down, suddenly stumbled out of my mouth.

'Dad *is* going to be OK, isn't he?' I probed, raising my head to glance at her. I didn't even need her to say anything as such, rather just wanted to look at her face and *see* the reassurance I desperately craved. But as my gaze met hers, there was nothing. The trademark twinkle of her sapphire eyes had gone, replaced by a vacant stare. Suddenly, she didn't look like my mum anymore. She was a scared little girl – just like me.

In that moment, in that silence, I knew.

*Dad was dying.*

My breath shortened. But denial followed hot on the heels of knowledge.

*No. It can't be true.*

I refused to believe it. She hadn't actually said it. She hadn't announced outright that he was going to die, so I could have it wrong. I *must* have it wrong.

I pushed her to say the words that I desperately wanted to hear.

'Mum. Mum. Dad's gonna be OK, Mum, isn't he?' I asked insistently, yet quietly.

Silence.

'Mum?' I repeated, anxiously.

Still silence.

'Tell me he's gonna be OK, Mum,' I pleaded frantically, repeating myself over and over until my words were barely more than a strained murmur, trying to make their way past the lump in my throat.

Then, finally, she spoke.

'Oh my baby,' she said, looking at me, then down at the floor.

No more words followed, but her gesture spoke volumes. Slowly, she shook her head from side to side, each sway shattering my world into a thousand more tiny pieces.

*No?!*

*No, my dad wasn't going to be OK?!*

*My dad was going to die?!*

Suddenly everything started to spin as if my body and mind were on two different boats being tossed about the ocean by a violent storm. Losing all coordination and stability, the ground moved beneath me. The safety and normality my family had always provided was wrenched away in an instant and I had nothing to cling on to.

*This can't be happening.*

*This can't be true.*

*This can't be my life.*

A barrage of emotions swept over me as I struggled to compute what Mum had just told me, my body unsure of what to do as my mind wrestled with what I'd just learned. I wanted to be inside. I wanted to be outside. I wanted to be alone. I wanted to be lost in a crowd. I wanted a hug. I couldn't bear to be touched. I wanted to scream. I wanted to be silent. I wanted to hit my mum in anger. I wanted to comfort and soothe her pain.

No matter how deeply I breathed, I couldn't get enough air into my lungs and one question churned over and over in my head.

*Where could I go?*

If my heart could be broken by my own mum, in my own bedroom, in my own house, then where was I safe?

I gripped the windowsill and tried to steady myself. Looking up into the dark night sky, I was sure I could see each of the stars dropping down in turn as my universe collapsed, piece by piece, in front of me.

Then my stomach lurched.

*I was going to be sick.*

I turned around and dashed out of my bedroom towards the bathroom, hand clasped over my mouth, almost colliding with my granddad at the bottom of the stairs. As our eyes met, I realised he knew. She must have told him she was coming to tell me. And now, from the look on my face he knew that I knew, too. My lip quivered and I burst into fresh tears.

'I know you're upset,' Granddad said. 'But how do you think me and your grandma feel? That's our son.'

His words felt like a slap in the face, their sting lingering. I was in free-fall and the place where I'd expected a soft, safe landing had turned to solid stone.

I didn't even know what to say in response.

I could only focus on what felt like betrayal. How long had they all known? Why were they keeping it a secret from me? Had they been laughing at how naive I was in believing he would get better?

*Silly little Rochelle hasn't realised what's happening yet.* I bet that's what they were thinking.

For the first time in my life, I felt on the outside, inside my own home. There was no one to give me the comfort I needed, no one with the emotional capacity to lend me the strength to deal with the enormity of the news I'd just received – they all needed theirs for themselves.

The sadness in the air seeped into everything – the walls, the carpets, the curtains – infecting each room with sorrow. The house shrunk around me, big emotions soaking up every inch of space, leaving me claustrophobic, struggling for breath.

I couldn't stay there a moment longer.

I had to get out.

I spun around and darted back to my bedroom.

'Clare,' I gasped, still fighting for air. 'I want to see Clare. Now!'

Clare had been my best friend since the first day of secondary school when the teacher sat us next to one another in English.

Without saying a word, Mum nodded and disappeared to grab her car keys, while I pulled a coat over my pyjamas. I was silent throughout the five-minute drive to Clare's. Motionless on the outside, inside waves of overwhelmingly raw emotion crashed upon my numb disbelief, over and over.

I couldn't even look at Mum as I climbed out of the car. On autopilot, I followed the route I'd walked so many times before. Into the house, up the sweeping Edwardian staircase, taking a right and dragging myself past two doors before I reached Clare's room.

Not even bothering to knock I walked straight in. Clare was there waiting, arms already open.

'Oh, Shell!' she cried.

Face crumpling and tears beginning to fall freely down my cheeks, I ran to her and everything came tumbling out.

'She… she said he's gonna… die!' I spluttered, dissolving into hysterical sobs.

It felt easier to talk to Clare. And safer too. After that evening's revelations I wasn't sure I could trust anyone at home to tell me the truth about anything.

Not that I actually said much. I couldn't. Because I wasn't *in* my body. My mind was hovering somewhere up above my physical form, detached from reality, whizzing with a million thoughts while the rest of me stared vacantly at the floor in front. We just sat, side by side, on the deep windowsill, legs dangling over the old cast-iron radiator in her bedroom.

After an hour or so with Clare, as the immediate shock began to fade, I snapped back into myself. Back into reality.

*What am I doing here?* I thought. *My poor dad. My poor mum.*

I felt nauseous with guilt. How could I have left her when she needed me the most?

As quickly as I'd needed to escape my house an hour earlier, I now had the most primal urge to be with Mum again. She – not Clare – was the only person in the entire world who could make this moment even a tiny bit better.

'I have to go,' I said to Clare. 'I'm sorry. Can you call my mum and ask her to come and get me?'

'Don't be sorry, Shell. Do whatever you need to,' she replied, kindly but also quite clearly out of her depth.

'Yeah, I think I should go home,' I repeated, shaking slightly as the adrenaline began to wear off.

Ten minutes later and Mum was there. We were already outside waiting – I was so eager to see her I'd made us stand by the front door the second I put the phone down. Unfurling from my tear-stained embrace with Clare, I flung myself straight into Mum's arms. I never wanted to let her go. She had to quite literally peel me off her so that we could both get in the car.

'See you at school tomorrow,' I shouted through the open window as we made our way back home.

That visit to see Clare was the first, but far from the last, time I sought sanctuary with a friend in a bid to escape the suffocating sadness of a home heavy with the burden of bad news. In fact, just two weeks later, at 2.03pm on Monday, 25th September, my mum turned up at school, found me in the common room and told me to pack up my books and come home. I wrote my name and the time in the signing-out book like a model schoolgirl, even though my hand was shaking with the knowledge of what Mum was about to tell me. Then, with a simple nod of her head, my universe shifted once again.

My dad was dead.

In an instant, I went from a fourteen-year-old girl to a fourteen-year-old woman.

The rest of the day passed in a blur. It was strange how much there was to do considering my world had just stopped. I went with Mum to pick up Hannah and Olivia from school, then we drove to the beach. Sitting on some big concrete steps, looking out at the empty autumn sandscape, we told them about Dad and cried some more.

'So, Daddy lives up there now?' asked Olivia, a puzzled six-year-old, pointing at the shadowy September sky.

But Mum had barely finished explaining to her that 'Yes, Daddy is an angel now, he lives in heaven,' before I was off again. School timetabling issues meant Mondays at 7pm were for my Psychology class.

It didn't occur to me not to go, and nobody told me not to. I didn't want to get into trouble and Mum was distracted with the girls, so there I was, four and a half hours after finding out my dad had died, still in my uniform, walking back to school for class.

As soon as the teacher dismissed us, I rushed to get outside.

I needed space. Physical and mental. This time it wasn't Clare I escaped to, but my friend Lizzie, who I'd known since I was nine. It was an instinctive reaction. I walked to her house unannounced, knocked on her door and asked if we could go for a walk along Southwold seafront. She didn't hesitate. My mind was too tired to talk as we huddled in the wooden porch of a beach hut, so we listened in silence to the melodic crashing of the waves instead. Constant. Ceaseless. Comforting.

It doesn't take a genius to see the pattern. My friend Clare was the person I wanted to see after my mum told me that Dad's cancer was terminal. My friend Lizzie was the person I wanted to sit with the night my dad died. And it was a similar story during Mum's illness.

Time and time again, I turned to my friends in moments of need, looking to them to steady me when life threw me off balance. There's a freedom in speaking to someone who isn't directly affected. A relief that you can indulge your feelings and sadness without censorship. I didn't need to worry that my gut-wrenching grief might also upset them in the same way I did when talking to my sisters or my mum.

Through everything, my friends have filled a space that I didn't even know was vacant until tragedy came to call.

## WHAT I WISH THEY KNEW

As Mum's illness progressed I found myself relying on my friends more than a millennial depends on Wi-Fi. At times, I wasn't sure I'd be able to go on without them. But it wasn't all plain sailing.

As helpful as it could be to talk to them about what was going on, their distance from the situation allowing me to unload my feelings without hurting them, it sometimes felt harmful too. You see, my situation was a passing raincloud on the landscape of their day. But I was the one stranded mid-monsoon, battered by downpours so heavy and so frequent that I was unable to even remember what clear skies looked like.

Despite all the best intentions in the world, so many conversations I had left me feeling more alone than ever. Talking sometimes felt pointless (at best) and sharpened my pain (at worst) and I became increasingly annoyed with the well-meaning platitudes that people rolled out.

*'I'm so sorry to hear your news.'*

*'I hope you're OK.'*

*'I'm here for you.'*

I got it. They wanted to be supportive, but as they opened their mouths, they would realise they had absolutely zero idea what to say. It's perfectly understandable. Even now, after everything I've been through with Mum and Dad, I still struggle to find the right words to comfort other people who have suffered a bereavement. I mean how exactly do you console someone whose world is in the process of spinning off its axis?

Most of the time, you can't. You just blurt something out, hope for the best and then tie yourself in knots for days afterwards worrying that you offended them. I know because I've been at both ends of the experience.

Given it's a universal experience, it seems strange there's such a lack of tried and tested guidance on what to say when your friend is dealing with a personal tragedy. I guess that's because there's nothing that anyone can say to make that kind of thing easy to deal with. If there was a magic phrase, chances are my friends would have said it to me over and over again.

But while there are no wonderful words guaranteed to make it all OK, there are definitely some that seem to make things worse. *Those* are the ones I wished my friends had known – so they could avoid them like carbs on the keto diet.

### 1. *'Just Think Positive'*

That one simple phrase, which came loaded with complex pressure, piled yet more responsibility onto my shoulders. It implied that last week's concerning test results were the direct consequence of me not being cheery enough. And that the outcome of next week's scan would depend on how often I cracked a smile. Was everyone expecting me to beat the growth in my mum's brain with a daily gratitude list?

While I understood it was said with good intentions, it felt dismissive. The more I was told to *just think positive*, the harder I found it to do.

### 2. *'I Know Exactly How You Feel…'*

As word spread that Mum's brain tumour was terminal, I had a steady stream of sweet messages of support and I genuinely appreciated people taking the time to wish us well. But then a vague acquaintance messaged on Facebook to tell me he knew *exactly* how I felt because his mum had high blood pressure and his dad had gout.

I wasn't trying to turn the situation into a game of *Trauma Top Trumps*, rating everyone on a heartbreak scale, but it irritated me to be told he knew what I was going through, when he quite clearly didn't. I was more than happy for people to share their stories; I just wish some of them didn't automatically assume they understood mine.

### 3. 'If I Can Do Anything, Just Ask' (and then disappear)

Throughout Mum's illness, my phone was peppered with messages that said:

*If there's anything I can do, just ask.*

What's so bad about that, you might think? The answer is, of course, nothing. The problem was not in the offering – that was plentiful and appreciated. But it meant the ball was back in my court, leaving me with another task I didn't have the headspace to deal with.

In the midst of coping with Mum's cancer, I couldn't always see what needed to be done because I was too focused on putting one foot in front of the other. What I really needed was something more tangible, an offer which required no thought from myself other than saying yes or no. Something like:

*I'm free at the weekend, so put your ironing to one side and I'll pick it up.*

*I'm at a loose end next Tuesday. I could sit with your mum while you have some time to yourself.*

*Don't worry about sorting dinner on Friday, I'll drop something in the morning for you to have.*

### 4. 'I didn't want to say anything and upset you'

Watching people tiptoe around the big bad thing that was happening didn't mean it wasn't there. In fact, watching them dodge and swerve the word 'cancer' simply drew my attention to it further.

It wasn't just in conversation either. The text never

sent, the card never written, the phone call never made. Nothing was as loud – or as hurtful – as silence. My anxious mind would take the spaces left blank by friends and family and fill them with my own story, whipping a missing text up into a whirlwind of despair in my mind.

Silence made me feel like my mum and dad were forgotten, when all I wanted was to be reminded of them.

At the time, I couldn't explain any of this to my friends. It felt selfish to even think about telling them how their well-intentioned attempts at helping, supporting or cheering me up went amiss. I understood they were doing their best to make things OK, when making things OK was an impossible task. I never wanted to make them feel bad for not being able to fix the unfixable. But looking back, it would have been helpful – for me and for them – if they'd known the way these simple phrases hit when I was in the thick of caring for Mum.

Even though some of my friends missed the mark, I always appreciated that they'd bothered to take aim. Their heartfelt gestures were little glimmers of light relief on my darkest days and there was no substitute for that.

## TRIBE MENTALITY

I'd heard of the fight or flight response, but I seemed to take it quite literally when Mum was ill. I was desperate to get away. Obsessed with the idea of jumping on a plane and travelling thousands of miles, far from the chaos and pain I was living.

One day, after posting yet *another* Facebook status about wanting to go on holiday, a notification popped up on my phone.

*Probably someone telling me to stop whinging,* I thought.

But it wasn't. It was a comment from my friend, Tonia.

*Why don't you come and stay in Qatar with me and Bunty and you can meet baby Freddie too?*

I barely recognised the feeling in my belly as I read the words. It had been so long since I felt it.

Excitement.

There was only one hurdle between me and having some time away: Telling Mum and the girls.

I waited until everyone was sat together in the lounge, watching TV, thinking it would be easier to tell them all at the same time, but now I felt like the Queen giving her annual Christmas speech.

'Sooooo…' I started, unsure of how to even broach the subject.

Nobody paid me the slightest bit of interest. Mum was too engrossed in that night's episode of *EastEnders* and the girls were both tapping away furiously at their phones, lost deep in a WhatsApp group chat.

'You know how I updated my Facebook status earlier?' I tried again tentatively.

'Oh yes, of course we do, Your Royal Highness. I plan my whole day around your social media updates,' chimed in Olivia sarcastically, not breaking her gaze from her screen.

'Good, coz… erm… well… you know how I mentioned wanting to go on holiday in my status…' I trailed off, the words catching in my throat. I felt sick from a nauseous combination of embarrassment, shame and fear. Embarrassment that I was seeking permission from my teenage sisters. Shame that I had dared to think I deserved a holiday, while leaving everyone else to it. And fear that Mum would think I'd been secretly plotting to escape her.

'Oh for God's sake, what is it, Rochelle? I'm trying to watch this,' added Mum eventually, exasperated.

'Tonia's said I can go and stay with her in Doha for a bit if I want and I was thinking of going,' I blurted out quickly before I changed my mind about asking altogether.

'Oh lovely!' replied Mum, 'When do you go?'

'Jealoussssssss!' shouted Olivia.

'Oh my God, why don't I have any friends who live somewhere fun?' added Hannah.

*That was easier than I thought*, I said to myself, surprised and still slightly in shock.

But even with their blessing, it took a few more hours and a big glass of wine to build up the courage to actually book. Eventually, with everyone else in bed, it was just me sat staring at an airline webpage. I took a big swig of cold Chardonnay and before I could talk myself out of it again, I clicked the mouse.

BOOK NOW.

There. It was done.

*No backing out now.*


Waking up the next day, rather than the usual medication or piles of washing, my late-night purchase was the first thing I thought about. I was more hyped than a five-year-old after a bag of blue Smarties.

'Are you sure you haven't been drinking today?' Mum asked, raising an eyebrow.

'Of course not,' I replied. 'I'm just looking forward to MY HOLIDAYYYYY!'

Olivia and Hannah rolled their eyes despairingly as if to say *you have officially lost the plot, Rochelle*, but I didn't care. The feeling of elation carried me through the day and I even managed to find some time to start getting some holiday clothes together. But as I was rummaging around in the deep, dark depths of my wardrobe, a thought hit me.

*What was I doing? My mum was dying.*

*And I was going on holiday.*

Suddenly, I became aware of a voice in the back of my mind. It seemed that Jessss-Ick-Arrrr, my irritating inner critic, was back.

'What an awful daughter you are Rochelle,' it said. 'Imagine leaving your family at a time like this.'

I started to argue back.

'But it's only for a week. The girls are more than capable…'

'Only a week!' the voice scoffed. 'Anything can happen in that time. How will you live with yourself if something happens while you're away?'

'B-but…' I stuttered, trying to find a comeback.

The voice started again.

'In fact, something probably will happen – and you'll deserve it too. Look at you, packing a case and swanning off in the middle of a family crisis. You better get ready to never see your mum again, because that's what happens to selfish people like you.'

I dropped the sun cream and bikini I had in my hands and slumped to the floor, the joy and excitement zapped out of me instantly.

*What kind of daughter am I?*


Whenever I had a wobble, Mum, Hannah and Olivia encouraged me to follow my gut. So I forced myself to fold away my doubts like an origami swan and went ahead with the trip.

*I think they were glad to be getting a break from me as much as I was from them.*

Even while I was thousands of miles away with Tonia, Mum was never far from my mind. I checked in about twenty times a day with everyone at home, still plagued by guilt for going on holiday. But the self-blame was counterbalanced by an inner knowing that I'd needed the break – before I broke.

By the time I boarded the flight home after seven blissful days away, I felt refreshed and well rested. I shuffled down the aisle to seat 33A, stopping only for an agitated lady with a bulging bag that refused to fit into the overhead locker. As I settled into my seat, I was lost in my own little world. Mum's next scan was due in four weeks and I was consumed by thoughts of what was to come over the next few months.

*Or years, if we're lucky*, I thought.

I couldn't help but hang on to the hope that somehow, the doctors had made a huge mistake. Or that maybe Mum would be like those people you read about in magazines, the ones who defy all the odds after a terminal diagnosis. I mean, was life really so cruel that it would take her as well as Dad? At the very least, I hoped they'd tell us that the treatment was working and we had more time with her than they first thought.

Part of me dreaded going back because I knew what was waiting. As soon as I put my key in the front door, it would be straight into the deep end of duties, restricted by responsibilities, trapped in an ongoing trauma, with barely anyone to turn to for help. But I couldn't stay with Tonia for ever, I had no choice but to put up and shut up.

Placing my bottle of overpriced airport water in the pocket in front of me, I took the blanket out of its plastic wrapping then flicked through the endless channels on the inflight entertainment, settling on a documentary with a narrator whose voice was both calming and commanding.

'There are said to be around one hundred uncontacted tribes left in the world...' he began, his smooth storytelling a soothing balm for my anxious mind. The narrator continued, explaining how humans all over the planet have been forming tribes for tens of thousands of years. Suddenly I had a light-bulb moment.

*That was it!*

We are made to work best as part of a group, a team, a village.

Having to lean on people *isn't* a failure. It's human nature. So why was I naively trying to cope with Mum's illness alone, only calling on one or two people for the odd favour? I wasn't built to function like that. None of us are. We're all far better off piecing together a patchwork quilt of support from a broad range of people and professionals.

Suddenly my attention to the documentary went from fleeting to fully engrossed. As the narrator described the way individuals take on distinct roles within the wider group, it had never been clearer. Humans form tribes for a reason: Different people taking charge of different things gets everything done.

*Maybe this was why I wasn't coping.*

I had so many friends around me, each with their own skills and strengths. All capable of helping me out with one of the range of things I had to get done. Yet I'd been looking for just a single person to come to the rescue and support me with it all. One person to fully understand my needs. One person, to take control, to make it all OK, to fix everything.

But it was an impossible task.

I was going through a unique, life-changing journey. How could any one person 100 per cent 'get' 100 per cent of what I was feeling? I barely knew myself. If even I didn't know what I needed, or how to react to what was going on, why did I expect anyone else to be able to do that for me?

Like a Magic Eye puzzle slowly coming into focus, I saw the pieces of my life falling into place.

I promised myself that when I got back, my mindset would change. No more leaning on a handful of friends for everything, then getting disappointed and frustrated when they didn't know what they were doing. Rather I would reach out to the *right* people, tailoring my requests for help so that I asked people for assistance in areas they were skilled at.

That meant, instead of ranting to a friend at random, one who had no idea about the subtle ways brain cancer can cause personality changes, I would DM Misha, a girl in the US who I followed on Twitter. Her mum also had a brain tumour, so there was a mutual understanding between us. She 'got' things instantly because she was going through the same thing, only on the opposite side of the Atlantic. Likewise, it made more sense to email a young carers' charity for support with practical stuff because they had the contacts and experience to get things done quickly. Then when I called an old friend, I could reminisce with them, rather than discuss the logistics of Mum's care.

As my new-found knowledge sank in, the tension I'd felt about returning home to my responsibilities loosened a little. I flexed my feet back and forth underneath the seat in front and rolled my shoulders down. My body softened, relaxing at the thought that it didn't have to all fall on me anymore. So much so, that one glass of wine with my inflight meal and I conked out, sleeping soundly all the way back to Gatwick.

After seven hours, twenty minutes on a plane and one surprisingly swift journey through security, I was in a taxi from the airport on my way home. After watching that documentary, the worry I'd felt packing my bags at Tonia's had dissipated, replaced by a new wave of hope... and the fact that I couldn't wait to see Mum, of course!

I practically leapt out of the taxi as it turned the corner into our road.

'I'm baaaaaaaaaack!' I shouted, half singing as I walked through the hall and into the kitchen. What I saw made my heart leap with joy. Hannah was standing by Mum's side, casting a watchful eye over her as she did something I hadn't seen her do in months.

Taking her good hand, Mum pushed up on the arm of her wheelchair and stood up.

Stunned, my jaw dropped, but she wasn't done.

She hobbled a few steps forward to the table, grabbed her tablets and popped them out of the packaging.

*ALL BY HERSELF!*

I couldn't contain myself and started clapping like a sea lion at the zoo that's just caught a ball on its nose.

'That's amazing, Mum,' I said, before sweeping her into a hug.

'You haven't seen anything yet,' said Hannah, smiling. 'She's been like this all week.'

I listened as she told me how Mum had walked a few steps here and there without her frame and how she was finding it easier to stand up out of her wheelchair.

I felt like a parent getting emotional about how their baby's gone from high chair to high school in the blink of an eye. It seemed like so much had changed in the few days I'd been away. The latest round of treatment had clearly made a difference.

Every time I saw Mum do something new, my overenthusiastic sea lion impression came bursting out. Buoyed by her progress and my in-flight revelation about how friendships are meant to work, I felt free enough to celebrate *something* for the first time in ages. I had an idea.

I was going to throw Mum a surprise party.

No, *we* were going to throw her a surprise party.

It was time to put this 'tribe mentality' to the test.

Mum's progress scan results on 1st July were her next big treatment milestone. I checked the date and it fell on a Friday.

*Perfect!* I thought.

We could bring friends and family together to celebrate how far she'd come and how much she'd overcome.

As the day approached, everything was coming together. Instead of taking it all on my shoulders and struggling like I would have done before, I thought back to that documentary on the plane and called in some favours. Working just like the tribes the narrator had spoken about, different friends focused on the specific tasks I'd asked them for help with, all working towards one common goal: Giving Mum a bloody good party.

Angie said she would sort out decorations, because nobody could position a balloon-arch and angle banners quite like her. Emma took charge of any questions on the Facebook event page I'd set up, giving directions and recommending nearby hotels for those travelling from further afield. And I transferred the money to Lauren so she could pay the venue and sort deposits.

As the night of the party rolled around, it was better than I could have imagined. I picked up yet another glass of fizz and looked across the room, smiling and soaking up the love around me. There was something so tender about so many people coming together from different cities and across different eras of Mum's life.

Somewhere in the crowd I heard a hearty laugh. It was a familiar sound, but one I hadn't heard in a long time. My ears led my eyes to Mum, sat with her friends Helen and Abbey, her head thrown back and shoulders shaking relentlessly.

She was having the kind of fun I didn't know it was possible to have with terminal cancer. It was as if, for a moment, she'd forgotten she was ill.

*This was exactly what I wanted for her.*

Overcome with emotion, I swallowed the lump rising in my throat. Tonight wasn't for tears, not even happy ones.

Distracted from my thoughts by my rumbling stomach, I turned to grab a paper plate. Browsing the obligatory beige buffet food, I'd only got as far as the staple sausage rolls, when I spotted someone else across the room.

*Wait, was that…?*

I squinted, wondering if the bubbles I'd been knocking back were playing tricks on me.

*I could have sworn that's… Yes! Wait, it is. It's Kim!*

I bounded over, mouth still full of pastry, clutching my glass, and tapped her on the shoulder.

'I wasn't expecting to see you here,' I said, as she spun round.

'Rochelle!' she replied, beaming and throwing her arms around me.

She'd texted me earlier in the day to say work had asked her to go to the Norwich office at the last minute. It was about an hour and a half away, so she wouldn't be in the area as she'd expected.

'I was about forty-five minutes into the journey when I decided I couldn't miss it…' she said.

'So you turned around and came back,' I said, finishing for her. 'Thank you so much.'

Happy tears threatened again, so I took another big gulp of Prosecco to hold them back. Everyone had really come through for me. And for Mum.

*The documentary was right*, I thought to myself. *Things are easier when you're part of a tribe.*

Mum went on about that party for weeks afterwards. She was genuinely stunned that so many people had made the effort to come and see her. I can still hear her words.

'But I can't believe it, everyone did that. Just for little old me.'

Seeing how much it meant to her also made me realise the importance of putting in effort with my own friendships. It's so easy to bumble along in your own bubble, stuck in a seemingly endless cycle of work-eat-sleep-repeat, especially when you're a carer.

It's the way the world is set up. But it's not the way life is meant to be lived.

We are meant to be part of something bigger.

We are meant to rely on others.

We are meant to mark occasions. Big and small, happy and sad.

We are meant to live the life out of our lives.

The idea of crowdfunding for practical and emotional support has stayed with me ever since watching that documentary. I'm slowly getting better at gratefully receiving what people are able (and happy!) to offer, no matter how small, to help me keep going. As soon as I embraced the idea in my own life, I noticed that people started stepping up and I felt less let down. Finding my tribe really did stop me from losing my mind.

# FRIENDSHIP NEVER ENDS (OR DOES IT)?

My breathing was sharp and shallow as I sat on the end of my bed, trying to psych myself up to have a shower and get ready to meet the girls in London. But each time I tried to lift my dead weight off the mattress, panic rose and my chest tightened.

*What was wrong with me?*

I'd organised this weeks ago. It was *my* idea, for God's sake.

I'd been looking forward to meeting up with Amelia, Becca and Jen, having a few drinks, escaping from being cooped up at home and seeing some different faces. After all, as the indisputable equation goes: Friends + Wine = A Good Time.

But now that the time had come, I couldn't face it.

*Stop being so pathetic, Rochelle,* I thought.

I'd travelled to the other side of the world by myself when I was seventeen with no problem at all. Yet at the age of twenty-five, here I was, shaking in my bedroom, freaking out about getting on a train for fifty-five minutes. I'd hardly slept all night because I'd felt so sick at the thought of going, and as soon as I woke up I had stabbing pains in my stomach.

No matter what my mind told me, my body wasn't going anywhere. As I picked up my phone and opened WhatsApp, I wondered if I even deserved the friends who were still making an effort with me. Three hours before we were meant to meet, I typed out a message that I knew was as familiar to the girls as it was to me.

**I'm not going to make it. I'm so sorry for being flaky.**

'SENT'.

As the message propelled out into the ether, a little nugget of disappointment hurtling towards three of my oldest friends, my lip began to quiver and tears started rolling down my cheeks.

*Who was I anymore?*

My personality was slowly fading away alongside Mum's health. Things that would usually be guaranteed to cheer me up, like an afternoon with the girls, no longer even raised a smile. The sociable me who loved to go out, meet friends and travel the world had vanished. All I wanted to do was stay within two metres of Mum at all times. Anything else, especially if it involved me going anywhere alone, would make me anxious and panicky, like a parent leaving their newborn for the first time.

Once the tears stopped, I stared vacantly into space, still not budging an inch from the edge of my bed. I'd been actively avoiding friends, one cancelled plan at a time, for months now. If I asked a psychologist, I was sure they would label it anxiety or depression, but it wasn't.

I knew exactly what it was.

I was embarrassed by who I'd become.

My mind was so consumed with thoughts of cancer, death and medical trials that I was sure I wafted sadness and grief wherever I went, the scent trailing behind me like perfume on a breeze. I wanted to hide away so I didn't force my *eau de melancholy* under anyone else's nose, especially those of my friends.

I knew they were happy to listen to me, but I wasn't. I was fed up of hearing myself constantly drone through the same depressive cycle in every interaction.

1. I cry.
2. The other person does their best to comfort me.
3. Nothing changes.
4. I stay stuck in this nightmare.

What was the point of signing up for any more rounds of the same? Even steering the conversation back to the other person didn't work any more.

'No, nothing new with me, you know – same old, same old,' I'd say. Each time hoping I could still be a good friend by focusing on them for the duration of the chat. But I no longer had the mental bandwidth to care about their 2lb loss at Slimming World, their annoying new boss or whatever else they told me about.

I was already taking on too many unwanted roles at home, so trying to play the supportive friend was one character too many. I couldn't keep up with all the costume changes. I was only one person. Me.

*Awful, horrible, selfish me.*

Sharing so many rites of passage would, I thought, bond me and my friends together for life. Take Charlotte, for example. At my seventh birthday party, we played such an intense game of tag that she ran through our kitchen's glass door and broke her arm. When we were nine, I dropped a box of 10,000 tiny beads from a craft set into my thick bedroom carpet and my mum made us pick up every last one with tweezers. At fourteen, on a school trip to Poland, Charlotte petted a stray dog and gave everyone on the coach home scabies. By sixteen we were in the library, doing last-minute revision, sharing earphones to a Discman, a packet of spicy Nik Naks and rhymes to remember the periodic table. At seventeen we were wondering if we were drunk after swigging a Smirnoff Ice, and by the time we were nineteen, on a girls' holiday to Turkey, we were sure – we were definitely drunk.

I presumed having so many mutually monumental markers,

from first kisses to first break-ups, would see us through thick and thin. But apparently a shared love of Colin the Caterpillar birthday cake and sending memes isn't always strong enough to hold things together.

As Mum's health deteriorated, friendships I thought were stuck tight with superglue turned out to be merely tacked with Pritt Stick. Not because my friendships were any less strong than other people's, but because they were tested more than most. We'd made it through spelling tests, driving tests and pregnancy tests, but when we faced the test of a dying parent, passing it together suddenly wasn't a given.

I found myself muting people on social media, archiving conversations on WhatsApp and leaving messages on blue ticks, never quite sure what to reply. The majority of my friendships became more diluted with each passing day. Time and changing circumstances meant that we both, blamelessly, stopped pouring our share of squash into the shared glass of friendship. Eventually, things became so watered down that neither of us were interested in taking a sip because there was no real flavour left to it anyway.

There were never any big dramatic arguments. We merely drifted until we were so misaligned that there was no chance of clicking back into place. As sad as it may seem, part of me thinks it wasn't such a bad thing. I started to see that the old bonds spluttering under new demands were clearing space for fresh friendships to flourish.

And they did.

Some friendships still grew – bloomed, even – in spite of the barren soil in which they'd been planted.

People like Chloé, who took the day off work to drive two hours to our house from north London to give me a hug, clean our oven, fill up the fridge, then leave. Becca, who spent hours researching specialist cancer clinics around the world. Emma, who would simply text three sets of days and times, ask me to pick one when I knew we'd be home, and then arrange a Tesco delivery of goodies. Hannah's friend Kira, who got her dad and his friend to spend the afternoon lifting sofas and building flatpack furniture so we could make a downstairs bedroom for Mum, and Rich, who always ended his texts with 'no need to reply' because he listened to me moaning about how much I had to do and wanted to make sure he could stay in touch without adding another thing on my to-do list.

In time, these friendships became even more special. My own micro army, standing on guard as I muddled through everything. Precious people who committed to being witness to my pain instead of trying to fix it. Friends who were willing to be inconvenienced at my convenience. Dear ones who understood the ebb and flow of our relationship and didn't panic that a change in dynamic meant the end for us.

After Mum's diagnosis, 'being Rochelle's friend' came with a completely different job description than it had eighteen months previously. Much like the manager of a restaurant and a football team share a job title but call for totally different skills, time, approach and responsibilities. Those who stuck by me had to make the commitment to be my friend, even when it was boring or uncomfortable. Not everyone wanted to fill that vacancy, and I didn't blame them.

Relationships are an intricate equation at the best of times but add the stress of an unfolding tragedy and they become so complex that even Einstein would struggle to solve it.

The Spice Girls were adamant that 'friendship never ends' but – dare I say it – I don't think Sporty, Scary, Baby, Ginger and

Posh got it quite right. Or maybe the catchy pop melody just didn't allow them to capture the full sentiment. It's the *concept* of friendship that never ends. Its importance is eternal throughout every season of your life. But the people with whom you share your friendship – that *does* change. It will continue to change over the years, new characters joining and leaving the stage as the plotline of your life plays out. And that's nothing to be afraid of.

# 8.

# Hope & Faith

## LETTERS TO HEAVEN

As Mum approached her second round of chemo, we had no idea how she would respond to it, or if it would mark the end of the line for her treatment. What I did know was that there was nothing I could do to make it any less brutal. So, in an attempt to combat my feelings of helplessness, I focused on what I *could* do, like finding ways to make the small window of time before chemo started enjoyable.

With some unseasonably warm weather forecast, I suggested a day trip to Southwold, the town we'd grown up in when Dad was alive. We gravitated back there time and time again, like boomerangs curving back to their starting place. But as we made our way, I realised my motive for this visit was prompted as much by my desperation as it was by giving Mum a pick-me-up.

It wasn't just the string of pastel-coloured wooden beach huts that fringed the shoreline. Nor the gentle clip-clop of Shire horse hooves transporting beer barrels through the narrow streets from one part of Adnams Brewery to the next. I wanted to visit because being in Southwold made me feel closer to Dad.

Knowing he had sat on *that* bench, watching me play in *that* park. Remembering when he sat at *that* table in *that* café. The town glistened with his fingerprints – magical, beautiful traces of his life that could never be wiped away. And I needed to feel close to him because, recently, the more I focused on Mum, the further my dad slipped from my head and my heart.

Even when I did think about him, my recollection of the past was tainted by the present, and my memories of him seemed to be fading.

*How could I remember the good old days, when life was full of new bad days?*

What's more, I was angry at him.

When he died, fourteen-year-old me had come to the conclusion that if he wasn't *down here* to look after me, Mum, Hannah and Olivia, then he must be *up there* looking after us. It softened the ache of grief a little to think of the situation as relocation rather than loss.

Deciding that Dad was still keeping us all safe made me feel lucky compared to other people. Not many of my school friends had their very own guardian angel looking out for them 24/7. But my faith in Dad's ability to look after us turned out to be a double-edged sword.

When Mum was diagnosed, my first thought was that there had clearly been a misunderstanding – Dad wouldn't let something like this happen to his girls. But as her cancer progressed, I grappled with the possibility that maybe he wasn't up there looking after us.

My entire belief system began to crumble around me when I needed it most. Had the oasis in the desert been a mirage all along? I felt foolish and naive, contemplating whether I'd been consoling myself with a falsehood for the best part of a decade.

That day, as we made our way around Southwold's familiar streets, I was overcome by rage.

'Dad – aren't you supposed to be fixing things for us? I thought that was the deal!' I mumbled, looking upwards to the heavens. I wanted to scream at him, to beat his chest with my clenched fists and roar, 'First you died and left us all and now you can't even be bothered to look out for us' to make him realise he needed to make this stop. But I couldn't. Instead, after we returned from our trip, I put pen to paper to try to make sense of it all.

*Hey Dad,*

*Pretty soon I'll have spent more time without you around than I got to spend with you here. Lots has changed since I last saw you and I've grown from your little girl to a lady (if you ignore that holiday in Zante…). I'm writing this letter because there's so much going on in my head right now, I feel like I'm going crazy. I'm not sure that Royal Mail delivers to where you are, but I hope somehow you get to see this.*

*I found a file the other day. It was filled with letters people wrote to you while you were in hospital, newspaper cuttings, and cards laid with flowers at your funeral. I pieced together a whole new side of you from the memories pressed between those pages, joining up the dots between old stories I half remembered and photos of moments I wasn't there to see first-hand. Flicking through, I realised how similar we are. So many words scrawled on those tear-stained letters were achingly familiar because they're the same words I've seen used to describe me in school reports, work appraisals and encouraging conversations with friends.*

*It made me so angry. Why aren't you here to tell me all those stories yourself? Why aren't you here to advise me, guide me, let me learn from your mistakes and make this whole thing easier? Maybe it's enough simply to know that I'm half you. Etched within me like a stick of seaside rock, I have those same qualities that everyone admired in you, running through me. Maybe not fully formed, but they're there. And in that sense, you've given me a leg up, because, if you were strong enough to make it through your trials then surely, by the laws of biology, I too can make it through mine.*

*You see, Mum's ill and they've said she doesn't have long left with us. We both know how bloody amazing she is and my guess is you miss her up there and want her back. But it's three against one, Dad – Me, Hannah and Olivia won't be able to cope without her.*

*I lost count of the amount of times you said, 'Look after your mum' to me and now I'm starting to wonder if you were talking about this moment all along. Did you somehow know this was going to happen? I promise I'm doing my best to look after her and I hope you're proud of me (at least enough to forgive me for my particularly bad taste in boyfriends so far). But can't you step in and do something?*

*I'm trying to follow your lead and make the most of the hand we've been dealt. I'm desperately digging around to find the positives and use them to build us a tunnel out of this darkness, but it's really hard some days, Dad.*

*After you died, a teacher at school told me that the word 'to heal' means 'to make whole again'. She said that in time, I would heal. I quite liked the thought that in a few years I would somehow fill the massive void inside of me that appeared when you went away. But the dictionary got it wrong. The wound of your loss hasn't healed. The little girl inside of me still needs her daddy every single day. In fact, as time goes on, I think I need you even more. As I pass new milestones in my life, I wish harder than ever before that I could reach for your hand to experience them with me...*

*I wish you'd been there to drop me off at uni in my first year, to reassure me when I quit in second year and to see me walk up on stage when I eventually graduated from a different uni three years later. I would have looked so much better in the photos if I hadn't cried that morning, thinking how proud you would have been. And I know that's going to carry on all through my life. You won't be there to link my arm and walk me down the aisle on my wedding day and you won't be there to hold your grandchildren when I have kids of my own. But as sad as I am not to have you here, Dad, in a way I'm glad you're not around to have to go through the pain of what is happening to Mum right now.*

*It hurts so much to see her like this and not be able to stop it. I know that as strong as you were, being unable to help her when she needed it most would have been torture for you. Nice one on dying first, Dad! At least you never had the pain of losing someone that you love – every cloud really does have a silver lining, doesn't it?*

*This probably sounds silly but when I was little, I used to think Grandma and Granddad named you purposely so that your initials were J.C.B. I imagined they secretly knew from the second you were born that you would grow up to be so strong that you could flatten any obstacle in your path. You were – you still are – my hero. It seemed there was nothing you couldn't do – you would always be able to fix things or at least find somebody who could. Remember when you even got hold of a turkey at*

*8pm on Christmas Eve, after you'd forgotten Mum asked you to collect it and you came home from work empty-handed? How did you even manage that?*

*I read something the other day which said some people believe we choose our parents. If that's true, then I think I found you in the catalogue somewhere between Richard Branson and Mr Miyagi. Enterprising, entrepreneurial, determined, visionary, hard-working, tenacious, charismatic, risk-taking, charming, intelligent, comforting, spiritual, full of perspective. That was you. It still is. You achieved more in your life than you would have dared to let yourself dream.*

*Dad, to me, you were a superhero. Invincible and capable of anything. But you weren't a superhero, were you? I know that now. You were just a man trying his best. And even your best couldn't out-do the cancer. Nobody's could. That night when Mum explained you weren't going to get any better, my world spun clean off its axis. The worst thing of all was that I expected you to be there to stop my wild orbit and set me back on course. I was waiting for you to come and wrap me in your arms, kiss me on the head and sort things out like you always had done before. But you didn't. You couldn't.*

*You know how you always used to call me, Mum, Hannah and Olivia 'my girls' and told everyone that we gave you reason to keep going? Well, now the roles have reversed, Dad. I need you to keep me going! Life is getting so muddled. The positives are getting more blurred, slowly fading away, whilst the negatives are crisp, clear images in sharp focus wherever I look. So, I'm turning to where you should be and thinking what you would be telling me if you were still here.*

*We went to your grave while we were in Southwold today. I was half-filled with despair and half-filled with reassurance* when I realised that at some point this will all be over. Whatever we do and whatever we achieve, it doesn't matter because, ultimately, we all end up in the same place that you are now. But then, as we stood there, all your girls together by your headstone, I realised I was wrong. Everything you did and achieved hasn't been lost because each of us three girls still carry such a large part of you. Olivia's eyes and Hannah's cutting one-liners, the way we know the lyrics to nearly every Motown song ever released... and how much we love Mum! All of those things were such a big part of who you were and now they're a big part of who we are.

It's comforting to think that even though I might not be able to see or hear you anymore, so many of the things that made you who you were still stick around in us three girls (thankfully minus the chest hair). I guess that as much as I miss you, I have to thank you, wherever you are, for leaving us with the lessons you learned so that we can use them when it's our time to be schooled by life. At times I worry I am forgetting you but now I realise you can never forget someone when they are a part of you.

You used to tell me that you loved me so much that you even loved every hair on my head (I never said it back because you didn't have much hair). So, I'm letting you know that every single one of those hairs on my head is trusting you right now. They're all trusting that this whole unbearable reality is somehow part of one of your crazy plans. Like when you converted a disused factory into a bowling alley, or when you and Mum started a pub with just 83p to your names. In the end, your mad schemes always worked out to be massive successes so I'm not gonna judge you and I'm not gonna say you've got it wrong – for now. Instead, I'm just going to wait and see what you've got planned out for your girls.

*And while I'm scared, like I am right now, I'm going to rewind to one of those lazy Sunday mornings at our old house. Mum cooking breakfast on her beloved Aga and me stood on your feet, my little hands clutching on tightly to the backs of your legs as you danced me around the lounge to music turned up loud…*

*For everything you have done and continue to do for me, I will love you always,*

*Rochelle xx*

*P.S. I'm sorry I sometimes get angry about everything and blame it on you.*

The letter was as much about me questioning my faith as it was trying to straighten out the jumble of thoughts that were clouding my mind. In the end, it brought me full circle. My decision was to do what I'd done for almost ten years – have faith in my guardian angel – my dad.

To believe that he was watching over us and trust he had a plan.

The idea of my dad as an ever-present guardian angel looking over me, was my way of bearing the emotional weight of losing him. It comforted me to think that he was on my team in the game of World-vs-Rochelle. If he was still up there rooting for me, still cheering me on, then he hadn't actually gone, and I hadn't actually lost him. I just couldn't see him.

## EVERYDAY ANGELS

When someone you love has a life-limiting illness, it often pushes you to your limits. So it's hardly surprising if you start looking outside the lines of 'normal life', searching for something bigger to make sense of it all.

*Or at least that's what I found myself doing while I was Mum's carer.*

Searching for signs, hunting for meaning and increasingly convinced that someone, somewhere was looking out for me.

During her illness I reached lows so low that I felt I couldn't go on. But I started to notice that each time I was about to reach those depths, someone would appear and say or do just the right thing at just the right time to give me the strength I needed to keep going. *Is this what people mean when they speak about angels?* I wondered.

It sounds pretty 'woo-woo' I know – but bear with me.

These 'angels' were normal people, in normal clothes doing normal jobs. But just like their heavenly counterparts, they appeared as if from nowhere, be it for a fleeting moment, a couple of weeks, or even longer. Take Sarah, for example.


I'd worked myself up into a guilty, frenzied mess over taking Mum for her first stint of respite care at the hospice. Driving us there, I felt as though I was dropping my child to their first day at school. On a different continent. In a country where they didn't speak the language.

The nurse practically had to shoo me out so I could actually get the 'respite' Mum's stay was meant to be giving me. But after I'd kissed her goodbye and was heading back to the car, the significance of what I was doing struck me like a bolt of lightning – I was *choosing* to leave my mum at the hospice.

*Why?*

One day soon there would be no way of ever seeing Mum at home again, so why on earth was I voluntarily picking to spend time away from her? By the time I reached reception, I was physically shaking, my heart and mind locked in battle. As I paused in the entrance foyer, my mind flitted back to one of the last times I saw my dad before he died.

'Look after your mum for me,' he said, quietly, his words taking all his strength as he lay in the hospital bed.

'I will, Daddy,' I promised, leaning down to kiss him on his forehead.

Was he looking down now thinking I was a failure? Was I doing the right thing? How could I claim to be looking after her when I was palming her off into a hospice so I could catch up on some sleep?

Was I failing both Mum and Dad in one easy move?

*I need a sign,* I thought.

Walking out to the car park, I cast my glance downwards and picked at the skin around my fingers. Anything to distract me from the guilt churning in my stomach. I was almost at the car when suddenly—

*THUNK.*

I collided with someone walking in the opposite direction.

'Oh my goodness, I'm so sorry,' I said, scrabbling around. 'I wasn't look—'

As I went to finish my sentence, I looked up to face the person I'd just knocked flying, when I realised it wasn't just *anyone*. It was somebody of real significance.

'Sarah?!' I exclaimed.

'Rochelle.' She smiled, extending her arms for a hug.

Sarah meant so much to our family. She had shared many a laugh with both Mum and Dad in years gone by and Mum even taught her children for a while. Sarah's husband was Dad's doctor during his illness and had known all three of us girls since childhood. And they had both been an invaluable support and constant loving presence in the months following Dad's death.

214

After one too many changes in telephone numbers and numerous house moves, we'd lost touch. But hers was a name that had always held a place in our family's heart, not least because of the memory of the amazing cakes she used to leave on our doorstep in the months after Dad's death, hoping to sweeten our grief a little.

'What are you doing here?!' I shrieked.

'I'm a volunteer here, my darling,' she explained.

Tears sprung to my eyes. There it was.

*My sign!*

Seconds ago, I didn't think there was anything in the world that could reassure me I was doing the right thing, but now everything had changed. Sarah looked at me as I welled up.

'What's wrong? Why are you here?' she asked.

*She had no idea Mum was ill.*

I explained everything and told her how bad I felt about leaving Mum at the hospice.

'You get yourself home. Get straight into bed, have a nap and I'll be here with your mum all afternoon,' she said, enveloping me in another warm hug. 'I'm going to go and see her right this second, so don't you worry. I'll even make sure all the other nurses here know what a VIP she is.'

There she was. An angel, turning up at just the right moment.

Walking to the car and forcing myself to leave Mum didn't feel any easier, but for the first time in months I breathed out a little longer and deeper, and my shoulders dropped a little from their default position by my ears. I took that one-in-a-million meeting as a sign that the same people who got Mum through nursing Dad would be around to see me through nursing her.

After my chance meeting with Sarah, I googled 'angels' and found myself transported to a world where white feathers appeared without so much as a pillow fight and floral fragrances wafted through the air with not a Glade plug-in in sight. It all came across a bit much too be honest. So many wacky 'woo-woo' stories left me thinking people's experiences were wishful thinking at best, or outright lies at worst.

But after a while, I wondered if the internet was doing angels a disservice. What if Reddit threads about esoteric encounters are the reality TV of the spiritual realm, showing a glossy, pumped-up, enhanced version of the truth? What if angels *do* exist but they're a lot more normal than we expect?

You see, throughout Mum's illness, Sarah wasn't the only 'angel' that crossed my path.

First there was the 'Taxi-driving Angel'.

He picked me and the girls up from the hospital the day we found out Mum had a brain tumour. We usually caught the bus to save money, but Ipswich's not-so-great night-time service meant we'd cab it home whenever we stayed late with Mum.

All banter and bravado, the driver chatted non-stop the whole ride home. When it came time to pay, he jokingly asked if Mum was ill from the stress of us girls. I laughed at first, but ended up spilling the story of what had actually happened. His empathy and kindness came as a pleasant surprise.

'You stay strong. I know you're brave enough to get through this,' he said.

Refusing to take my money for the ride, instead he made me promise that I'd use it to get a taxi back to the hospital to see Mum the next day, rather than taking the bus. And that's exactly what I did.

That night me and the girls hugged and cried as the news sank in. Then the next morning I took a taxi to see Mum.

Despite always using the same taxi company, I never saw that particular driver again, so I never got the chance to thank him. If he reads this, I hope he knows that I'll never forget the kindness he so freely gave me, on a night when I needed someone to be kind to me more than ever.

Then, there were the 'Blink and You Miss Them Angels'.

People like the guy who dashed across the street, battling the Christmas crowds in Ipswich town centre, to open a door for us. He must have spotted me struggling in the pouring rain to carry bags, open the door and get Mum's wheelchair up the small step and into the shop.

To him, it was nothing. To me, it meant everything.

After a day of being jostled, cut up and left to struggle by people too absorbed in their own lives to notice us, it was the gesture I needed. I didn't know his name, I can't really remember what he looked like. But when I needed an angel to remind me that the world wasn't all bad, there he was and there he went, all in the blink of an eye.

Finally, there were the 'All-Knowing Angels'.

The team at The Joseph Foote Trust (now part of The Brain Tumour Charity) were a constant support throughout Mum's illness, checking in with us, letting us know they were there when we needed them, without ever being pushy. There were no restrictive office hours, no off-limits questions, no forms, no procedures. Just kindness.

Phoning to see how we were doing, I explained it had been a particularly bad day for us as a family. We'd found out Mum's tumour had grown and the big decision about whether to try chemo loomed.

'I feel like the only thing that cheers Mum up at the moment is watching property programmes and *EastEnders*,' I joked, thinking nothing more of my off-the-cuff comment.

But less than twenty-four hours later, I got another call from the charity. I had no idea how, but they'd arranged for us to go and look around the *EastEnders* set! A few days later, as we posed outside the Queen Vic and knocked on Dot Cotton's door, Mum's trademark sparkle returned to her big blue eyes for the first time in months.

To be able to make her smile like that, when she'd just been reminded that her body was failing and soon she would have to leave her three girls, could surely only be the work of angels.

Every step of the way, there were people like these who I came to think of as heaven-sent. They somehow glided into my life without drawing attention, patiently waiting in the background until I needed them to step in and lift the pressure. Turning up at the precise moment when my knees had buckled and I was about to fall, they appeared a split second before it was too late. Some were strangers, present for a fleeting moment, others were familiar and stayed for longer, but to me, they were *all* angels.

## HELPLESS YET HOPEFUL

A photo of Dad hung at the bottom of the stairs. Everything about it glowed – his deep, mahogany tan, the orange and reds of the dusk skyline, the cold amber beer in his hand, and the soft glint in his eyes as he glanced back over his shoulder at Mum who was taking the photo. You could feel the warmth of the evening air and sense the relaxation, just him and his girl on an endless summer night.

At the end of every day, as Mum started the difficult climb upstairs to her bedroom, she would look at that photo and whisper to it.

'Goodnight – love you.'

I sometimes wondered if she did it as a way of asking Dad to give her the strength to get up three flights of steps. But on the night of what would have been their twenty-eighth anniversary, a tiny tear trickled down her cheek as she looked at it.

I felt helpless. Helpless to bring Dad back so that he could help her deal with her death, the way she had done for him. Helpless to stop Mum's cancer, or to make the treatment any less awful. Helpless to stop the black hole of emotion that I knew she fell into each night, thinking about leaving her three young daughters to fend for themselves. Helpless to find the words that would make things any better. Helpless to fix anything.

Even when I tried to distract us by doing something 'normal', things seemed tainted by Mum's illness. I could never quite pull it off. There was always a tweak or an adjustment that needed to be made, reminding us that however hard we tried, things would never be the same again. A simple cinema trip now required designated accessible seats. And an impromptu meal became impossible because we couldn't sit in booths and had to wait ages for a table where Mum's wheelchair wouldn't block a walkway.

I ached to be able to *do* something that would allow us all to forget, just for a moment, what was happening. To taste just a slice of the life we would have been living if Mum hadn't been ill. But there were all kinds of hurdles to clear before we could even *make* the kind of plans I longed for us to enjoy together. Which was why I was up early, on stand-by for *The Call*, the one which would tell me if Mum's radiotherapy had worked.

After an hour spent telepathically willing the neuro-oncologist to hurry up and ring, my phone started buzzing and No Caller ID flashed up on the screen.

'Hello, Rochelle speaking,' I answered, tummy flipping as I awaited the impending verdict.

'Is that Mrs Bugg's daughter?' the consultant asked.

'Yes,' I replied.

After listening to a load of medical jargon, which I was sure was about 78 per cent Latin, I asked him to repeat it back to me in words I'd have some chance of communicating to everyone else. As I took in his words, my heart soared. This time, aside from reduced blood circulation in the brain that had caused Mum to have several mini-strokes, it was mainly *good* news.

*The radiotherapy had stopped the tumour from growing.*

*The tumour had shrunk a little since the last scan.*

With all the signs looking positive, there was only one last question on my list, one that had been whirring in the back of my mind for months. We'd been wanting to go away for a while now, but we needed his say-so before Mum could travel. I couldn't wait any longer to find out.

'Is Mum fit to fly?'

I almost cheered out loud at his response.

'Yes, I don't see why not. Short-haul, in the EU. That would be fine at this stage,' he confirmed.

The windows to my heart, which had been clamped shut for months, were suddenly flung open. A gust of fresh air rushed in, clearing the cobwebs of claustrophobia that had been slowly suffocating me. It was the news we'd all been waiting for.

Operation: Mega Holiday could finally commence.

I galloped down the stairs, two at a time, and found Mum and Hannah sitting in the kitchen. Hannah was painting Mum's nails to make her feel pretty.

'We have some breaking news, ladies,' I began, making completely unnecessary but equally uncontrollable theatrical arm gestures. They both stared at me, eyes narrowed, as they wondered if I'd had too many of the Starbucks double espresso shots I kept in the fridge.

'Where's your suitcase, Mum?' I asked by way of a hint, but Mum wasn't playing along.

'I don't know. Hannah's painting my nails,' she said bluntly, using her good hand to shoo me out of the way because I was blocking the TV. Undeterred I carried on.

'I just spoke to Dr Michaels. The scan's come back,' I said, before pausing for effect.

'He said we can go on holiday!' I exclaimed.

In that instant, I had their attention.

Unintentionally in unison, their shoulders dropped and they threw their heads back, both taking a long, deep exhale as if they'd just crossed the London Marathon finish line. I'd known it was the news we all wanted, but I didn't realise how much it was the news we all *needed*.

The next week saw a flurry of research to find the perfect, accessible holiday destination, then another three weeks later and we were on a flight to Alicante. Looking out of the plane window, then around at our little family, each on a budget bright orange seat, I smiled.

*We've made it, at last we bloody made it.*


The first few days of the holiday passed in a deliciously dreamy blur filled with excessive quantities of tapas, generous jugs of sangria, snoozes in the sunshine and cooling dips in the pool. I could already see that the break from the hamster wheel of treatment and the change in scenery was lifting Mum's spirits, or *maybe* that was just the handsome Spanish *señors*. As my feeling of helplessness started to drift away, I became a bit bolder and more ambitious. Mum was doing so well, maybe it was time to try a little something new.

A mobility scooter.

We'd been going for walks along the beach most days, but I thought it would be nice for her to regain a bit of independence (and give my arms a break from pushing her wheelchair). Collecting the scooter from reception, I smugly congratulated myself on having had such a good idea. But we barely made it out of the hotel grounds before my self-assured smile became a panicked grimace.

'Mum, be careful,' I said, as she swerved worryingly close to a giant terracotta plant pot sitting in the lobby.

'I *am* being,' she yelled.

*She's just getting used to it,* I thought.

I rested Mum's bad arm, the one she didn't have much control over, on the scooter's front steering panel so she could focus on steering using her left hand and my smugness returned. After a few minutes she was whizzing ahead, and I scorned myself for being so unfit that I couldn't keep up with her. But then I realised that Olivia and Hannah were lagging too.

'Is it me or is Mum getting further and further away?' asked Hannah.

'I thought it was just me,' Olivia and I both replied in unison.

Terror set in, as did my doubts about this 'great' idea.

'Oh, bloody hell,' I said, rolling my eyes as I suddenly realised what had happened.

Mum's right side was now essentially a dead weight and her arm had slowly started to slip down the control panel, turning up the speed dial as it did. She was now, quite literally, firing on all cylinders and going full pelt down the otherwise sleepy Spanish street.

'We need to get her!' I shouted, the three of us breaking into a sprint to catch her up, slip-slapping and stumbling in our Havaianas.

'Oh my God!' I exclaimed, watching on, horrified, as Mum veered off the pavement and on to the road. She was heading straight for the oncoming traffic, swerving all over the place to a chorus of car horns. From her body language, I could tell she didn't have a care in the world. Seemingly convinced the beeps were cheering her on, she sped up with every new toot, oblivious to the fact she was leaving a trail of destruction in her wake.

Running hard, we finally made it to within her earshot and Mum turned her head towards us.

'Put the brakes on,' Hannah screamed.

Mum looked bemused by the sight of her three sweaty, panting daughters chasing after her.

'What?' she said with a shrug.

*This is officially the worst idea you've ever had, Rochelle,* I told myself.

'I'm just gonna move your bad arm here, Mum,' I said repositioning it so her hand was resting in her lap. 'It keeps turning the speed dial up when you have it there.'

In a manner that only Mum could, she looked at me, took her good arm and used it to lift her bad one up and put it back on the steering panel, slouching like she was a seventeen-year-old boy cruising for girls in his Fiesta.

Before I could do anything to stop her, she shot off again.

As she made it to the main promenade that ran the length of the beach, the three of us in hot pursuit, I said a prayer: *God help us all.*

I didn't know whether it was her dodgy vision, or she was just

on a mission to get to the bar, but she had gone full-on *Fast &
Furious* on us. Oncoming traffic and pavements crowded with
tourists didn't seem to register with her in the slightest. She
was intent on zooming at full speed with no regard for traffic,
people, dogs, children, café tables or waiters' legs, let alone the
Highway Code.

I made it close enough behind her to hear a German tourist
give her a mouthful of abuse after Mum ran over her handbag.
But before I could apologise on her behalf, I heard a massive
crash, quickly followed by the shouts of a chorus of irate Spanish
shopkeepers. I looked ahead and gasped.

She'd managed to take out the entire sunglasses display in one
of the seafront shops. Luckily for me, but not for their profits,
the fake Ray-Berries and Golce & Dabbana glasses stopped her
in her tracks.

'All right there, Lewis Hamilton?' I said, jokingly, as I finally
caught up with her. 'I think it's time we put you and this scooter
into retirement. Don't you?'

'Probably, yes,' she said, giving an awkward grimace as her
eyes darted towards the angry Spaniards surrounding her. 'Let's
go back.'

I let out a sigh of relief, until I realised. We were thirty
minutes' walk from the hotel.

*With no wheelchair.*

We tried taking it in turns to jog alongside the scooter, using
one hand to pull the 'go' lever and steer at the same time. But
in the 30°C heat and taking up the entire width of the busy
pavement, the approach was a spectacular failure. Especially
when Mum kept trying to join in with the steering.

I stopped and covered my face with my hands. What could
we do?

*Think, Rochelle, think.*

Then it came to me. I turned to Olivia and looked her dead in the eyes.

'What?' she asked, suspiciously.

'For once you're gonna wish you weren't the skinniest sister,' I smirked. For a moment she looked at me confused, then she clicked.

'No way! Not a chance! I am *not* sitting on her lap and driving her back,' she said.

'Oh yes you are,' I shot back.

'But there are loads of hot guys. I will *actually* die of embarrassment. No way. Not happening,' she whined.

'Liv, there's literally no other way,' I pleaded.

Ten minutes of huffing, bickering and eye-rolling later, she gave in. Sitting on Mum's lap, she started the engine and they scooted off back to the hotel. As she pulled ahead of us, she turned her already-beetroot face towards me and Hannah.

'If I see anyone hot, I'm getting off and leaving Mum by herself, just so you know,' she shouted.

I shook my head again in despair but then breathed a final sigh of relief.

'Thank God we only hired it for the day,' I said, as Hannah and I dissolved into hysterics.

By the time we got back to dinner that evening, we were *all* laughing about our disastrous trip earlier, even Olivia. It turned out that this wonky, slightly broken, not-quite-to-plan moment had brought us more fun and joy than any of the grand, expertly orchestrated, picture-perfect gestures I'd attempted over the last few months.

That day taught me to look for the perfect moments that hide within every imperfect experience. I won't lie, when I was picking up sunglasses from the floor and struggling to remember my A-level Spanish to apologise to those shopkeepers, I did *not* appreciate the experience in any way, shape or form. When I nearly tripped over my own flip-flop and my shorts were disappearing up my bum as I tried to keep pace with the Queen of Speed, I did *not* for a second pause to consider how I would one day look back and laugh. But I do now. And I hope Mum does too, wherever she is.

I like to think that in those final weeks when Mum was lying in bed, tired and unresponsive, she was playing back all the best bits of her life. If she was, I bet she was remembering that day on the mobility scooter and the 'too good to be true' cheap holiday to Turkey where they moved another family into our room while we were out on a day trip. I reckon she was replaying all the times she had to pretend to enjoy the disgusting attempts at cookery I brought home after Food Tech lessons at school, and the Christmas that her and Grandma drank so much Baileys that they were huddled in the kitchen panicking there was no meat on the turkey – only for my dad to walk in and tell them they were trying to carve it upside down!

As helpless as I felt during Mum's illness, I always remained hopeful because we still had some life left to live together, however limited it was. We still had good times and bad times to see in by one another's side. And that is the greatest gift you can give someone. To be with them as they use each of the colours in the palette – even the unpretty ones – to paint the richest, most vibrant life they can during the time they have left. Even when you feel helpless, you can still, always, be hopeful.

# 9.

# Death & Dying

## THE LONG GOODBYE

I untucked three chairs from underneath the table and arranged them across the width of the balcony. Me, Hannah and Olivia sat in a line, legs outstretched, feet resting on the railing in front of us, looking out across the lights of the town twinkling below.

Sorrento was every bit as stunning as we'd imagined, more so, in fact. Tourists mixed with locals, spilling out from trattorias on to pavements while the balmy summer air buzzed with chitter chatter and the sound of spoons scraping the last sumptuous strands of spaghetti from the bottom of bowls. It was like walking through a postcard brought to life.

Save for a few 'technical difficulties' with Mum's wheelchair, we'd even managed to navigate the quaint yet uneven alleyways, although it usually left Mum looking like a nodding dog on a car dashboard.

'She doesn't seem to mind after a few limoncellos,' Olivia

laughed one night as we tried to get Mum up a hill with *Coronation Street*-style cobbles and what felt like an Everest-esque incline.

Me and the girls had been working together all day, anticipating her needs and predicting one another's moves to make sure the holiday ran as smoothly as possible. But with Mum now safely in bed, wiped out from a busy day, it was finally time to relax. We sat for a while, giggling and gossiping, waiting to digest the ridiculous amount of mozzarella-smothered food we'd managed to eat earlier. But as one hour blurred into the next, eventually there was a lull in conversation. We each floated away into our own thoughts, following the twists and turns of our minds for a while, until Hannah suddenly spoke.

'I know this probably sounds really strange,' she started. 'But I wish that Mum had cancer somewhere else.'

'How do you mean?' asked Olivia.

'Like, somewhere other than her brain,' she explained.

In that instant, something in *my* brain clicked. It was the answer to a question I hadn't even realised I'd been asking myself for months.

I often found it hard to answer when people asked me how Mum was doing.

'Yeah, she's doing well, thanks,' I'd say with a smile.

But I don't think I ever sounded 100 per cent convincing. You see, I wanted to be positive and talk about how radio-therapy had given her some strength back in her bad hand. To be upbeat and focus on the fact she was still able to make it up and down the stairs from her bedroom to the kitchen each day. I wanted to be grateful for all the things Mum *could* still do, but there was always something niggling away at me. I'd just never been able to work out quite what – until Hannah's comment. She finally helped me pinpoint the unsettled feeling that had been chipping away at my positivity.

*Mum was different now – and she had been from the very beginning of her illness.*

From the moment I moved home to care for her, Mum was there physically, but her emotions and reactions had begun breaking up like a mobile phone signal heading into a tunnel. It had started with small, silly things like the way her laugh changed and how she began to reply to everything, however funny or however serious, with 'Oh bless.' Seemingly overnight she went from the person who always knew what to do and how to sort things to Little Miss Panicky, thinking it was a national state of emergency if we ran out of milk.

Then there was the out-of-character bluntness.

'Rochelle, you're useless at helping me up the stairs,' she said one day. 'I want Hannah to do it. I like her more.'

Her words smarted like a splash of scolding water. I quickly reminded myself that she didn't mean to be so tactless, that the *real* her would feel awful for offending me, but my attempts at self-reassurance barely soothed the burn.

And let's not forget the selective hearing. She'd started ignoring you if she wasn't interested enough in what you were saying. She'd even done it in the restaurant that night.

'Mum, do you want water or Coke?' I asked.

*Silence.*

'Mum?' I repeated, unsure if she'd heard.

Still nothing.

'MUUUUUMMMMM!' I barked.

'Yes, I can hear you,' she snapped suddenly.

'Why aren't you saying anything then?' I pushed. 'What do you want to drink? Water or Coke?'

'Well, I'm not going to answer, am I, because I want wine!' she replied.

The four of us usually ended up in hysterics at her tumour-induced quirks. Like when she confused her words and we had to decipher what she was talking about. We'd go back and forth, me throwing out guesses, her shaking her head and offering up mimes like it was a game of charades. But I still found the personality changes tough.

I was grateful that she hadn't become angry or violent like some people with brain tumours do, and I knew cancer was never a welcome visitor whatever part of the body it chose to make its home. But there was something so unnecessarily evil about picking on someone's brain. It was horrible enough to watch Mum deteriorate physically, without the tumour gnawing away at who she was as a person as well.

Every now and then we'd get a brief glimpse of the fun-loving, dynamic woman who was still somewhere inside of her. Like when we'd caught her hiding behind her biggest sunglasses hoping that nobody would notice her gawping at the group of very attractive Italian men in very small swimming trunks (we did, because we were doing the same). Or the way she'd been sending us on near-hourly trips to the gelato shop around the corner from our hotel, as if on a one-woman world record bid to try all 160 flavours by the end of the week.

But in a way, that hurt more.

It served as a reminder of just how much of my mum – the wonderful compassionate, loving, vibrant, sharp, humorous, force of brilliance that she was – had already gone.

When my dad was ill, he went through a very obvious physical decline with his illness, but he was still *Dad* until very close to the end. It may have taken him more effort to make one of his jokes or do one of his stupid impressions, but he still did. He still could. Yet I started missing Mum months before she died, even while she was still with us.

Losing Mum to a brain tumour felt like losing her twice. In her double-decker death, first I had to watch on helplessly as the woman I'd known all my life emotionally slipped away, like grains of sand through an egg timer. Then, before I had a chance to get to know the woman who was left, I lost her too – this time physically. By contrast, when Dad was eventually diagnosed, the oncologist gave him just six weeks to live.

I used to think we were 'lucky' with the way that his death played out. Of course, I wished I'd had longer with him, but I saw it as a blessing to be given just enough time to say everything that needed to be said without suffering for too long in intolerable limbo, waiting for the dreaded to happen, once we knew the diagnosis was terminal. I considered the speed of his illness to be the ONE thing I was grateful for. So second time around, with Mum, I was angry that the universe couldn't even give me that.

Watching Mum live through her death was a kind of exquisite agony. The slow-motion unravelling of her life was both a blessing and a curse. In a strange way, I could see how her journey was the kindest, most gentle way this awful situation could play out. A gentle fade rather than a sudden power cut. Mum's misdiagnosis with the stroke gave us a transition period to get used to her not being well, without the overwhelming scariness of a terminal illness. Then her gradual decline allowed us to adjust, ever so slightly, to what life would be like once she was gone.

Having lost Dad so suddenly, I appreciated the extra time we had to spend with Mum. Being so acutely aware she wouldn't be around for ever pushed us to do more, to travel more, to laugh more, to talk more, to take more photos and to make more memories. Life simultaneously became more precious and more painful because we were armed with the knowledge that each time we did something, it could be for the last time. I was both heartbroken and grateful for knowing I needed to appreciate every last moment and not let it pass me by.

Yet still, without realising, both times I slipped into the 'if only' trap, driving myself crazy imagining how things could have been different and less painful.

*If only I'd had longer to prepare.*

*If only I didn't have the torture of watching them in pain for so long.*

Looking back, I can see those thoughts were worthless because bereavement isn't a competition and there are no winners. Having lost someone relatively quickly and someone relatively slowly, I can safely say they are both equally as difficult and equally as precious.

For me, the time spent living with someone's terminal diagnosis is the most difficult part of all. It is impossible to heal from something that isn't yet over, so the knowing and waiting can feel worse than actually losing them. After the bombshell news drops, each passing hour you're struck by more shrapnel – fragments of unbearable shock, frantic disbelief, desperate panic, bewildered struggle and deep sickness lodge in your heart as you try to process what you've been told.

Both times, finding out my parents were going to die left me gasping for air, slowly suffocating in a room full of oxygen. Although I was inconsolable when the time came to say goodbye to them, it was a different sort of sorrow. The finality of death somehow brought with it a bittersweet sense of peace after the frantic scrambling to find a cure and desperate wishes for the doctors to realise they'd made a mistake. There was nothing left to argue with, rationalise or cure. All that remained was the challenge of acceptance.

## CAUSE FOR ALARM

We pulled into the gravel-covered car park of the quiet countryside church where Dad was buried and as I put on the handbrake, I was suddenly sucked under by a wave of unfamiliar emotion. We visited his grave every year on his birthday. Everything looked the same as it always did, but today something felt different. What was it?

Then I realised.

*This is the first time we've been here since we found out Mum's cancer was terminal.*

Head spinning, I clumsily pushed Mum across the car-park gravel and on to the stony cemetery path. But almost immediately I was jolted from my spiral of stress.

*CRUNCH.*

The chair ground to a halt. A dam of pebbles had built up in front of the tyres, causing the wheel to stop turning. Mustering all the strength I could, I shook and shimmied the wheelchair – and her – until I loosened the stones and the wheels started spinning again.

'Stop jiggling me, I feel sick,' Mum moaned as we bounced over the uneven surface.

'Stop being so overdra—' I started, but before I could finish, Mum was shouting.

'Rochelle. Bloody. Bugg!' she yelled as she was tipped to a near forty-five-degree angle. Clutching the side of her wheelchair with her good arm to make sure she didn't fall out, Mum launched into an expletive-filled rant. I gasped, realising I'd just accidentally steered her into a rabbit hole and nearly out of her chair. But as the immediate panic faded, the four of us dissolved into laughter.

Whatever we did as a family always turned into a comedy of errors at some point. I'd have put money on Dad being up there, laughing at the state of us, and, truth be told, I was glad. The light relief was a welcome distraction from the dark, depressive thoughts racing through my mind when we'd arrived. But as we stood by Dad's graveside, the laughter stopped and silence fell.

I could physically sense everyone's fears hanging heavy in the air. And as my mind started running wild, I wondered what was running through Mum's?

Was she looking at the new graves that had been dug since our last visit?

Was she thinking that she would soon be joining them in the ground, too?

Was she staring at Dad's headstone, knowing that one day her name would fill the space next to his?

*Because I was.*

I couldn't help it, my brain looped straight back to the spiral of anxiety I'd been distracted from earlier. Was Mum judging how well I cleaned the grave and arranged the flowers, because she knew that soon she'd be lying there, too?

These paralysing thoughts were nothing new. Like a stalling engine that couldn't restart, whenever I tried to divert my mind onto a positive track, I'd splutter and come to a standstill, frozen in fear. Even at night, horrible thoughts would sneak into my slumber and terrorise me out of sleep. Waking in the early hours, I'd be trembling, crying, panting to catch my breath as

I tried to outrun the scenarios my subconscious dreamed up in its desperation for answers.

The same questions buzzed around my head, day and night. Questions like the ones hovering now, haunting me while I stood silently staring at Dad's grave.

*What about if Mum dies in the middle of the night and she's alone?*

*How would I ever forgive myself?*

*What about the day she goes?*

*Who do I call?*

*What do I do?*

*What does it feel like to be with a dead body?*

*Where will they take her once she's died?*

Stood there by the grave, panic rising in my chest and anxieties sounding like a near-constant alarm in my head, I tried to stifle any external signs that I was struggling. But as the inevitable drew ever closer, it was becoming harder and harder to conceal.

Towards the end of Mum's illness, those alarms became impossible to silence. They wailed in my head non-stop. Good scan results or a nice day out might muffle them, but only slightly, and any relief was only temporary. But most terrifying of all was knowing that it wouldn't be long before the drills were over, and the alarms would signal a real emergency.

At the time, I was convinced I was going crazy, but that's because, stood at Dad's graveside that day, I knew nothing about the effect of ongoing trauma on the brain. I lacked the reassurance I now have of understanding my reaction was far from unusual. In fact, it was almost to be expected.

I wasn't going crazy at all. That screaming alarm was basic biology. My brain's way of letting me know it was stuck in protection mode.

In 'peace times' – when there is no immediate threat to deal with – the parts of the brain work together in harmony to assess and process threats. But in times of stress, these roles can get a little mixed up.

*The result?*

Trauma, whether a one-time event or a prolonged situation, can leave you in a hyper-vigilant state, fixed on high alert, consumed by the need to look out for and identify any more threats. Your mind struggles to get on with daily duties because it's constantly on watch for what is going to go wrong next, deeming what were once simple, easy tasks as too much, too risky or too dangerous.

And that's exactly what happened to me.

During Mum's illness, my internal alarm was constantly sounding. I was forever on high alert, waiting for the next bad thing to happen.

It wasn't until after she passed away, when the alarms turned off and my ears began to adjust to the normal volume of the world, that I realised how intrusive and distracting they had been. As they did, I wondered how I'd put up with the tinnitus of trauma for so long.

I wish I'd known that the invisible army of anxieties invading my brain weren't predictions of the future, but simply sent by an overactive brain trying to protect itself by thinking through every possible eventuality. If I had, maybe, just maybe, things would have seemed a little less scary and a little more manageable.

## GIVING UP –vs– GIVING IN

I gently kissed the bump on Mum's head. I still couldn't believe what she'd done the day before, falling while she was using her walking frame and somehow managing to get her head trapped between a chair and her bed.

'Are you feeling any better, Tumble Tina?' I asked.

'Yes, I'm fine,' she said with a smirk. 'Can you get me in my wheelchair and take me to the loo?'

She seemed to have bounced back just fine, so I didn't feel quite so bad for teasing her over her comedy fall. But I could tell that the knock to her confidence was worse than the one to her head. She hadn't wanted to use her walking frame since, not that she would admit it, of course.

*I'm just tired today.*

*It'll be quicker if you push me.*

But I knew that it was because she was scared to. During the day, it wasn't too bad, but now – at night – me, Hannah and Olivia were on high alert, just in case she called one of us. It wasn't so much the added responsibility that I minded, more what it meant for the bigger picture.

Was this the start of a new stage in her decline?

Another step towards that unwelcome destination we all knew was coming?

The falls, the new symptoms, being able to do less for herself – the more things changed, the more I wanted them to stay the same. Even if that meant still having a mum who was dying of a brain tumour.

How was I supposed to know what it all meant?

I was at Mum's side for each appointment and every treatment session, and while I always had questions, I didn't always feel I could ask them. Some topics of conversation seemed out of bounds with Mum there. It was so hard. What was I going to say?

*'So, do you think Mum is getting closer to dying then?'*

How could I ask a consultant that with her sat next to me?

Even if I did, and risked upsetting her, the medical professionals were so careful not to say the wrong thing, or to make any promises. Conversations often sounded more like I was listening to them read out terms and conditions. Every opinion and prognosis came with such comprehensive small print that I wondered whether they even meant what they said.

Trawling through my mental list of anyone I might be able to put these uncomfortable questions to, I suddenly remembered Andy.

He was the founder of The Joseph Foote Trust (now part of The Brain Tumour Charity) and I'd stumbled across him on Twitter during one of my mammoth research sessions. He started the charity after losing his young son to a brain tumour. I'd spoken to him a few times before, and by the end of each call, I always felt relieved that someone *got it*, even if he couldn't always tell me what I wanted to hear.

I helped Mum go to the loo and then tucked her back into bed, as she was feeling tired. Once I was sure she'd started dozing, I slipped upstairs to my bedroom, grabbed my phone and dialled Andy's number, desperately hoping he'd be free to talk.

Thankfully, after just a few rings he answered. He greeted me warmly, but I barely gave him a chance to say another word before I swiftly launched into all the ideas, questions and doubts I'd been adding to the 'Secret List of Hope' I had stored in my mind.

'Who should I be going to for second opinions?

'Is there a cure I don't know about?'

'Is Mum having scans regularly enough?'

'Should I be pushing for more treatment options?'

'Is there something I should be doing that I'm not?'

After listening patiently to my overwhelming outpouring, Andy talked me through the specifics of Mum's type of cancer, explaining how tumours grow and describing the different ways treatments work to try to kill the bad cells.

The facts he gave me were, thankfully, missing the caveats and small print that the information from Mum's consultants came with. It was empowering. He was sharing the knowledge I needed to evaluate for myself whether something was worth pushing *for* or pushing *away*. Instead of banding around percentages, long medical names and scary words, he explained everything in a way that was relatable without being patronising.

A wave of gratitude washed over me. His patience felt like a gift, but I knew that his knowledge didn't come from a textbook, rather from painful, first-hand lived experience. He'd been through it all himself with his son, Joe.

An hour passed, but rather than trying to hurry me up, Andy allowed me to keep talking for as long as I needed. Free from the time pressure of an allocated appointment slot, I asked all the questions I'd held in for months, either because I hadn't had a chance to bring them up or I hadn't felt comfortable enough to.

'They misdiagnosed Mum with a TIA – a mini-stroke – at the beginning. Several times, actually,' I started. 'If I went and demanded a second, third, fourth opinion, do you think they would have found the tumour sooner and been able to treat it? If I'd caused more of a fuss, do you think she would have had a better chance of being cured?'

Andy told me that misdiagnosis was par for the course with many types of brain tumour and asked if I knew the name of Mum's specific diagnosis. I stumbled over syllables, trying to make sure I pronounced the words 'anaplastic astrocytoma' correctly. As I made it to the end of the medical tongue twister, he explained that 'anaplastic' meant the tumour was actively growing, and that Mum's type of cancer was aggressive – typically a grade three or progressing to a grade four. An early diagnosis was unlikely to have made much difference.

His words lifted the weight that had been hanging heavy in my heart for close to a year. *I wasn't to blame for them missing the tumour for so long.*

Moving through the mental list of worries that were whirring away in my mind, I went on to the next.

I'd recently heard about a clinic in Texas, in America where they'd apparently cured lots of patients with brain tumours. It was extremely expensive so I'd lay awake every night for the last week wondering how I could start fundraising to fly Mum over there for treatment. I asked Andy his thoughts and listened expectantly as he let out a long sigh, filled with recognition and understanding.

He explained how he'd flown all over the world – to Moscow, Mexico, Japan and beyond – investigating potential treatments when Joe was diagnosed. He visited scientists and tracked down doctors offering every type of lotion and potion as a cure. But, acutely aware that there are con artists out there, trying to make a quick buck off people's desperation, he made sure to ask detailed questions and demand verified proof.

Andy admitted that he too had heard the same success stories from the clinic that I had, but I knew from the tone of his voice, that he didn't think Mum would be one of them. All the hope that had been building in my heart, dissolved in an instant when he told me, apologetically, that the type and grade of Mum's tumour meant he doubted that even their treatment would be able to help.

Swallowing down the lump in my throat, I shook my head at the phone. 'No, no, it's fine. I need to know this stuff,' I replied in an upbeat tone that I hoped masked just how deflated I felt. Tracing further down my internal list of hope, I finally reached another burning question. This one was less about wishful thinking and more about reality, and it terrified me. *What do I do when Mum dies?*

I knew that I would never be *ready* for it to happen, but I wanted to be *prepared*. I had no idea what it would be like. What was I meant to do when that moment came? What should I expect?

But I couldn't quite bring myself to say the words. 'And what about when … you know … *it* happens?' I asked, tentatively nudging the conversation into a devastating direction.

Andy gently told me that the last steps of the journey against a brain tumour are usually light, bright and peaceful. He explained that as the tumour grew, Mum would gradually become more and more sleepy. She'd be compos mentis when awake, but nearing the end, that would likely only be for about ten minutes a day.

I immediately thought of Mum, lying curled up asleep in her bed. I'd just heard the *Loose Women* theme tune coming from the TV downstairs. That meant it was about 12.30pm. How long had she slept already today? How long did we have left?

Then, after a little more prompting and prodding from me, Andy told me – in the kindest and most tender way possible – that, from what he knew, he thought that we would lose Mum.

Somehow, I was caught unawares by what I'd already known for months. While my brain had long since accepted the doctor's diagnosis, it seemed my heart had not. I physically felt the last few fine threads of hope float away.

*No more 'one in a million'.*

*No more 'you never know'.*

*No more 'stranger things have happened'.*

It was definitive. Mum had no more options. There was no hidden hope and no miracle cure I'd missed. Sat on the same bed, in the same room where I'd already received and delivered so much bad news. The place where I'd spent endless hours clinging onto hope that there was a way to avoid what everyone else considered inevitable. Here I was again, filled with despair. But this time, there was also an unexpected light of reassurance.

As heartbroken as I was, there was comfort in knowing that everything I'd been thinking, planning, hoping, researching and wondering was completely normal. That Andy had done it all, too. To my anxious brain, his words were reassuring and relaxing, like a loving father rhythmically rocking his restless baby to sleep.

We were making the right choices.

*I* was doing the right thing.


For me, that call was a milestone. An unexpected turning point in my way of thinking. Hearing Andy's wise words settled the hurricane inside of me, when nobody else could. Because I knew he'd been through what I was going through. There was no ulterior motive or targets to meet. He had listened to the story in full and not fobbed me off when I mentioned a newspaper cutting about a new treatment or clinical trial.

Some consultants were dismissive, leading me to burrow down further into self-doubt, unsatisfied with their responses. And when I spoke to some medical professionals, the incompleteness of their answers to my questions often left me wondering if I was doing all I could for Mum, unsure of whether I was fighting hard enough for her. But Andy and the team at The Joseph Foote Trust changed all that. They listened and they understood.

Up until that call, I was haunted by the thought that I wasn't doing enough, or I wasn't doing things right. I was always the A* kid growing up, the one that didn't fail, do badly, or retake. If I ever showed any signs of worry, people's response would always be the same.

*Oh, you don't need to worry, you always do well.*

Speaking to Andy, I could see that I'd been taking a similar approach to Mum's cancer, applying the same expectations, thinking it was *my* job to make sure everything worked out OK. But after our call, I realised that my shoulders were aching from all the responsibility, when much of it wasn't even mine to be carrying. I finally understood that it wasn't down to me to cure the cancer. There was nothing I could or should have been doing, thinking or saying that would have made everything better.

Being a carer is totally different to anything else you go through in life. There are no rules to apply, no test to take, no textbook with the answers in the back. Hard as you try to find one, there is no correlation between the outcome of a loved one's illness and the effort you put into looking after them.

In many respects, that chat with Andy wrote the last page of the *Hope and Fighting* chapter in the story of my caring journey. It allowed me to judge for myself what I should be putting my energy into chasing and what would be futile to pursue. His honest advice laid to rest all the secret hopes I had for a happy ending and helped me write the first few lines of a whole new chapter.

*Enjoying and Savouring.*

In a bizarre way, it was a relief. I finally understood that what was happening was inevitable, and not down to me needing to do more research or ask better questions. It just *was*.

That realisation allowed me to give myself permission to surrender to what was always destined to happen and shift my focus from fighting reality to getting on with making the most of it. It taught me one of the most important lessons I learned as a carer.

## Giving up isn't the same as giving in

*Giving up* is stopping when the going gets tough, even if you know you've got it in you to keep fighting. It's quitting when you know that, with a bit more effort, you could still walk away victorious.

*Giving in*, on the other hand, is surrendering to destiny and graciously accepting that some things in life are out of your control. It is making the conscious decision to start swimming with the tide after struggling for so long to swim against it. And it brings with it a surprising beauty and sense of peace.

When a loved one has a terminal illness, never *give up* but don't be afraid to *give in*.

## ONE OF THESE MORNINGS

I couldn't quite put my finger on it, but I knew that something had changed. In the same way that nip in the autumn air lets you know the final chapter of summer has been closed, even when the sky is still blue and the days are still warm. There hadn't been one, definitive moment of change, no cataclysmic shift. Rather it was a subtle intuitive knowing. A winding down and the start of a long exhale.

I knew Hannah and Olivia felt it, too, although none of us mentioned it. Perhaps we were all in denial, despite, deep down, it being undeniable. There was a sense – a *knowing* – that we'd begun the last level of this heartbreaking video game. And it was this knowing that prompted me to make the call.

'Could you arrange for the Marie Curie nurse to start sitting with Mum overnight?' I asked the district nurse.

'Of course,' she replied gently. 'I think that would be a good idea.'

'Thank you,' came the words from my mouth, but I only half meant them. Truth be told, I had hoped she would argue with me, tell me it was too soon to get them involved. Her immediate agreement spoke volumes. I knew what it meant. Marie Curie nurses were not a long-term arrangement, they had one sole purpose.

*To help in the final few days of a person's life.*

Two days later, the doorbell rang. I peered through the peephole and saw a slim woman with a short, efficient blonde bob stood on our doorstep. She looked like she spent her evenings shimmying away at a Zumba class, not keeping a watchful eye on dying patients, but then I spotted the small artificial yellow daffodil attached to her pale blue tunic.

*This must be Sandra,* I thought.

As my hand hovered over the door handle, I tried to push away the lingering unease in the pit of my tummy. Nothing had ever been this well-organised or speedy during Mum's illness. Why now? How did they manage to arrange this so quickly?

*What do they know that I don't?*

'Hello, I'm Sandra from Marie Curie,' she announced warmly as I opened the door.

'Nice to meet you,' I replied, walking her the few steps from the hallway to Mum's makeshift bedroom in the lounge.

'Mum, this is Sandra,' I said, crouching slightly so that my face was level with hers and stroking her hand.

'She's going to be around tonight just in case you need anything. If we don't hear you, you can tell her and she can come and get us. OK?' I continued.

Mum gave a barely audible grunt.

*She'd heard me.*

I turned to Sandra and flashed a smile that confirmed she had Mum's seal of approval, but as I did, I noticed the serious expression on her face. She seemed concerned.

Inside, panic started to rise, but outside I focused even more on the practicalities, talking Sandra through where everything was in excessive and completely unnecessary detail.

'The remote control for the TV is here. You use this one for the Sky but then you need this one to change the volume. And there's a downstairs toilet just there. There's a small sink in there if you need it too. And I've left out a tray with tea and coffee in the kitchen. But there's also drinks in the fridge, so if you need anything, just help yourself, don't feel like you need to ask,' I rambled without pausing for breath.

Like an estate agent trying to sell her a house she didn't want, I spoke at Sandra non-stop to prevent her from saying anything I didn't want to hear.

'Thank you, I'm sure I'll be fine,' she said, nodding politely as I was finally forced to take a breath.

Then she reached out to pick up Mum's notes from the

metal holder hooked over the bottom rail of her bed that we'd borrowed from the hospital. Transfixed, I couldn't break my stare as I watched her leaf through them with pure concentration, concern etched deeper into her face with each page.

I already knew what she was reading. I read Mum's notes every time someone wrote in them. Whether it was a care worker, a GP or a visiting nurse, as soon as they left I'd go straight to the increasing wedge of papers stuffed into the holder at the end of the bed, eager yet apprehensive to see what they'd said, as if it was my end of year school report.

But they never revealed anything new. It was like watching a film when you'd already seen the spoilers on Twitter. They all outlined the same plot. Mum was ill, she was going to die at some point, but for now she was still alive.

Still, it was strange to see someone reading them for the first time.

After what felt like an eternity, Sandra put her hand on my shoulder and I suddenly realised that I'd been holding my breath, like an *X Factor* contestant waiting for Simon Cowell to tell them if they've made it through to the next round.

'Can I speak to you in the kitchen?' she asked, turning towards the door as she spoke.

'Of course,' I answered, following her.

Closing the door gently behind us, she turned and looked straight at me.

'You do know your mum is really quite ill, don't you?' she started softly.

I frowned indignantly.

'Yeah, of course. That's why I called Marie Curie,' I stated bluntly, slightly irritated.

I was about to ask her if she'd had a long day and add that she wouldn't be here if my mum was well, but before my impulses got the better of me, she spoke again.

'I just want you to be prepared because it looks to me like it might be tonight or tomorrow morning,' she said, breaking the news as softly as she could.

'Oh. R-right...' I stuttered.

All the blood in my body instantaneously drained downwards and pooled, pulsating, in my feet.

'Um, OK. Right,' I repeated, trying to process what she had just said.

*Mum might die tonight.*

Suddenly I was in free-fall, as if I'd been pushed backwards into a never-ending black hole. All I could hear was silence. Raw, deafening silence. Until Sandra spoke again.

'I think I've got my bearings with everything, so I'll go and sit with your mum now and you can have a moment to yourself,' she offered, her words punctuating the air and puncturing my heart.

I felt like all the air had been sucked from my lungs. Legs like jelly, and gasping for breath, I turned and stumbled into the hall. Palm flat against the wall, I made my way upstairs, tracing my route with my hand.

*I had to tell Hannah.*

She was stuffing clothes into her bulging wardrobe as I made it to her room. Collapsing on the end of her bed, I took deep deliberate breaths to try and get enough oxygen back into my body.

'What's wrong?' Hannah asked, arms still full of dresses and hoodies.

'Um, Span, the nurse has just said she's worried about Mum,'

I began. 'L-like she thinks sh-she might not have... long left at all.'

I stammered as my mouth tried to form words my brain hadn't yet comprehended.

'How long?' Hannah asked, joining me at the end of the bed.

'Like... as in... tonight or tomorrow type of not long,' I said.

As soon as the words left my mouth, I wanted to force them back in. 'But I dunno. I mean Mum was a lot better yesterday than she's been in weeks – sitting up and even talking. So maybe the nurse is over-reacting a bit,' I offered, even though I'd read it was common for terminally ill people to have one last 'really good' day right before the end. As much as I was trying to soften the blow to Hannah, I knew I was trying to convince myself too.

*Mum was going to be fine. This wasn't the end.*

'Yeah, well, maybe she just doesn't get how Mum usually is,' Hannah offered.

'Yeah,' I agreed, leaning into denial.

'You watch, the nurse is gonna make us stay up all night thinking Mum is gonna die, then we'll be knackered tomorrow,' she joked and we both laughed uneasily.

Despite all that we knew and everything we'd been through, the thought that Mum could *actually* die soon was so overwhelming that it seemed ludicrous. We quipped sarcastically, convinced that by this time tomorrow we'd be laughing about 'that stupid nurse' who thought Mum was about to die. But deep down something inside me stirred again.

*A sense of knowing.*

'I'd better call Olivia,' I said, heading to my own bedroom.

She was at Nandos with friends but pulled herself away from her peri-peri chicken for long enough to pick up. Her reaction was the same as mine and Hannah's.

'What do *you* reckon, though? Do *you* think it's serious, or is the nurse just a bit thick?' she asked.

'I'm not sure,' I replied. 'But you should probably come home. Better to be safe than sorry.'

It was just gone 11pm when I heard footsteps coming up the stairs. I hoped they were Olivia's and that I'd missed the clonk of the front door, but in the pit of my stomach, I knew.

*They belonged to Sandra.*

I'd just come out of my bedroom as she reached the landing. Immediately our eyes locked.

'I think it might be a good idea if you come down and sit with your mum now,' she said.

Her powerful message was delivered with a gentle tone. It was time.

*We were about to watch our mother die.*

'OK,' I mumbled.

Suddenly, I was painfully aware of how ill-equipped we all were to deal with what was about to happen. Hannah's door was ajar, so I pushed it open and gave her a slow, silent nod that said everything she needed to know. By the time we were downstairs, we heard the front door open and a bag drop to the floor in the hall.

*Olivia had made it home.*

'Hey,' she said, anxiously surveying the scene, scanning our faces for a vague sign of reassurance that everything was going to be OK. But there was nothing we could give her.

It wasn't going to be OK. Not this time.

*This was it. It was happening.*

I tilted my head as an invitation for her to join us.

'Look, Mumma. Liv's here now,' I said, stroking Mum's arm. 'All your babies are here now.'

I grabbed another chair so that all three of us were arranged around her bedside, Hannah and Olivia each holding one of her hands while I rubbed her arm. As we sat there, clinging on to her, my mind wandered. Surely the laws of physics made it impossible for her to go anywhere while we were holding on to her so tightly? It was three against one. However strong she was, she couldn't leave while she had her babies trying their best to keep her here.

*Could she?*

As we sat around her, she didn't make a sound, but I remembered that Hannah had read your sense of hearing is the last thing to go, long after all the other senses. So, as I tickled Mum's arm gently, we carried on speaking to her, making silly jokes. If she could still hear us, I didn't want her to listen to me crying. I didn't want Mum to be scared. I didn't want her to think that we couldn't cope, and I didn't want her to feel any guilt about going to be with Dad.

I just wanted her to drift away peacefully, safe in the knowledge that we would be strong and do her proud.

'Your three babies are here with you, Mumma. You're safe, just relax. We all love you. We're all here by your side. You just breathe nice and slowly. Go and give Dad lots of cuddles from us,' I said.

But it was the last thing that I really wanted. I wanted her to stay with us for ever.

As I tried to soothe her, I felt as if I was being physically torn in two. I was willing her to go so she didn't have to fight anymore, but at the same time every fibre of my being was aching for a miracle, some kind of magic that would make her stay with us.

The intensity of the moment made it feel as if we were

trapped in our own little bubble. I'd completely forgotten that the TV was still on in the corner of the room, until flickers of light from the screen caught my eye.

I looked over and smile cracked across my face.

'Look what it is, Mumma. It's our film!' I said, brushing my thumb against the pale back of her hand. '*Miami Vice.*'

The faintest hint of a smile rippled across her face as I spoke, the corners of her mouth making a microscopic movement upwards. Goodness knows why, but it had always been a cult classic in our family. Perhaps it was the combination of Colin Farrell, Jamie Foxx, sunshine and speedboats that won us all over, or simply that it was one of the only movies we'd all watched at the cinema together.

As I picked up the remote, I heard the lyrics of the song playing in the background of the scene and had to swallow down the tears.

'*One of these mornings, it won't be very long, they will look for me and I'll be gone.*'

I'd never taken any notice of them before, but as they hung in the air, I turned off the TV, looked back towards Mum and realised how painfully fitting they were. In that moment, it became clear that Mum had seen enough – of the film and of life down here with us.

Her breathing had been really rapid for about forty minutes, but suddenly even that seemed to pick up pace. I couldn't explain how or why, there was just a feeling, a palpable sense that the illness was leaving her. That the end was coming.

Her cheeks, which had been puffed up by the steroids for months, slowly started to deflate, showing off her beautiful cheekbones. The lines in her forehead, earned from years of worry about us girls, disappeared, leaving just perfectly smooth, radiant skin, as if all the subtle imperfections collected throughout her life were being silently airbrushed away.

Then, in a split second, her breathing changed from short, sharp, shallow breaths to slow, laboured ones. She was barely able to open her mouth to let any air in. We stayed by her side, talking rubbish to her, making bad jokes and trying to keep our tears at bay.

As we did, I breathed in deeply, desperately trying to make sure I'd remember what she smelled like, and gripped her hand extra-tightly so that I could remember what it felt like to have her fingers intertwined with mine.

We weren't *saying* goodbye to Mum, we were *feeling* goodbye to her because, for all their millions of uses, words had no place at a time like this. Knowing glances, eyes speaking in silence, soft forehead kisses and gentle hand-holding were the only language we needed.

A silent panic that somehow also managed to be peaceful descended across the room. We knew what was coming, but it was OK, it was just us girls with our mumma – quiet, relaxed and for the first time in months, without pain.

After about ten tranquil minutes, Mum suddenly took in a really deep gasp for air.

Then silence.

After another desperate gasp, her sparkling blue eyes wide open staring at us, we huddled round her even more closely, knowing what was coming.

'It's OK, Mum,' I said, holding her hand and stroking her arm. 'We're here.'

Blue eyes still sparkling, Mum suddenly winked.

One... two... three... Three times.

*One for each of us girls.*

Then she gasped deeply inwards.

Still clutching her, we were suspended in time, waiting, willing her to exhale. But there was nothing. Our darling mummy had fallen asleep for the last time, gently drifting away to be reunited with the love of her life somewhere up there.

Even though she was still in front of me, I could *feel* that Mum was gone. There had been a profound yet invisible shift in the room. Something had been removed. It was as noticeable as taking all the seats from a car. She had gone from a person to a body.

*How could this happen?* I wondered.

How could I *feel* her absence when the familiar contours of my mum were still physically present?

Struggling to process this unfathomable fact, I thought about the way people say a picture paints a thousand words. If that was true, then feelings must paint an entire gallery of pictures, each describing a dictionary's worth of words capable of telling the story of someone's entire life.

Still holding onto Mum, the three of us started to make declarations and promises that came from the very depths of our souls.

'I promise to make you proud, Mum.'

'I love you so much, thank you for being the best mum I could have ever had.'

'I promise to look after Hannah and Olivia as best as I can.'

'You don't need to worry, Mum. We are going to be OK. We are going to make you proud.'

I knew she couldn't hear me anymore – or maybe she could, just from somewhere else. But it didn't matter, I needed to speak those words out loud in the world. I needed to say them. Hannah and Olivia did, too. As we went round, one by one, Mum's chest suddenly jerked upwards again. We all leapt back startled, open-mouthed yet holding our breath. A storm of the most extreme emotions shattered the calm in the room.

*Fear, hope, disbelief...*

Had she come back to life?

Then, as my ear tuned in to a familiar gentle whirring sound, I realised. It was the pressure mattress on Mum's bed, which inflated every hour or so to prevent bedsores.

'It's the bed,' I managed to say.

The three of us exhaled in unison as if we were trying to blow away the heart-stopping surge of feelings coursing through our bodies. Then someone laughed. I can't remember who started it, but before we knew it we were all laughing. And crying. Crying laughing. And laughing crying.

'Only us! That would only happen to us!' Olivia spluttered.

The whole moment was so surreal. My brain scrambled to find something solid, to identify a truth on which I could rely and use to orientate myself. But I couldn't.

*She was still lying here.*

*She was still warm.*

*She still felt like Mum.*

*She still looked like Mum.*

But she was gone. How could that even happen? How can you be here one minute and not the next? As we sat with her in a state of disbelief, her physical presence comforted me. As long as she was still in our line of vision, we could kid ourselves that she was just sleeping.

*Please God, let her just be sleeping.*

But no amount of hoping could make my silent prayer come true. After about ten minutes, Sandra reappeared in the room with a solid reality check.

'It's probably time to think about washing and dressing your mum,' she said. 'Would you girls like to do it? Or if it's too much I can do it for you. Whatever feels right for you all.'

The question caught me off guard. After spending ages panicking about Mum dying, I'd never really stopped to think through the practicalities in detail. For all my worrying, I still didn't know the answer to the question that now lay in front of me.

*What do you actually do when your mum has died in your front room?*

But when faced with it, there *was* no question about what was right, wrong, or usual procedure. We didn't stand by Mum's side for so long to leave her at the last hurdle.

'We'll do it,' I said, firmly and without hesitation.

Tears were streaming down my face as I carried a bowl of warm water, a flannel and a small hand towel to Mum's bed. We took off her nightie and between us began washing her. It was the most difficult thing I had ever done, yet at the same time my heart was bursting with pride.

I knew this was the most precious, most important job I would ever do in my life. Being able to do this one last thing for Mum was the biggest privilege we would ever receive, washing every last trace of the illness away from her. It was somehow beautiful, a true labour of love.

After we'd dried her, we picked some clothes to dress her in, settling on her favourite russet top, which she loved because it made her blue eyes stand out even more than they already did. It was the first time in so long we'd seen her in anything but a nightie.

'She looks perfect,' I said.

'I know, it's like she's ready to go out somewhere,' agreed Hannah.

'Maybe for dinner somewhere nice with us girls,' added Olivia.

After we were done, we sat with her a little longer. None of us wanted to leave her by herself but suddenly, Sandra reappeared.

'Are you ready to call the funeral director?' she asked, in her gentle, reassuring tone.

'Um, yeah, OK, I'll do it now,' I said, bluffing unconvincingly before looking at my sisters, bewildered. Nobody had told me about this part.

I hadn't realised that I would have admin to do right now.

Nobody had told me you needed to call a funeral director there and then, when it happened. Nobody explained that was what happens to someone's body after they died. I looked at the time and date on my phone screen. It was 3am on Good Friday. At a loss for what to do next, I did the only thing I could think of. I opened Google on my phone and typed in:

*Funeral Director Ipswich 24 hour.*

There was no time to trawl reviews and as far as I was aware there was no Compare The Market for undertakers, so I clicked on the first link and called them. I can't even remember what I said; I can only recall the words of the stranger at the other end of the line.

'No problem, madam, we will be there shortly. Sorry for your loss,' he said, before hanging up.

An hour or so later, there was a solemn knock at the door.

*It could only be one person.*

I was strangely touched by his decision to knock instead of ringing the bell; it seemed somehow more respectful, more dignified. But I knew what that knock meant and no matter how respectful and dignified it was, it signalled the arrival of the moment I never wanted to come.

For a second, I considered just ignoring it.

*Maybe if we didn't let anyone in, we could block out the world and it would all be OK,* I thought.

We could stay here, the four of us together and nothing would have to change. We wouldn't have to deal with the pain.

But I knew that wasn't an option.

Slowly, I got up from the sofa next to Mum's bed where I was huddled, legs intertwined, with my sisters. It felt like the longest walk in the world as I made my way to the front door and unlocked it with a trembling hand. Two men were waiting outside, both dressed in black. Behind them, in the dim glow of the streetlights, I could just about make out some kind of stretcher.

My legs started to shake as I realised what was about to happen. *They were about to take my mum away for ever.*

Two total strangers I just found on the internet were going to take my mum's body and drive it away to God knows where. It might have been how things were meant to work, but I couldn't watch. Instead I ushered them in and pointed to Mum, before escaping to the kitchen with Hannah and Olivia. I just couldn't bear to see them take my mumma away, knowing that she was never going to come home again.

Another ten minutes passed, before there was a familiar solemn knock on the kitchen door.

'Come in,' I responded. The undertaker walked in confidently yet with his head slightly bowed.

'We are all done here, madam. All that's left for me to do is to give you these,' he said, handing me an envelope filled with leaflets about what would happen next.

'That should give you the information you need for now,' he added. 'Give us a call in your own time, when you're ready.'

With that, he was gone.

Holding the white A5 envelope, bulging with folded sheets, I began to absorb the absurdity of it all. In my mind, I began to shout at Mum.

*Is this a joke? Is this the trade-off we have to make with you gone, Mum? You go and I'm left with an empty bed and some leaflets telling me to make sure I register your death within five working days?*

Exasperated, I chucked the leaflets on the dining table, the papers splaying across its marked white surface. Outside I could hear the faint sound of the undertaker starting the engine of his car.

*The car with my mum inside.*

But before I was able to process everything that had just happened, Sandra slowly pushed the kitchen door open and popped her head around. I managed a half-smile in a feeble attempt to let her know she could come in, but she stayed in the doorway.

'I don't want to intrude, girls, but if you're all right I'll be off now as there's nothing else for me to do here,' she said.

'Define what you mean exactly by "all right",' quipped Hannah and I felt something welling up inside me again.

*Was this sad, or was this funny?*

At first, I wasn't sure, but it soon turned out to be both. In a dizzying combination of exhaustion and disbelief, the three of us burst into a hysterical combination of laughter and tears. As we did, Sandra simply nodded, gathered her belongings and slipped out quietly, closing the front door behind herself without saying another word. To this day, I don't know if she was offended by the outburst, but I imagine she'd seen similar scenes so often that she knew what to do for the best. Like Mary Poppins, she knew when to magically fly away without causing a fuss, when we were able to carry on without her help.

As she left, I sat on the sofa, my head pinned back as if held by G-force, kept there by the impact of the rollercoaster of emotion of the last few hours. Staring out of the window yet looking at nothing, I wondered if it was all real.

Did that just actually happen?

As the hours ticked by, I drifted between the rooms of our house, feeling lost.

*Utterly, utterly lost.*

As I floated around, my mind wandered, too. The only time I jolted back into myself was when I'd suddenly think I needed to go and check on Mum, as I had done so many nights before. But as quickly as the thought entered my head, I would realise...

*She wasn't downstairs to check on anymore.*

The tears flowed, steadily and constantly, but I didn't know why. Nothing about the night's events had sunk in. I still couldn't believe it.

She couldn't be gone.

She was my mum.

She was always there for me.

*Maybe she'd just gone out somewhere for a bit and she'd be back soon?*

In the hours and days after Mum died, I struggled to get my head around what had happened. If my heart had broken into a million pieces when Dad died, and each of those pieces broke into a million more when Mum was diagnosed, I wasn't sure there was anything left to break. But there must have been, because after Mum died it ached more than any metaphor or simile could do justice. My chest had been cleaved open and I was exposed to the coldness of the world with no choice but to face it alone, without Mum by my side.

# 10.

# *Moving On*

## WHERE'S THE 'FUN' IN FUN-ERALS?

A week after Mum died, in some ways everything had changed; in others, nothing had changed at all. Mum's mobile was still on charge, her freshly washed nighties were still in the ironing pile and her medication was still sat out on the side. Kind messages and flowers from friends were still coming, only now they were addressed to us girls – not Mum. There was still lots of paperwork to be sorted and calls to be made. Only now, instead of arranging delivery of equipment, collecting prescriptions and letting in the carers, I was asking them to take back the equipment, dispose of medication and cancel the carers.

But when the driver collected Mum's equipment, the difference was visible. Her walking frame and shower chair were gone, and in the living room – Mum's makeshift bedroom for the last few months of her life – there was just a big, empty space.

Just like after her diagnosis, when the adrenaline kicked in I went into do-do-doing mode. Olivia's eighteenth was just a few days away, so we decided to wait until after that to have the funeral. Despite losing Mum, we still went ahead with the weekend in Leeds we had planned to mark her big birthday. Organising a funeral and a party at the same time wasn't something I ever imagined myself doing.

*Bet I'll get confused and organise a stripper for the wake!* I managed to chuckle, knowing Mum would appreciate my inappropriate humour.

Ticking off the simple, clear-cut chores from my checklist, was strangely soothing. Ordering flowers, wrapping presents and choosing hymns was so much more manageable than the lone task I knew would linger on my to-do list once these jobs were done: Try to move on from Mum's death.

Powering through my list distracted me from what had just happened and, to my surprise, offered some light relief. You see, it turned out that arranging a funeral can be full of bizarre, macabre moments that are so ridiculous, they are, well... funny.

First was my trip to the funeral parlour. When the woman working there handed me a menu, I didn't even open it before asking for a gin and tonic. It was just what I needed to calm my frazzled nerves and ease my grief.

'Umm, err...' the funeral director stuttered, dressed all in black and trying to stifle her laugh. 'If you just take a look at the menu, madam,' she said, trying to maintain her composure.

'OH MY GOD!' I exclaimed, opening it up. 'I thought it was a *drinks* menu!' I gasped, looking down at the fold-out brochure filled with different styles of coffin. What started as a giggle soon turned into hysterics. The more I thought about how wrong it was to be laughing at caskets, the funnier I found it.

'Afraid not,' the funeral director said, smiling. 'But that's not a bad idea, you know. Maybe we should start. You wouldn't be the first person to want a drink going through all this!'

Then came the rigmarole of choosing what to bury Mum in. Feeling like celebrity stylists, Hannah, Olivia and I had browsed her wardrobe making and vetoing suggestions.

*Too booby. Too strappy. Too uncomfortable.*

In the end we tried to build the outfit from her feet up, with Olivia selecting a pair of nearly new black boots from the back of Mum's wardrobe.

'Nah, Mum always said those pinched,' Hannah said.

'Well she's probably not gonna clock up many miles in them, is she?' Olivia retorted. She'd barely finished the sentence before her shoulders started shaking and tears were running down her face. At first I thought she was upset, but then she let out a giant snort.

'Imagine her coming back to haunt us because she got a blister,' Olivia joked, setting us all off.

Now I understood why they say, 'You either have to laugh or cry'.

But it wasn't just morbid humour getting me through – it was Mum herself.

Trying to pick a picture of Mum for the Order of Service, I fanned out hundreds of loose photos that nobody had ever had the patience to put into albums. As I looked through, one in particular took my breath away. It was from her and Dad's wedding day, a few weeks before he died.

Wearing a pale blue shirt, Dad was sitting in a wheelchair, attached to a drip. His six-foot-two frame now weighing a little over seven stone. He was frail and delicate, the yellow tinge of his jaundiced skin, making his dark eyes look even bigger and even sadder. Mum was stood next to him, crouching slightly so her face was level with his, her piercing blue eyes frosted with tears. Wearing a bright, patterned dress she'd grabbed quickly one afternoon on the way to pick us up from school, she hadn't had time to choose something special, get her hair done or to bother with much make-up. But the love between them leapt from the photo.

To think what she must have been going through as she looked at Dad and said, 'I do' in the hospital chapel. For richer, for poorer. In sickness and in health. The vows she took that day summarised a life she had already shared with my dad. Looking at that picture immediately put all of my hurt into perspective. If ever human strength could be captured in a photograph, I was looking at it.

If Mum could get through that, I could get through this.

When Olivia's birthday came around, we allowed ourselves to let go. Rather than being tainted with sadness as I worried they might be, the celebrations were more intense – we had just made it through living hell, and nobody was going to stop us from celebrating (not even the hotel manager who told us to keep the noise down). Olivia's eighteenth came at the perfect time, a brief moment when our brains knew we were able to enjoy our freedom, but our hearts had yet to catch up and drag us into the grief that was coming.


On the morning of Mum's funeral, I found myself sat at the kitchen table wondering what to write on the card for the flowers.

*Why had I left this so late?*

These were the last words I would ever write to my mum and here I was, rushing them like a piece of overdue GCSE coursework. I'd intended to do it the night before, but I couldn't.

All the words I could think of meant that she had actually gone.

*For ever*.

Sighing, I put the pen down and turned up the radio. As I saw the hearse pull up outside, a song I recognised floated over the airwaves. It was Ben Howard.

*'Keep your head up, keep your heart strong.'*

Looking at the hearse, adorned with the flowers we'd selected, I took a deep breath.

*That's all you've got to do to get through this funeral, Rochelle*, I told myself. *Keep your head up. Keep your heart strong.*

Eventually, I processed out of the house with Hannah, Olivia, my grandma and my ex-boyfriend, who had come along for moral support. As we hovered in the driveway, deciding who was going to travel in which car, our neighbour walked over.

'Hi girls, haven't seen your mum around for a while, how's she doing?' she enquired.

Silence fell as we looked from the neighbour, to our sombre black attire, to the hearse parked at the front of the house, and back again.

In the end, it was Olivia who articulated our dumbstruck silence.

'Not great. We're just on our way to her funeral,' she replied in her typically terse tone.

Then it happened. Powerless to stop myself, I burst into the most inappropriate fit of giggles in my whole entire life as I absorbed the absurdity of our neighbour's question.

It was the comic relief we needed as we started the journey towards the church.

But there was no escaping the bittersweet sadness of the funeral itself.

The service passed in a blur of tears and smiles, as people

shared their memories of her. By the time we arrived at the cemetery for the burial, after driving from the church, grief was weighing heavy in the air. Waiting at the graveside for the hearse to arrive, I turned to one of my old uni friends who was standing beside me. Staring straight ahead, I nudged him.

'Things have changed a bit since the old days, haven't they?' I said. 'What happened to nights out in Tiger Tiger, strawpeedoing £1 bottles of Smirnoff Ice?'

The question invited banter, but he knew what I really needed.

'Come here, Bugg. Give me a hug,' he said, stretching out his arms.

I went to turn to him, but the heel of my shoe didn't turn with me. I'd sunk into the muddy ground next to the open grave. Suddenly, my foot came out of my shoe and I lost my balance.

'Whoooa!' I shouted as I tumbled, heading straight for the grave.

A loud gasp rippled around the crowd of waiting mourners, all convinced I'd collapsed, overcome with grief. Luckily, I just about stopped myself from falling in, but a deafening silence fell as hundreds of sets of eyes watched me, on my knees, trying to brush my dress down.

'And I'm not even drunk yet!' I muttered to my friend, as he helped me up.

The macabre, ridiculous 'you couldn't make it up' moments carried me through those first few weeks after Mum died. That and all the prepping and planning for her funeral.

I'd always thought the timing of funerals was a bit odd. No sooner has your heart been ripped in two, than you're suddenly forced into a new job as a sombre party planner. Grief hits and – as you struggle to even get yourself dressed each morning

– you're being asked to make decisions about flowers, songs, readings and coffins.

But when the sad task finally fell to me, I realised there is a method to the madness. There's a strange comfort that comes from keeping busy. Organising a funeral gives you a temporary focus, providing the mirage of a safe shore to keep swimming towards as you navigate the unfamiliar waters immediately after someone has died. It's only after it's all done that things really change.

You see, as quickly as life altered the night that Mum died, it soon did again after her funeral. Friends and relatives who had been crowding around our grief suddenly seemed to be mysteriously missing. One minute we were inundated with people, cards, flowers and supportive messages. The next, our phones went quiet, the doorbell hardly rang, and the postman rarely delivered anything but bills.

A few days after we'd laid Mum to rest, everyone seemed to vanish. Where once people had busily swarmed like ants around the crumbs of our life, suddenly there was nothing but a silent void.

*Poof!*

Just like that. Not a single lazy one was left dawdling home in a sugar-coma haze. I didn't know where they'd gone, there was no line marching away, and they didn't ask me to hold the door open for them while they embarked upon their mass exodus.

They just disappeared.

It was much the same after Dad died.

Like a *Coronation Street* cliffhanger, some people are drawn in by death, attracted to the intensity of it all, enthralled by the overwhelming emotion on display. They love the drama – on the condition they're not caught up too closely in the centre of the chaos – and tune in, safe in the knowledge that they can turn it off, go to bed and leave it behind when they've had enough for one day.

I've found that once the intrigue and 'glamour' of a death passes, often so too does much of the support. People disappear quickly and mysteriously, leaving you not only empty from your unthinkable loss, but also dazed and confused by the whirlwind of attention that swept in, swept up and swept out so very quickly. With the most difficult days of your grief still ahead, you feel more alone than ever – just you against the world.

## BACK TO THE FUTURE

I squinted through the shop window to judge the queue and see if I had time to grab a coffee before my parking was up. But as I looked back, I caught sight of a familiar face heading towards me. Our eyes locked before I had chance to look away.

It was Beverley, one of Mum's old work colleagues. My stomach sank.

*There was no getting out of it – I had to stop and talk.*

With nowhere to hide, I braced myself as she made a beeline for me. I plastered a fake smile on my face and then she pulled me into a hug so tight, I wondered if we were permanently bonded together. It wasn't that I didn't like her, she was lovely. I just dreaded conversations these days, because I had no answers for people's inevitable questions.

'How are you, my darling?' she asked.

'Yeah, you know. I don't think it's quite sunk in yet. But everything is just about under control,' I replied, wheeling out the same go-to phrases I'd been using for the last six weeks since Mum died. Recently, I'd been saying them so often to so many people – friends, family, customer service agents I'd had to inform that 'the account holder has died' – that they rolled off my tongue without me thinking or feeling a thing.

Truth be told, I wasn't feeling much at all these days, and it was strange. I was the kind of girl that shed a tear or two at a low-budget Netflix Christmas movie, and when I watched *The Notebook*... Don't even get me started.

Yet now, at one of the most difficult points in my life, I seemed to have developed the emotional depth of a frying pan. I wasn't exactly on top of the world, but I wasn't wallowing in a pit of depression either.

It was a month and a half since Mum had died. Surely grief should have caught up with me by now? Wasn't it about time it started wreaking more havoc than a Jägerbomb-drinking stag do on a bar crawl in Magaluf?

But it hadn't, and I couldn't work out why.

I knew that everyone deals with bereavement differently, that there's no right or wrong, no set of rules on how to cope. But I was surprised by how long it was taking for the numbness to wear off and the grief to kick in. I was in standby mode, waiting for someone to either power me back into action or switch me off at the mains entirely. I understood better than most that life is too short to spend just existing, but I didn't know how to move things forward. Even when I tried to coax grief out of its hiding place, I was left none the wiser.

*Come on then, if I'm gonna crash and burn, can we get it over and done with so that I can start building myself back up?* I would think.

But nothing. All I felt was intense frustration from being at a standstill, unable to muster the mental or physical strength to move anywhere.

I longed for some guidance on grieving. The teen magazines

I used to read said it takes half the amount of time you were in the relationship to get over your ex when you split. Is there an equivalent equation for losing a parent? I wondered.

But then Beverley asked me The Question and I was snapped out of my self-reflection.

'So, what are you going to do now?' she probed.

She wasn't the first to ask. Over recent weeks, I'd noticed that people's questions had stopped being about how I was feeling and instead become about what I was going to do next. It was clear that the rest of the world had moved on, the page had been turned between Act I and Act II of my life and I had no choice but to get on with writing the rest of the story. The problem was, I had no idea what I wanted the plotline to be.

Even before the sentence had fully left her mouth, my mind started racing through the list of questions I'd been putting off answering. What we were going to do with Mum's clothes? Where were me, Hannah and Olivia going to live? Would we stay together in the family home or go our separate ways? A host of big, scary decisions loomed over us, like a storm cloud over a summer picnic. We needed to salvage what we could from the wreckage that had been left after Mum's cancer had torn through our lives, but how?

Should the three of us try to carve out our own lives or should we cling tightly to one another and build a new life together? Should I step back into my old world where I was my own priority, or look for a path that worked for my sisters as much as for me?

For days after bumping into Beverley, The Question ricocheted through my mind, bouncing around the options like a pinball in a machine. I knew I had to get back to 'normal' life but what even was that now? It's tricky for any twenty-something to know what they want to do with their life, but it's infinitely harder to decide when the people you would usually discuss things with aren't there anymore.

The pressure to make the 'right' decision was so much greater because I had no backup.

Struggling to choose my next steps, I tried (and failed) to explain the pressure I was under to my friends. I wanted them to understand the emotional and financial responsibility I felt.

'Would you rather walk across a tightrope with or without a harness and safety net beneath you?' I asked, to illustrate my lack of parental backup.

'Yeah, but my parents don't give me money.'

'Yeah, but I moved out of home when I was sixteen.'

'Yeah, but I don't get advice from my parents for every decision I make.'

Their responses made me feel as if I'd simply been spoilt before and was now complaining about being in the same boat they'd been rowing for years. But they misunderstood my question. I wasn't asking if they used the safety net or relied on the harness. I wanted to know if they'd prefer to walk the tight rope *with* or *without* them. Even if they didn't admit it, the answer was always *with* because even if they never fell, knowing that safety equipment was there gave them peace of mind and the confidence to go further and faster.

We all have to walk the tightrope of our own life and it's not easy for any of us to keep our balance. But after Mum died, the stakes were higher for me, because I was facing life without the practical, emotional or financial safety net of having my parents around. It's a comfort that is *so* taken for granted by most that it is almost imperceptible.

For most, it means knowing that if you fall in life, you have someone you trust who will be there to catch you, to break your fall, or at the very least to help you back up. I no longer had that. The same friends who told me they knew how I felt were the ones who dropped their kids off with their grandparents for the weekend so they could do the overtime they were offered. The same friends whose mums did their laundry when their washing machine broke, and whose dads gave them money for a dining room table when they moved into a new house with their boyfriend.

Now that I'd lost two key players on my team, not only did I have to work harder, I was also alone in taking responsibility for any screw-ups along the way.

A week after bumping into Mum's old colleague, I was still no closer to answering The Question.

One evening I caught myself on a marathon Google session, comparing round-the-world flight tickets and trying to decide whether to travel South America top to bottom or bottom to top. And that was after I'd just spent the last three days drawing up a business plan for an idea I had, filling out application forms for jobs in Dubai, Australia, London and Barcelona, and sending off for information about a uni course.

*I had to tell myself to stop.*

With each passing day, I felt increasingly lost. Lost as if I'd been abandoned in a foreign land and told to find my own way back, without even knowing where I was trying to get to. Lost like one of those people you see on the news who wandered away from their tour guide in the rainforest and spent three years eating leaves and drinking their own wee to survive before finally being found by a local tribe. So lost, I doubted even a map, coordinates and a compass would help.

I watched as my sisters clutched on to fragments of their

life before: university, relationships, friendships. But the more *I* looked, the more I couldn't find my way.

I knew that I needed to throw myself into something, I just didn't know what. Caring for Mum had been so restrictive in so many ways, dictating where I could go, what I could do and when. Now that I could do anything, rather than feeling free like I'd imagined, I was overwhelmed by the choice. It was as if I'd been on the cabbage soup diet for years and now I was at an Eat All You Can buffet, unable to decide what I wanted.

I was angry at my own lack of action.

'I know how precious life is but I'm still not making the most of it,' I ranted to my friend Becca.

'You know there's an actual thing called *analysis paralysis*, right? When you've got too many options, you overthink things, so your brain freezes and does nothing,' she explained.

Finally, I understood why I was finding so much choice more difficult than having none at all.

I was so busy turning my head every which way, trying to see everything that was out there, that I forgot to look at what was right in front of me.

I quickly realised there was no need for me to take a giant leap. It was OK for me to take things one step at a time and trust that I would end up where I needed to be. Now that I was no longer a carer, I had control over what I did, when I did it, and what's more...

*I could change my mind!*

It sounds simple, but it took me so long to see it. Knowing that picking option A didn't mean I was ruling out options B, C, D and E for ever made it much easier to move forward. Once I took away the pressure to make a *quick* decision, I was finally free to focus on making the *right* decision.

I told myself to keep my eyes open for a sign and trust that I would get the answer I needed. A few days after my conversation with Becca, it came.

I picked up a book that had been sat on my bedside table, untouched, since it was delivered – *A Field Guide To Getting Lost* by Rebecca Solnit. As I absent-mindedly leafed through the pages, a section jumped out at me – a quote from historian Aaron Sachs.

*[Explorers] were always lost, because they'd never been to these places before. They never expected to know exactly where they were. Yet, at the same time, many of them knew their instruments pretty well and understood their trajectories within a reasonable degree of accuracy. In my opinion, their most important skill was simply a sense of optimism about surviving and finding their way.*

I read it again, and then a third time, allowing the profundity of the words to sink from my brain down into my bones.

It was not only OK for me to feel lost – it was inevitable.

When you go through a massive life-changing experience like losing someone you love, your entire landscape alters instantly. When we lost Dad, my world suddenly looked different. When we lost Mum, it became unrecognisable. Horizons shifted, landmarks disappeared, and the shore was nowhere to be seen. I was forced to start a journey I'd never made before, so how could I possibly expect to know the way?

Over time, I have learned that when you find yourself in new territory, there's no 'right path' to follow, so you don't need to worry about getting it wrong. Simply trust that you have everything you need to find your way again.

In the same way the people in that book relied on their familiar instruments, sense of direction, previous experience and sense of optimism, now, so too do I. As long as I head off in the vague direction in which I want to go, keep putting one foot in front of the other and remain hopeful that good times lie ahead, I am pretty much guaranteed to make it.

Now, when the weight of grief starts dragging me down and I feel lost, I trust that my inner satnav is calculating my route and will give me the directions I need to get back on track. However many wrong turns, diversions and fuel stops there might be, I can finally relax because I know I am on my way to the right destination.

## SO TELL ME ABOUT YOURSELF...

I rolled my eyes as I read the next question on what felt like the millionth job application I'd filled out that week: *Give an example of a time you've had to make a difficult decision.*

Before becoming a carer, I would have breezed through these forms with well-rehearsed examples from past roles. But now, their questions drove me crazy. My definition of 'difficult' was very different to what it had been when I was last looking for a job two years previously. What I really wanted to write in the empty box with a 500-word limit was:

'*Helping my mum decide whether it was worth going ahead with another round of chemo that couldn't cure her and would make her feel like death, but would buy her a few more months? No? Not difficult enough? What about choosing what clothes to bury my mum in? Is that the level of difficult you were looking for?*'

But of course, I didn't.

It had been seven weeks since Mum's funeral and I still felt lost, I still felt sad, and I still missed my parents. What I *didn't* feel was 'ready to get a job', but for finances' sake, I knew I had to make the leap back into the world of work. It was time for me to start taking part in life again and begin building some kind of a future for myself, albeit while I was still sorting through the rubble of my emotions.

While caring for Mum, I would daydream about having a normal job where I could switch off come 5pm, go for after-work drinks, book annual leave for guilt-free holidays, and watch the money build back up in my bank account. But now that Mum was gone and these had become very real possibilities, I felt overwhelmed, like a frightened animal that had just been released from captivity.

I was still programmed into carer mode, as if I'd been put on a tag, the invisible electronic monitor around my ankle keeping me to a curfew and within a certain range. If I dared to stray too far, it was as if sirens went off in my head and full-on panic mode set in.

I was finally 'free' to get my old life back, but I was no longer convinced I was capable of it.

Plus, it wasn't just about me anymore. I couldn't do whatever I wanted, wherever I wanted, like before. I felt I had to stay living in Ipswich, at least until Olivia finished school. So I threw myself into an online job search, restricting my parameters, persevering with lengthy application forms, sending off my CV and hoping nobody noticed my copy and paste covering letter.

It wasn't long before I was asked to interview for a marketing role, but it was a junior position and paid less than the one I'd left in London when Mum first fell ill.

*Maybe this is what you need though,* I thought.

After all, it was a quick fifteen-minute commute from home and a job I could do with my eyes closed.

*You don't want something challenging right now, Rochelle,* I tried to persuade myself. *Doing something easy might help you get back into the swing of working in an office again.*

Mustering up as much fake enthusiasm as I could, I replied to the email offer.

*I would be delighted to attend the interview on Wednesday at 2pm.*

Two days later, I squeezed myself into the same black dress I'd worn for Mum's funeral and made my way to my meeting. It seemed morbid, but it was the only smart thing I owned after two years of living in leggings. Arriving, I did a last-minute make-up check in the toilets, then played on my phone while waiting in reception.

'Rochelle Bugg,' a voice called after a few minutes.

A woman appeared and ushered me towards a nearby office.

I walked in to find a rotund middle-aged man reclined in a leather office chair. His desk was littered with papers, in a nondescript room overlooking a bleak, grey industrial estate car park.

'Monty,' he boomed, extending his hand without moving from his seat.

'Lovely to meet you, I'm Rochelle,' I replied, stretching across his vast desk to shake his hand.

My stomach churned as I took off my jacket and dug my portfolio out of my bag. It was a strange feeling. I was nervous because this was my first interview in so long, but at the same time I couldn't have cared less. After all, what could he possibly say that would come anywhere close to being as difficult as the last two years of my life?

This was far from my dream job.

*I just needed to convince him that it was.*

'I see you've been out of work for a while,' Monty boomed,

before I'd even had chance to take a sip of the tepid water his PA had left for me.

*What an opener!*

'Well, I was my mum's carer for nearly eighteen months until she passed away,' I explained, determined not to let a tear get anywhere even close to my eyes.

'I see. So you stayed at home with her for a bit, did you then? That's nice,' he retorted.

*That's nice?*

I wanted to reach over the table and punch him, but I fought the urge as he continued to speak.

'You're lucky I'm considering your application. I want someone who can really hit the ground running as we have some big projects coming up,' he said, flicking through the plastic pockets of my portfolio. He barely looked at me as the words kept pouring from his mouth.

'I wouldn't usually touch someone who has been out of the workforce for so long,' he continued, condescendingly. 'But you've got a good degree and I like what I see here.'

As he wafted his hand over my work, I felt myself go red, but I couldn't work out if I was angry or embarrassed. Monty continued to deliver his assumptions about me at thunderous volume, pointing out all of his own commercial successes over the years as he did, and very quickly I began to feel less than I was.

As if I didn't match up to him or his expectations.

Suddenly, I wished the pain I felt from losing my parents was physical. That it was possible for him to see the scars and the hurt I carried around each day. If he could, there was no way he'd be lauding his assumed superiority over me. In fact, he'd be begging me to work for him, amazed by my strength and resilience.

Or would he?

Self-doubt surged up inside of me. I'd assumed that my past experience would make me a shoo-in, but now I wasn't so sure. He was probably right. Everything had no doubt moved on by leaps and bounds since I was last in an office. What if I didn't even know how to do anything anymore?

Eventually, Monty came to his conclusion.

'Well, I think we've chatted enough. I've asked everything I need to,' he said. 'I like you and I'm willing to take a chance on you.'

Unsure of what to say, I waited for him to continue.

'It's a bit of a risk on my part, taking you on, so what I propose is that you come and work for us, but given everything I've mentioned, I just don't think we'll be able to stretch to the salary that was offered in the job description,'

'Oh, right, OK. So, what would you be able to offer?' I managed, fumbling over my words.

'I'd be happy for you to start right away on, say' – he wrote a figure on a piece of paper and pushed it across the desk – 'and we could think about a review in six months.'

Taken aback, I fell silent. That was a few thousand less than the role was advertised for. I might have been out of work for a while, but I still had experience and relevant qualifications. It didn't seem fair.

*But what if he was right?*

*What if I really was a risk?*

If I didn't take this opportunity, other people might not be so kind. Who was to say I'd even *get* another interview with such a big gap on my CV? What if no one else was willing to take a chance on me?

Swallowing down Monty's version of events, I nodded and ignored my gut feeling.

'Thanks, that sounds good,' I lied.

'Great, my PA will sort the paperwork and we'll see you bright and early on Monday,' he said and smiled.

Getting back in the car and heading home, I told myself I should be proud of securing a job in a little under two weeks. But deep down I knew this role would be unlikely to bring much cause for celebration.

'How did it go?' asked Hannah as soon as I walked through the front door.

'I got it,' I replied in a downcast and dejected tone.

'Whaaaaat? That's great! Well done!' she added, encouragingly.

'Hmmmm, we'll see,' I said, thinking back to my last job in London and wishing I was going back there instead. Then I slinked off upstairs to buy some new work clothes online.

*At least it's given me an excuse to go shopping. That's one good thing to come of today*, I thought to myself.


# WORKING 9–5

I expected to be physically exhausted going back to the routine of a 9–5, but I wasn't prepared to be emotionally wiped out by it, too.

On my first day, I locked my computer, got up from my desk, grabbed my bag and headed out to waste my lunch hour in the nearest café. But as I did, I instinctively reached for my phone to call Mum's mobile.

*I'll just give her a quick ring to let her know that it's going OK and everyone seems nice*, I thought to myself.

Then I realised.

*She's not going to answer.*

The colour drained from my face. I felt silly and embarrassed, checking over my shoulder to make sure nobody saw I'd just tried to call my dead mum!

*How could I have forgotten ?*

Hand shaking, I put my phone back in my bag as a wave of sadness washed over me. I was suddenly snapped back into my unwelcome reality – and it wasn't the only time that week.

By Friday of the first week in my new job, I was ready to scream. If one more person asked me, 'Where were you working before you came here?' or 'Do you live on your own or with your parents?' I was certain my head would explode. I almost felt bad as I watched my new colleagues' faces drop in horror as I repeated my stock answers with zero emotion.

'I was caring for my mum until she passed away about ten weeks ago.'

'I used to live in Leeds but my mum got cancer, so I moved back here to look after her for a while.'

'No, my mum died in April so it's just me and my two sisters at home.'

I must have sounded like a robot, but it was the only way I could get through it. It wasn't their fault, but the whole thing was so awkward. I'd pray that they'd drop the subject as soon as I'd told them, but nine times out of ten they'd try to be nice and follow up with something they thought would be comforting.

'Aw, that's so sad but at least you've got your dad,' they'd say.

Sometimes I would just lie and agree, simply because I couldn't face watching their silent panic when I told them that my dad was also dead. Sharing personal traumas with a stranger while still sounding professional just wasn't an art I'd quite mastered.

After less than a month in my new role, I was physically and emotionally exhausted. I thought this job was what I wanted – or at least what I *needed* – to get back to the 'old me'. But something had changed. Or rather *everything* had.

The 'old me' was gone for good.

I was very different to the twenty-five-year-old who'd got a call to say her mum had had a mini-stroke. I looked different, I felt different and I thought differently. And as that understanding dawned on me, I knew I'd have to learn all over again who I was, what I enjoyed and what I wanted to do with my life.

In a strange way, being a carer upped my expectations of what I looked for in a job. Even when I'd had the 'perfect' life for someone in their early twenties – a great job, living in a lovely flat with my boyfriend, a life full of eating out and cocktails, mid-week cinema trips and weekends where I drank too much and danced like I thought I was J-Lo circa 2001 – I would sometimes catch myself thinking, *Is this it?*

Was there nothing more? Is this what we do? Go to work all week, ticking off the days until the weekend when we spend too much money on nights out that we don't remember? But I never once had any of those feelings when I was at home caring for Mum. Being able to help her had made me feel so proud.

I never thought I'd say it, but I missed being a carer. I would have put money on me being glad never to have to push another wheelchair, count out pills, sit in hospital waiting rooms, or watch daytime property programmes – but I missed it massively. Not the bruises and boredom and backache, but the sense of purpose.

It was by far the most fulfilling thing I had ever done, so, the day she died, it felt as if I'd been made redundant as well as orphaned. Caring was never 'just' a job. However tired or sad I was, there had been a greater driving force making me get up and carry on.

*My mum needed me.*

Now that she wasn't there calling my name, I found myself struggling for a reason to get up and carry on. I'd lost my purpose.

How was I meant to fill the gap that had been left now I didn't have her to look after? She had been the sole focus of my life day in, day out for nearly two years. My reason to get up, my motivation to carry on. What could I possibly do that would come anywhere close to being as worthwhile as that?

It certainly wasn't this office job. I knew it wasn't where I wanted to be or what I wanted to be doing. But I didn't feel like I had much choice as the shockwaves of Mum's death continued to tear through my family, collectively and individually.

I quickly sank back into the routine of early mornings, breakfast news and eating my toast as I was walking out of the door, to make sure I got to the office on time. In a way, having that sense of normality back was great, but as my brain started to refill with Outlook folders, keyboard shortcuts and choosing what sandwich to go with my Meal Deal, I realised something:

I didn't want to forget the valuable lessons I had learned from losing Mum and Dad.

Everyone acts as if the goal after you lose someone is to get over things. They think the aim is to find the light at the end of the tunnel and forget you were ever in the dark. And while I never wanted to relive the pain of losing my parents, I knew that if there was anything good to come from these life experiences, I needed to grab on to it and not let go.

About three and a half months into the marketing job, something happened to remind me that I had changed irrevocably as a result of my experiences. That there was no way I could just pick up where I left off – and that maybe I shouldn't.

It was 3rd October – Mum's birthday. Only this year it was the first time we'd faced that milestone since she'd died. I was on my way to work as usual, hoping that by keeping busy, the emotion of the day wouldn't get to me. But as I was walking out of the door, biting into a cereal bar as I went, the house phone rang.

*Who could be calling this early in the morning?* I asked myself, feeling vaguely panicked.

Taking the bar out of my mouth, I grabbed the handset and pressed the green button.

'Hel—' I didn't even finish my greeting before I was cut off.

'Shirley? Shirley is that you? It's your mum. I'm just calling to wish you a happy birthday,' came the voice at the other end of the line.

I froze instantly, each and every atom in my body turning to ice as I stood motionless, unable to make a sound.

*It was Nanny.*

My mum's own mum had called her to say happy birthday.

*Her dementia.* I realised. *She's forgotten.*

Suddenly I was snapped out of my thoughts.

'Shirley! It's your mum. Are you there?' she asked again, but I still couldn't manage to formulate a response.

What could I say?

*Sorry, Nanny, Mum can't come to the phone because she's dead.*

'Nanny, it's Rochelle,' I managed to croak eventually.

'Oh, hello darling, is your mum there? I want to wish her a happy birthday,' she questioned.

All I could hear was the sound of blood pulsating in my ears. I gasped for air as I realised I'd been holding my breath since I answered. In the end I settled on a non-committal response.

'No, she's not here at the moment, Nanny.'

*Not exactly lying, but not exactly telling the truth either.*

'Oh, well, will you tell her that I called?' she asked, concerned that Mum might have thought she'd forgotten.

'Of course I will,' I said, sitting myself down on the bottom stair as my legs started to wobble. 'I'm really sorry but I'm going to have to go because I'm late for work, but I'll give you a call a later, OK?'

I hung up before she even had chance to reply, dropped the phone at my feet, then slumped against the bannister, crumpled like a piece of scrap paper ready to be thrown into the bin.

For a moment I was numb, in shock as I struggled to process what had just happened.

Then they started.

At first it was just one, involuntary. I didn't even know it was happening until I felt the wet blob careering down my cheek. But more followed, until rivers rolled from my eyes as I whimpered and wailed at the overwhelming sadness of life.

*My life.*

For a few minutes, I lost myself in the grief, but then I caught a glimpse of the clock. I was due at work in ten minutes. There was no way I would make it on time. Snapping back into myself, I bent over to grab the phone from the floor and dialled the office number.

RING, RING.

*Please don't let him be in yet*, I prayed silently.

RING, RING.

I wanted to leave a message and be done with it, but I had no such luck. Monty answered.

'Morning,' he barked.

'Hi, it's Rochelle. I'm really sorry but I'm not going to be able to make it in today as I'm not feeling too good,' I said.

My stuffy nose must've betrayed the fact I'd been crying.

'Why? What's wrong with you?' he probed sharply.

I took a long, deep breath in as I juggled my options.

*Lie, or tell the truth?*

Ever the good girl, I decided to tell the truth. Before I knew it, I was regaling the whole story as calmly as I could. Once I was finished, I waited. The silence seemed to go on for an eternity and I knew immediately.

*I'd made a big mistake.*

'Well, look, it's five to nine now,' he said eventually. 'Splash some water on your face, jump in the car and you can be here for half nine. I won't say anything about you being late.' He served up the offer as if he was doing me a grand favour.

At first I felt attacked by his bullish forcefulness, but then something inside me clicked.

*This wasn't right. This wasn't how you treated people.*

'Um, Monty, no, I, erm…' I said, stumbling over my words.

'What do you mean?' he snapped.

'Look, I really don't think I'm going to be much use if I come in today. My mind just isn't with it,' I said, suddenly feeling a little more composed. 'I'm up to date with everything – ahead of schedule for that big trade show, in fact.'

With every word I grew a little bolder.

'I just need a day to myself to get my head straight and I'll be back in first thing tomorrow. I can come in early and say late for the rest of the week,' I proposed finally, begrudging myself for talking as if I'd done something wrong and needed to make it up to him.

'Well, that's going to be your call, Rochelle. I can't force you. If that's what you want to do, you can either take today unpaid or use your annual leave to cover it,' he retorted.

Suddenly, I was furious as well as heartbroken.

I rolled my eyes and clenched my jaw in a bid to hold in my anger. He was trying to punish me for not doing what he wanted.

'Yep. Whatever. I'm really not that bothered. I'll sort it tomorrow,' I jibed in a clipped tone, desperate to get off the phone before I told him what I really thought.

I hung up and immediately let out a throaty, animalistic growling sound, my jaw locked together and hands balled into fists.

*Who did he think he was?*

In the few months I'd been in the job, I had outperformed the previous person in my role, contributed ideas and exceeded my KPIs. Did he really just see me as a slacker, trying to get a day off for fun? Surely everyone knew that grief didn't stick to a schedule? That you couldn't predict the impact it would have on your mental health. There's no set calendar for working through a bereavement. It's not as if I could have planned time off for my surprise emotional breakdown and booked it as annual leave.

I could have easily phoned up and pretended to have food poisoning from a dodgy takeaway and been paid for the day, no questions asked. But I chose to tell the truth, explained I needed a day. *Just one day.* And this is what happens.

All the talk about mental health being just as important as physical health. That's all it was – talk.

Rob from sales had called in sick on Monday. Everyone knew it was because he was hungover from a stag weekend in Dublin, but he'd still been allowed to take *that* as a sick day. Monty brushed it off as Rob 'just being a lad'.

But somehow when it came to me, it was different.

Why should I work at a place where a hangover was deemed more worthy of paid sick leave than dealing with your mother's death? Right there and then, I decided.

I was going to quit.

After all, what was the worst that could happen – when the worst had already happened?

# MOVING ON FROM MOURNING

As much as I knew in my heart that it was time to quit, it took a little while for my head to catch up. Desperate for a distraction from decision-making, I went to visit friends in Leeds.

After filling up with fuel, I drove off the garage forecourt and turned on to the motorway. But barely ten minutes into the long drive home to Ipswich, after my much-needed weekend away, a wave of emotional and mental exhaustion washed over me. Tears started silently trickling down my face, but I couldn't pinpoint one particular reason why.

*There were so many.*

As all the undefinable reasons spun round in my head, my tears turned from low sobs to gut-wrenching wails. For the four-and-a-half-hour journey home, they didn't stop. Making their way from deep in my tummy, pulling my heart out of place and dragging it up into my throat, my primal howls forced rivers from my eyes. And for the first time since Mum had died, seven months on, I could *feel* the hurt.

The anaesthetic of shock had finally worn off.

It was a feeling that I knew all too well. Instantly, I was fourteen years old again, transported to the end of my bed, crying and holding a picture of my dad, knowing that I would never see him again. That exact same hurt was coursing through my body now and the same question was ringing in my ears.

*How is it possible to feel so empty and yet so full of pain?*

By the time I arrived back in Ipswich to an empty house,

I didn't know where I belonged. My weekend away had made me realise that so much had changed and nowhere felt like home anymore.

The world I'd left in Leeds a few years before no longer existed, with some friends having moved away and others having moved on, settling down and having kids. But being in Ipswich didn't feel right either. It used to be a retreat, somewhere I could escape busy Leeds life, a welcoming place where Mum would be waiting for me with a freshly made bed and home-cooked food. Yet now the town felt claustrophobic, restrictive and full of painful reminders of the last two years.

My sisters and I had stayed living in the family home since Mum died. It felt like the right thing to do, at least until Olivia had finished school. But no matter how much I believed that the three of us needed to stick together, the current arrangement just wasn't working.

I'd morphed into a strange sister/parent hybrid. I had responsibility for everything – from sorting legal matters and earning money to pay bills, to cooking and cleaning – but influence over nothing. Hannah and Olivia didn't seem to respect or respond to anything I said.

Whatever I asked them to do around the house was met with a 'Yeah I will… in a minute' followed by the slam of the front door as they went out again without lifting a finger. When I told Olivia that I didn't like coming home from work to find her 'friends' (who I'd never seen before) helping themselves to what was in our fridge and wandering around the house like it was theirs, she'd just rolled her eyes and walked off.

*She wouldn't have dared do that to Mum.*

It was if I'd become a single step-mum to teenagers, resigned to a life of bickering and bitching. But in many ways, I only had myself to blame. I'd volunteered for the role, automatically presuming I had to fill it just as much as my sisters assumed I'd step into it.

Yet despite expecting me to take that role on, they didn't respect me, even when I took a stand. I went on a housework strike once, hoping it would make Hannah and Olivia step up. But they didn't. All that happened was I ended up eating my cereal out of a wok – with a ladle – because they were the only items in the entire kitchen that were clean. I knew they were struggling too, but I was at breaking point.

Since becoming Mum's carer, I'd been abandoning myself one micro-action at a time. Going with *their* Netflix choice, ordering the takeaway *they* wanted and picking up after *them*, all just to keep the peace. It had become second nature to put other people first, deciding what I wanted from within the confines and parameters set by others, fooling myself into believing it was all my choice. But by this point, I was beyond fed up and something had to change.

*For my own sanity, if nothing else.*

I loved my sisters with all my heart, but as much as I wanted to be near them, I needed my own space too. I longed for time by myself to make choices that were truly mine. Realising what needed to be done, I called a family meeting. That Saturday morning, I made pancakes and as we sat around the kitchen table, plates drenched in syrup and dotted with blueberries, I explained to Hannah and Olivia how I was feeling.

'Things aren't working like this,' I said. 'I feel like you two leave me to do everything.'

'I agree. Things aren't working,' Hannah said.

'Why's that?' I said out loud, before adding, in my head:
*You're having everything done for you.*

'You're so bossy, Rochelle,' she continued.

'Yeah, you try and control everything,' said Olivia.

'Well, I feel like you just take me for granted,' I retorted.

Silence descended as our differing thoughts met for the first time. This wasn't just not working for *me*. It wasn't working for any of us.

'So what are our options?' Hannah asked.

'Maybe we could rent out this house and each find somewhere else to live?' I suggested. 'That way we'll still have Mum's as a safety net, if we change our minds.'

'That seems like a good plan,' Olivia said. 'I might not go to uni anymore like I was planning to. I was thinking I could get a job here and move in with Arron.'

For her, staying in Ipswich made sense. That way she could still be near her friends and boyfriend.

'Jamal and I have been talking about moving in together too. I might go to London to be with him,' added Hannah. Before Mum got sick, she and I had been due to move to the capital together, so picking up where she left off made sense too.

'OK,' I said. 'Have a think, talk to them and then we can decide.'

But as we all left the table, a tacit agreement in the air, I suddenly thought, *What about me?*

Where would I go?

And there it was again. The Question was back.

What was *I* going to do next?

I was at the point in my grief where I needed to put some of my troubles down. They were too heavy for me to carry around for the rest of my life. I knew it was time to move on from mourning, but I didn't know where I was meant to be moving on to.

Leeds was the obvious option, but even though I'd had a

lovely visit to see friends, I didn't belong there anymore. In the same way, I couldn't go back *physically* to my life before Mum got ill, nor could I go back to who I was *mentally* and *emotionally* before all of this happened.

My hurt was now a part of me, running so deep that it had embedded itself in my body. It was in the calcium that hardened my bones and in the blood that coursed through my veins. Woven into the fibres of my muscles and riding on the coat-tails of my nerves. I was no longer the same person, so I couldn't expect to slot back into my same old life.

In the same way that whistling winds blow across desert plains, causing dunes to collapse and be reformed, my experiences had reshaped me entirely. I was made of the same sand, but I could now be found in a different formation, in a different place, with a whole new inner landscape to explore.

But whenever I focused on the future, all I could think about was the past. Contemplating my next step, I was confronted by everything that I'd lost and all that I would miss – Dad not being at my graduation, Mum never meeting her grandchildren, no longer having anywhere that felt like home. The crushing weight of it all hit me.

In time, I found the only way to free myself from the weight of sadness was to not only reflect on what I *had* lost, but to pause and think about what I could still lose.

*My sisters, my health, the roof over my head.*

It may sound counter-intuitive but it actually bolstered me. A wave of gratitude for what I still had washed over me and motivated me to make plans to move on.

As the weeks passed, I tossed various ideas around as to what to do next. Yet despite all the logical options – places I'd lived before and cities where I had friends – one random idea refused to stop rattling around my mind.

*Manchester.*

But I'd only ever visited a handful of times and I didn't know anybody there. Was I being selfish thinking about upping sticks to the other end of the country and leaving my sisters without me nearby?

All I knew is that I couldn't get the idea out of my head. It was still hovering in the corner of my brain when my friend Nilesh called. We'd worked together a few years before, back in Leeds, and he'd just got a new job and was looking for someone to live with.

'Where's the job?' I asked.

'Manchester,' came his response.

My eyes widened and I raised my eyebrows in amazement. Was this another one of those signs I'd started looking out for?

'Really?' I shrieked, checking he really had just said what I thought he had.

'Yeah,' he replied. 'I'm going up to look at flats next week. Do you wanna come?'

Deciding it was time to take a risk, I responded immediately.

'Cool. Sounds like a plan!' I said.

It really did, a chance for a new start. But after a few weeks of planning, the seed taking root, I started to panic.

*Was I being reckless?*

Losing a loved one leaves you overcome by the extreme emotions of grief. Having your understanding of life turned on its head can mean you start seeking out experiences that truly make you feel alive. Realising how quickly life can be taken away gives you an urgency to get out into the world and see everything, feel everything, touch everything, taste everything and hear everything. You're suddenly tempted to do something wild, something you'd never normally do.

*Get a tattoo, travel the world, have a baby and get married – all in one week!*

Was moving to Manchester just another one of those crazy plans?

Working in Monty's soulless office from nine to five each day felt so mundane and stifling. But was that just because being a carer had numbed me so much that I couldn't be satisfied with 'normal' life? Did I want to do something huge because that was the only way to match the intensity of the past two years? You see, even though that extreme situation was often uncomfortable, it had also become familiar, my new benchmark.

I was unsure. Was grief throwing me a lifeline, or throwing me off track?

I was too confused to tell, so I made myself a promise:

*I can make the most of this opportunity for a fresh start, but I can't do anything whilst I'm drunk on sadness that I can't undo once I've sobered up from my grief.*

In the end I made my decision.

I was going to hand in my notice and give a new life in Manchester a try. I printed off my resignation letter at home and went into the office extra early so that I could leave it on Monty's desk without anyone seeing.

At 9.56am came the inevitable email calling me into his office.

Five minutes later, 10.01am, I was biting my tongue, trying not to argue back.

'Look, you know I'm not a man who minces his words so I'm going to be straight with you. You're making a mistake,' he barked. 'If you were my daughter, I'd be telling you not to do this. Not to move away. Not to leave a good job. Not to leave your sisters.'

My blood began to boil.

But I *wasn't* his daughter. And he *wasn't* my dad.

How dare he presume to know what my parents would be telling me to do right now?

His lofty tone suggested he thought his words were having a profound effect on me. And they were – just not the way he'd hoped.

*I'd never been more certain that I was making the right decision.*

'Thanks for your thoughts. I'll let you know if I change my mind and want to stay,' I retorted, hoping my comment was seasoned with enough sarcasm to get him to shut up, but not so much that he refused to give me a reference.

The things you learn from caring for and losing a loved one are not always immediately apparent. It often takes a while to uncover the lessons, but when you do, they're incredibly powerful. Losing Dad at such a young age brought home the realisation that we don't always get as much time here as we think. His death taught me to get out there in the world and do and see as much as I could – before I couldn't. It made me realise there's no need to be afraid of anything because one day it will all be over anyway.

Life is a game – sometimes I will win, sometimes I will lose, but ultimately it will be the taking part that counts. Leaving Monty's office that day, I didn't know if my gamble would pay off, but I knew I was going to give it a good go.

You see, as much as everyone says that life is too short, losing both my parents made me realise that life is also too long. Too long to waste it living the same day over and over again in a job you hate. Too long not to buy that ticket or apologise to that person. Too long not to read that book or take that course and too long to never spend time pursuing your passion or working towards that goal.

Life is too long and too beautiful and too bursting with opportunities to numbly fumble your way through it with half-hearted experiences. Yes, life is too short not to take risks and follow your dreams, but equally life is too long to spend it unhappy, unfulfilled or living other people's dreams that have been sold to you as your own.

After four weeks and six long journeys up and down the M1 from Ipswich doing viewings, Nilesh and I walked into a warehouse conversion in Manchester's trendy Northern Quarter, slap bang in the middle of town.

*This was the one.*

Before we knew it, we were signing on the dotted line.

'I guess that's my decision made,' I said, handing the pen back to the estate agent.

'It is,' said Nilesh. 'But just because you're a girl that doesn't mean I'm gonna let you have the en suite room, you know.'

'Err, yeah you are!' I said jokingly. 'It's the law. Girls always get the en suite.'

'I'll leave you two to it,' the estate agent chuckled.

As we left the apartment, I took one last look at the blank canvas for my new life and smiled. Moving on was hard, but it felt good to know I now had a space that was mine, where I could get my life back and remember who I was, without the pressure of having to fill Mum's shoes.

The feeling I got when I walked into that flat made me appreciate that often we don't know where we're going until we get there. It's only once we've arrived that we realise we've been heading there all along.

Sometimes things 'click' and feel inexplicably right, like deciding to take the house the second you walk through the door, or speaking to someone like an old friend, despite having only just met. I think of these moments of recognition as a nod from the depths of your subconscious, or perhaps from the heights of the universe, letting you know that you are on the right track. They're a sign telling you to keep going down the road you were always meant to follow.

I think it was that deeper knowing which meant I persisted with my madcap Manchester move, despite it having no rational foundation. But that doesn't mean that things clicked into place without any conflict. My move up north felt right in so many ways, but as I unpacked the boxes in my new bedroom, a part of me still felt guilty for moving on.

*Does this mean I don't care about Mum anymore?*

*Is my fresh start also the start of me forgetting her?*

As the months after her death went by, I had more and more days where I 'only' missed Mum a few times a day, not 24/7 as it had been. I began to worry it meant that soon I wouldn't miss her at all. Would it get to the stage where I only thought of her once in a while, like that old school friend I hadn't seen since Year 9?

Taking a break from unpacking, I scrolled through Instagram and saw a quote by Hafez which stopped me in my tracks:

*Ever since happiness heard your name, it has been running through the streets trying to find you.*

In that moment, I realised that happiness still hadn't quite found me, but it was down to me to allow it to do so. I couldn't keep hiding from happiness, worried that meeting it once more would mean I was forgetting Mum in some way. I wasn't a bad person for wanting to move on after losing someone I love. I wasn't disrespecting my parents or glossing over their existence. I was just moving forward.

Society always wants us to label things as either this *or* that, but so often they are both this *and* that at the same time.

Just because a zebra is black, it doesn't mean it's not white too.

I've realised that so many of my struggles and so much of my guilt around moving on after Mum's death came from not knowing I could hold two contrasting emotions at the same time.

*I can be healed and still healing.*

*I can live a normal life and still be affected by my loss.*

*I can leave the past behind but still remember my parents.*

*I can move on with my life and Mum and Dad can come with me, too.*

*I can love someone and also disagree with them.*

*I can be happy and excited for the future and still be sad about the past.*

*I can see the silver linings in my experience and also resent that it happened at all.*

*I can see that things will never be the same again and they can also be good again.*

*I can be in the darkness of grief and I can still have enough light to see.*

*I can heal from my loss and still never forget what happened.*

*I can see that things can go differently to the way I planned and still turn out OK.*

People say you die twice: once when your heart stops beating and again when people stop saying your name. I know I'll never stop saying my parents' names, so I don't need to worry that they will ever be forgotten, even if I have moved on with my life.

# 365 DAYS

I picked up the remote control and flicked through the channels aimlessly, more interested in the satisfying click of the button under my thumb than the scenes playing out on the screen. I was restless. Agitated. Claustrophobic. Sad. I was so many things and I knew exactly why.

It was the first anniversary of Mum passing away.

I'd been fine all day. I'd known it was coming, after all. But at about 9.30pm my reaction changed, and it caught me completely off guard. I shifted in my seat, fidgeted, got up to make a drink, sat down again with it, and didn't touch a drop. I tried to distract myself in a hundred different ways, but my mind was intent on focusing on one thing and one thing only.

*The time.*

My eyes kept finding themselves drawn to the clock on my phone so I could calculate exactly what would have been going on at the same time 365 days ago.

Ever since Mum was diagnosed with that hideous brain tumour, I had been writing my way through things. It was my release, my outlet, my way of unscrambling the thoughts in my head and processing them into some coherent reflection of the pain, emotions, helplessness and confusion in my mind. Maybe that was why the urge to reach for my laptop seemed so natural, despite not knowing what words would appear on my screen as my fingers weaved across the keyboard.

Without meaning to, I started writing about the evening Mum died. I had been so involved with her care that everything, particularly her last night, was stored in my mind for ever in wide screen, Technicolor, surround sound, HD, 3-D. The entire world had moved in such slow motion when we said goodbye to her, that my brain had time to remember every last detail. Yet I never thought about those details. Or was it that I couldn't?

Part of me believed that if I did, I might not be able to carry on because the enormity of my grief would eclipse any hope I had left inside of me. But tonight was different. For the first time since we lost her, every single specific found its way out of the recesses of my mind. I couldn't stop myself from replaying that night, minute by minute, knowing it was all happening at exactly this time last year.

*Three hundred and sixty-five days ago, I was living my worst nightmare.*

Rarely in life does something so monumental happen that it's instantaneously etched onto your memory, through every layer of your brain, right to your very core. But this was one of those things. It was immediately imprinted through every cell of my being, like a stick of cheap Blackpool rock. The sound of the Marie Curie nurse's footsteps as she came to my room. The green of her eyes as I caught her gaze at the top of the stairs. The phone call in hushed voices as I asked Olivia to come home. The irritating hum and whirr of the medical mattress on Mum's bed. The strange colour of Mum's hands as her body started to shut down. The raspy rattle of her breathing which I could feel against my cheek as I leant in close over her.

The memories invaded not just my mind, but my body too. Advancing like an unbeatable army, taking the air from my lungs, forcing burning tears to spring from my eyes and dragging me, defeated, back to relive it all over again.

Typing away, I watched the time tick by in the corner of my screen. In my mind's eye, I hovered, hawk-like, over the scene from Mum's final night.

**11:53pm** The three of us were sat around Mum's bedside knowing what was coming at any moment, yet never truly believing for a second that it would actually happen.

**01:16am** Soon Mum would take her last breath.

As the clock marched on, I stayed immobile, transfixed by where its numbers eventually led me…

**02:06am** The moment Mum made one last scrambled sigh for air, before winking at each of us in turn and finally letting go.

It seemed ridiculous to relive it in real time – surely one round in the ring with death is enough? But I trusted that my brain knew what it needed to do to unravel the knots of grief in which it had been bound for the past year. I hadn't slept properly for the last two weeks and the nightmares that haunted me in those final few months of Mum's illness had returned.

Maybe I needed to remember it all before I could let it go?

I realised in that moment, as I committed Mum's final moments to the page in front of me, that remembering was OK. Because the fact that I *could* look back on it meant that I was still here. Somehow, I had muddled through. The world had continued to turn, and I had managed to keep up with it. My first year without Mum or Dad had been about survival.

*Could I survive?*

*Would I survive?*

The answer was yes, I could – and I had. If I could do that, if my heart carried on beating even after it had been broken beyond all repair, then anything was possible. I could achieve anything I set my mind to.

That was what the next year would be about. It was time for me to decide what I wanted from the world. Where I wanted to go, what I wanted to do and who I wanted to be.

I had survived and now it was time to thrive.

# 11.

# *Healing*

## FAIRY LIGHTS

Carefully balancing my kebab in one hand, while opening the front door with the other, I drunkenly stumbled into the house, kicking off my shoes. As I sat down, a WhatsApp message flashed up on my screen.

**You home safe? So good to see you back to your old self xx**

I pulled a half-frown, half-smile at the glowing screen, and wondered if my friend knew something that I didn't.

*Back to my old self?*

Was I? Was that really it? Was I over losing Mum in just six months?

If I was, it was news to me. But then how could I tell? I had no idea what being 'over it' looked like.

How would I know when I'd gone from *healing* to *healed?*

As I sat in the pitch black, too lazy to get up and find the light switch, and with a stray piece of lettuce from my kebab

303

stuck to my knee, I thought about how Mum's death had been like a power cut. A sudden shutdown leaving me consumed by darkness. But instead of sitting around and waiting expectantly for the electricity to come back on, I'd set about doing all that I could to make it happen quicker.

I took things to extremes, trying all I could think of to hurry it along. I spent thousands on a juicing retreat in Spain, waited for ten hours at Alexandra Palace to hug an Indian saint on her visit to London, scoured the internet for recommendations for psychics, got tarot readings, tried reiki healing, and even started putting crystals in my bra.

Each time, I hoped it would be 'the thing', the one to flip the grief switch off and turn the lights back on. But my efforts were in vain, because healing from a bereavement doesn't work like that.

I didn't need to be extreme. What I needed to be was *consistent*.

Recovering from the loss of someone you love is not one big, dramatic light-bulb moment. It is the meticulous process of lighting a long string of fairy lights, one at a time. Alone, each tiny bulb doesn't seem like much, just as each small act of healing seems minor and insignificant. But illuminated together you suddenly see just how much light there is in your life once more. You stare at each of the tiny bulbs in amazement and realise that you did the impossible.

You survived the un-survivable!

No doubt the steps you took will have been so small and so gradual that you'll barely have noticed you were moving, but that's exactly how it works.

My healing has been made up of thousands of minuscule shifts. It's come from sharing good times, cold cocktails and loud music with friends, and it's come alone, reading thought-provoking books and heading on spontaneous solo travels.

Healing has happened with early-morning sunrises watched from plane windows and late-summer sunsets after picnics in the park. It's been uncovered with morning walks through bluebell fields, afternoons lost in old photo albums, and long evenings enjoying snuggles on the sofa.

Healing, for me, is knowing that Mum and Dad once breathed the same air as I do now; it's remembering that the sun which shines on me today is the same one that warmed their bones and tanned their skin. It comes from understanding that everything that matters will last – my memories, their values, our love. And from realising that their legacy didn't end when their lives did because they left a spark in myself and my sisters that pushes us to do and be all we can.

Healing – one small glimmer of light at a time – is a slow and steady process, but one day, you will look back and be able to see how far you've come.

## GRIEF TSUNAMI

Apart from the fact my mum had died just a few months earlier, it was the most normal of 'normal' days. Standing in the queue in H&M, I was waiting to pay for a dress I didn't need but had convinced myself was essential.

Hovering by the tills, my eyes fixed on the mother and teenage daughter in front of me. At first I only noticed the plastic handles of their shopping bags digging into their fingers, but I soon started eavesdropping on their idle chit-chat. Momentarily, I was sucked into their world.

'What do you fancy for dinner tonight?' the mum said.

'Can we get a takeaway?' the daughter asked hopefully.

'OK,' came the reply.

'Can we get Chinese from that place with the really nice ribs?' the daughter continued, pushing her luck.

I didn't hear the mum's response because, suddenly and without my permission, I felt the tentacles of the past creep around me and drag my mind back to the days when that same scene played out – but with me and my mum in their roles. The days we would sneak off – just the two of us – and drive to Norwich, where she would treat me to some new clothes and I would nag her until she agreed to take me to the place *I* really wanted to eat.

'Can we go to the Pizza Hut buffet, Mum?' I'd ask, over and over until she finally relented.

It had been years since I'd thought about those days, but as the long-forgotten memory popped up like a daffodil in springtime it was both comforting and confronting. Suddenly, there on the H&M shop floor, I missed her more than ever. Seeing that mother and daughter, doing what I had once done with *my* mum, reminded me just how lonely I felt.

While my day had been perfectly 'normal', my life at that point was far from it. I was confused, bewildered and scared at having to face life by myself. Overwhelmed by the choices and changes up ahead, there was only one thing that I wanted to do.

*Run into my mum's arms.*

I desperately ached for even the slightest sliver of time to talk things through, just the two of us. But I couldn't and I had no idea how to fill that void. When your whole life is built on one woman and that foundation crumbles beneath you – how are you meant to stay standing?

It took all my strength not to collapse to the floor right there next to the tills. I didn't even see the happy mother and daughter leave the shop. I just focused on putting one foot in front of the other, paid for my dress then trudged, trance-like, back to the car park. In a daze, I dumped my shopping bags in the boot, climbed into the car and started up the engine with the stereo on full-blast.

Despite the volume of the music, I barely noticed my Spotify shuffling through tracks until, about halfway home, a solitary line leapt out of the speakers and into my heart.

I'd never heard the song before, but the voice was unmistakably Ed Sheeran, singing about the tsunami tides of longing he felt for someone he missed.

In the months since losing Mum, that one lyric, hidden in the middle of the melody, was the first thing I'd heard that came close to capturing the infinite emotions that were sloshing around inside of me. The ones I was struggling to make sense of.

Losing Mum was so catastrophic, so big and so overwhelming that it had shaken my entire world to its core and wiped out everything I had ever known.

Just like a tsunami.

And just as tsunamis trigger physical earthquakes, so bereavement triggers psychological earthquakes. The after-shocks of grief, like my one in H&M, can be as sudden and damaging as the original catastrophe, striking at any moment, knocking you down before you've had a chance to regain your balance from the last.

But as the ripples from my earlier upset began to fade, I realised that I had survived it. I was still standing. By the time I unpacked, made dinner and sat down to eat with Hannah and Olivia, I had all but forgotten about the mother and daughter whose tender interaction had shaken me to my core. As we ate together, laughing and joking, the sadness slipped from my consciousness, just like the spaghetti tumbling from my fork as I twirled it around my bowl.

After dinner, as we sprawled on the sofa, I grabbed my phone and started scrolling through Facebook, more out of habit than anything else. Endless inconsequential updates and targeted ads rolled past my eyes, until suddenly, there it was.

A video of Mum that I hadn't seen for about a year.

She was lying on the bed with her customised eye patch riding up because the elastic had lost its stretch from too much wear. Hannah was sitting next to her and leaned over to give her a kiss.

The jolt to my heart took my breath away.

The scene was so familiar and so real, that for one brief, beautiful moment I forgot Mum wasn't in the other room anymore. I pressed play over and over again, desperate for some kind of connection with her after all these months. But then the aftershock of reality hit, and I was engulfed by grief for the second time that day.

This was just a precious memory, trapped in my iPhone with so many others. She wasn't next door. She no longer existed on this planet. And this video was the only way I would ever get to hear her voice again.

Right there, in the middle of an otherwise unremarkable evening, I began longing for my mum – not in a dramatic, staged *telenovela* way, but in a simple way. I longed to know she was in the same house as me, to hear the dance of her voice through the air, to feel the touch of her fingers wrapped in mine as I held her hand, to sense her heartbeat as she pulled me in for a hug.

I was homesick for my mum. I missed her in the same way I did while on my first school French exchange trip. The same trip when I'd learned that the French don't say 'I miss you' like we do, but rather *Tu me manques,* meaning 'You are missing from me'. Body tightening, I realised how much more fitting that was because what I was feeling was physical, not emotional. A part of me went when she did. She was missing from me and I didn't feel safe without her. Now everything I did, everywhere I went, every thought I had, my mum was always missing from me.

*Would I ever stop noticing that she wasn't there?*

The hurt started sneaking out of hiding, freeing itself from the marrow of my bones, unbinding itself from the fibres of my muscles and coming together to form an infinite whirling pool of sorrow in the pit of my stomach. My face contorted into a pained expression and I couldn't catch my breath as a wave of sickness rose in my throat.

A solitary tear finally escaped, meandering slowly, snake-like, down my face, taking the familiar route from my eyes, across my cheeks and hovering on my chin momentarily, before crashing and falling. More followed, hot and steady, tracing that same well-worn path. But there was no noise, no howls. I silently gasped for breath while my face remained paralysed in its expression of grief.

I don't know how long I sat there, the concept of time abandoned to the tsunami of my tears. I prayed they would wash the pain out of my body. But they didn't. Crying until I was sick, I hoped I could purge myself of the agony. But I couldn't.

I was yet to learn that the tsunami of my grief was only just beginning.

# COCKTAILS AND ROLLERCOASTERS

The thing that surprised me most wasn't *when* things caught up with me, but rather *what* things caught up with me. In the months following Mum's death, I knew a taste of grief was on its way, but when it arrived, it was like being served an entirely different drink to what I thought I'd ordered.

I expected neat shots of pure sorrow, but instead found myself woozy and nauseous from an endless cocktail of emotions. My grief was a bespoke blend, shaken and stirred to my own unique experiences, memories, predispositions and vulnerabilities – as was everyone else's. Each of us sat sipping our own distinct drink.

Just as a barman would struggle to extract the gin from a Martini he'd made, it was near impossible for me to separate or pinpoint all the thoughts and feelings inside of me. I was going through a potent mix of extreme rage, the deepest sorrow, punishing guilt, crippling longing and paralysing fear – emotions all far more intense than I'd experienced before, and all happening at the same time.

Everything was dredged from the bottom of my soul, shaken, then served up for me to down. Disbelief, exhaustion, regret, pain, abandonment, anger, confusion, love, gratitude for the good times. The lethal cocktail went straight to my head and it was all too much to stomach.

I knew I needed to find a way to sober up from my emotions. *But how?*

Setting out on a quest to navigate my way through grief and back to myself, I came across the Kübler-Ross Grief Cycle online. Looking like something that from a physics GCSE textbook, its colour-coordinated categories and neatly labelled sections helped me feel as though I had the slightest clue – and more crucially, control – over my healing. It outlined the five sequential stages of grief:

1. Denial
2. Anger
3. Depression
4. Bargaining
5. Acceptance

It's called a cycle, but I came to see it as more of a continuous rollercoaster. Essentially, it says that after a bereavement, first you'll freeze, then you'll go up, then down, then even more down, followed by up, up a bit more, then just about OK again. When I first saw it, my reaction was dismissive.

*I'm far too complex to go through such a standard process with something as personal as grief. No way does this apply to me.*

But when I thought back over the months that had passed since Mum's death, well – as much as I don't like to admit that I'm predictable – let's just say this Elisabeth Kubler-Ross woman knew what she was talking about.

Having already lost Dad, I arrogantly presumed my brain was pre-programmed to work through grief like a pro. Three or four months after we lost Mum, I thought I was doing pretty well. Another month or two later and I thought I had actually got there, I knew what the finish line looked like and I was heading straight for it. But then along came another wave of feelings – prompted by that mum-and-daughter duo in H&M – and I realised I was barely past the halfway marker, let alone close to the end of the race.

You see, what I hadn't bargained on, and what the Kübler-Ross graph didn't account for, is what happens when you lose someone to a terminal illness. Namely that you get a Buy-One-Get-One-Free ticket for the rollercoaster of grief. You go through all of the stages once *before* the death, in relation to the diagnosis and the illness. Then, without a chance to stop, put the handbrake on and enjoy the stability of the 'acceptance' stage, someone whacks their foot on the accelerator and off you go through the cycle all over again. This time *after* their death. Once more you're sent through the stages of denial, anger and depression because the person you love is no longer around.

Only you're not always aware your carriage has started rattling along the tracks again.

Coming up to a year after Mum passed away, I started getting angry at everyone and everything around me. People driving too slowly, shop assistants who didn't have what I wanted in stock, people who texted me too much and people who didn't text me enough. The broken strap on my bag, the council who didn't empty the bins over the bank holiday, and the world because it took away my mum.

I'm not usually an angry person. Moody? *Yes*. Irritable? *Guilty as charged*. But the stomach-burning, chest-tightening, fist-clenching anger that overwhelmed me during that period of my life was new. It wasn't until I looked at the Kübler-Ross cycle that I realised I hadn't turned into an awful person. Much to my relief and reassurance, I was simply making my way through the *Anger* phase.

Likewise, I was alarmed when I first noticed my lack of interest in anything, and the way I'd started alternating between insomnia and sleeping for days on end. I panicked at my sense of helplessness and the way I'd started to wonder what the point of it all was. But then I remembered I was probably heading into the *Depression* phase.

Without the Kübler-Ross Grief Cycle, I probably would have thought I was going crazy, but the diagram helped me realise there are no shortcuts or fast-tracks when it comes to healing from a bereavement. And that's a bitter pill to swallow because, in the depths of mourning, a single emotion can be so overwhelming it feels as if you've been possessed by a body-snatching alien.

Whenever I felt sad, afraid, angry, hopeless or lost, I had to remind myself that I *have* emotions, but they are not who I am as a person in my entirety. This is something my friend Mussarat told me back when Mum was still alive.

I was in a blind rage after a mix-up with some of Mum's scan dates.

'She's not getting the treatment she deserves,' I seethed. 'People are so incompetent.'

As my blood boiled and I rambled on about how unfair it all was, Mussarat stopped me in my tracks.

'Is your hair angry?' she asked.

I half-laughed and looked at her like she was cracking up.

'No,' I said.

'What about your little finger? Is that angry?' she continued.

'No,' I repeated.

'Your feet then? Are your feet angry?' she asked finally.

I pondered for a second or two, before answering. 'Angry about squashing them into heels on nights out maybe,' I joked. 'But definitely not angry about Mum's scans.'

'OK, so *you* are not angry,' Mussarat explained. 'You simply *have* some anger right now.'

For me, that was a lightbulb moment. Emotions aren't a part of us; they are outside of us. We move through them, but we don't become them. It's a slow and gradual process, but you need to learn to feel your feelings without letting them define you.

While the Kübler-Ross graph is brilliant in so many ways, my journey has not been the smooth curve the diagram suggests. There was a clear beginning to my bereavement, but there is still no end point, no final destination: there is no expiry date on grief.

It's never-ending. Like a car journey when you're desperate for a wee. There's no finish line to cross. No certificate upon completion.

As the time since Mum's death has multiplied – from four days, to four weeks, to four years and beyond, the rollercoaster of emotion keeps cycling round, again and again. Each time I am faced with a fresh dose of grief, the ups and downs have gradually become less pronounced, less intrusive and less jarring. While the peaks and troughs are no longer quite as dramatic, they never stop coming.

The aftershocks of grief still catch me off guard, even during moments I presumed would be joyful, like moving into my own house, or dancing the night away at a friend's hen do. Both were years after the bereavement, at times when I thought I was *over it*, but the hauntingly familiar loneliness and abandonment returned just as fresh as ever.

But that's OK.

Going through the motions is still progress, helping smooth a few more of the pain's rough edges.

Those who haven't suffered a bereavement often imagine the hurt remains way back there in the past experience, but, in fact, it's ever-present. To an outsider, years have passed *since* the pain of my mum's death. However, from *my* perspective, I've been living for years *with* the pain of it. And those are two very different things, just like being thirsty *five years ago* is not the same as being thirsty *for* five years.

As carers who have – or will – lose someone, this knowledge is extremely powerful. It is a reminder to remain proactive in mending your broken heart, a prompt to preserve your parachute of self-care for when you inevitably start heading for rock bottom. Whether you're being swept up in a tsunami of grief, or rattled by one of its aftershocks, you need to keep your support structures in place for longer than you might think to survive.

# Afterword

## SNAKES AND LADDERS

Throughout Mum's illness, I worked on the presumption that once she was gone I would go back to a vague version of my old life and I'd be happy again. I knew there would be tears and sadness, but ultimately, I assumed I'd pick myself up and carry on from where I'd left off. As if caring for Mum was nothing more than a diversion that would eventually loop back around to where I was happily heading before she fell ill.

But the reality was very different.

After me, Hannah and Olivia moved out of Mum's house to go our separate ways, I headed to Manchester and did what I always said I would – *focus on getting my old life back.*

Twelve months after losing Mum I stopped blogging, because I worried that continuing would seem attention seeking, that people would think, *'Yeah cool, that was ages ago. You can't keep harping on about your dead parents, Rochelle.'*

Yet in truth, things were far from over.

A whole new stage in my grief was only just beginning. And it was one the Kübler-Ross Grief Cycle didn't seem to mention.

*The Aftermath.*

Of course, in typical me style I thought I was fine. After that first year without Mum, I assured myself that I was *there* with the healing – but that was before I realised that the fallout from a bereavement is like an iceberg. Grief spreads far deeper and wider than anyone could possibly know from looking at the surface. I thought my task was to melt a small pile of frost that had missed the summer sun, when in reality I was harbouring a frozen mountain of hurt big enough to sink the *Titanic*.

In Manchester, I embraced 'normal' life and enjoyed many Prosecco-fuelled, bar-hopping, laugh-filled times, meeting new faces and making new friends. I tried to build a support network there and reconstruct something that vaguely resembled a family, while working hard to set up my own freelance writing business and working full-time in PR.

I was doing just *fine*.

But two and a half years after moving there, something started to shift inside of me.

One day after work, I went to the gym, the place packed with people, filling up the long line of treadmills. As I studied the row of robotic-looking runners and tried to find a free machine, I realised this was how so many people spend their lives.

*It was how I was spending my life.*

Staring blankly ahead, running on the treadmill, turning up the speed, yet not actually going anywhere. No matter how steep the incline or how fast I was running, I was still standing in the same place, just getting increasingly tired from it all.

Jogging on my machine, I wondered if the life I'd created was what I truly wanted. I was doing well at work, I'd got a pay rise and my bonuses were getting bigger, yet I wasn't any happier. The more money I earned, the more I spent on things I didn't really need. I started ordering a bottle of wine instead of a glass, buying lunch at Prêt instead of Greggs and suddenly needing YSL mascara when Rimmel had been just fine for so many years.

In trying to keep up with my 'new' life, I was sliding too far away from my old one. By being 'normal' and doing the same as everyone else, I thought I wouldn't notice how much I was missing my parents. But instead all I achieved was to get worryingly close to overlooking everything that I had learned from losing them. I was starting to forget all that death had taught me about life.

Like everyone else on those treadmills, I was so focused on running, on having to keep going and not sliding off the back that I forgot there was an option to slow down the treadmill of life. I'd become so preoccupied with always being on the go, it hadn't even occurred to me there was an option to stop the treadmill, to get off and to walk over to another piece of equipment or to leave the gym entirely.

Suddenly, I felt silly.

I'd done what I said I'd never do and forgotten the searing clarity and invaluable perspective that being a carer had given me.

*Life is one big game and we need to stop taking it so seriously.*

I'd been sucked into a routine, eyes looking down at all times – at my phone, my keyboard, my wallet – doing or buying something else that I thought was going to make me happier, thinner or richer. I'd forgotten to look up. And I'd forgotten to look inside myself.

If I didn't do that, how would I know what I really wanted to be doing, what really brought me happiness?

*I had to get off the treadmill.* Metaphorically speaking and literally too, because my workout had left me knackered!

In the weeks following my revelation, I started slowing down the speed of my 'new' life, so that I could step safely off. I quit my job, booked a plane ticket, packed a case and headed to Bali for a month.

It was time to become a walking *Eat, Pray, Love* cliché.

I finally took the time I needed to realise just how much I'd overcome. To give myself the space, quiet and freedom to lay my many demons to rest. I went to Bali to reflect, to process, to write, to learn and to let go. To set free painful memories and finally heal.

Sitting in the warmth of the dusk sun as it sleepily stretched across Bali's rice paddy skyline, I took out my notebook and pen. I didn't know the storyline yet, but I was *finally* ready to start writing the next chapter of my life.


That was just over five years ago and I'm still deciding where that storyline will take me. That's why I wrote this book. You see, nobody ever seems to write this part of the story. The part that comes after The End appears on the cinema screen. The part that's messy and screwed up, difficult and painful. The part which doesn't fit the timescales you read about online and drags on long after everyone else thinks you should be over it.

To me, getting back on track after losing a loved one is like learning to walk after a serious leg injury. Immediately after the accident, all you can do is focus on survival, stem the bleeding and numb the pain. Then comes a period of immobilisation – physically, emotionally, or both – as you process what has happened and your body adjusts until, after a while, you feel strong enough to start using your leg again. As you build back your strength, each small step you take looks so easy from the outside, but you know it takes a super-human effort.

'Look! I'm walking! I must be fine!' you tell people (and yourself).

You assume that your regained movement means life is back to normal, ignoring your limp and overlooking the fact you can't walk as far as you used to. It's not until you are *truly* healed, when the limp has disappeared and pain has subsided, that you realise you even had them in the first place. It's only then you appreciate just how much effort it had been taking for you to walk.

Even though you thought you were *fine* as soon as the bleeding stopped. Even though you thought you were *fine* when the initial pain and shock subsided. Even though you thought you were *fine* when you could manage a few small shuffles forward. It is not until you really are *fine* that you realise you never were before.

The same could be said of me since Mum died.

I'd been acting as if I was fine for years, not realising that I hadn't quite regained my balance after being knocked sideways by her death. I'd been so bullishly intent on moving forward, so keen to *get on with things*, that I'd often been blind to the path of grief that I'm still walking and that I will continue to walk for the rest of my life. I recoil in embarrassment at some of my ill-informed choices over the last few years, the relationships that were doomed for failure and the decisions that were rushed into. But I suppose that's what happens when you don't know who you are or where you are – you become more vulnerable to attack, from everyone and everything.

Some of my misplaced optimism right after Mum's death still makes me laugh.

*If only I'd known how things were going to pan out.*

But maybe it's for the best that I didn't.

I presumed that the day we buried Mum was rock bottom, the point from which things could only get better. I had no idea that some of the hardest struggles were still to come. Everything I saw as an anchor, every relationship I felt was rock solid, every truth I believed to be unshakable, all changed.

Nobody had explained that the emotional turmoil of a death ripples far beyond the loss of a person and that grief does such very strange things to families. I had no idea that some people grab at material possessions in an attempt to fill the huge void that's been left, or that others actively encourage the void to grow as a coping strategy to help them forget the past ever happened at all. But the toughest realisation of all has been to learn that everyone reacts differently to death and that I have no control over how other people cope.

As the years since we lost Mum keep passing, I realise that nothing is as I thought it would be. Some people I presumed would be holding my hand have turned out to be the ones trying to cut it off. And others I thought were there to support me were actually seeking out my vulnerabilities so they could twist my need for love and stability for their own gain.

But, slowly, I am accepting that it's all OK, because I am OK.

*I am still here.*

I've gradually started to realise that I'm allowed to do things for me, that I'm allowed to be my own priority. After being a carer that can be a difficult concept to get your head around. But it's one that's beginning to sink in. 'Normal' life has resumed and enough time has passed for me to carve out a new path for myself. But it has not been easy.

*My God, it has not been easy.*

The day I first found out Mum was ill, I woke up happy. Yes, I had my worries – silly things like wondering who would get the bigger bedroom in the flat I'd just signed up for with Hannah – but no real problems. I got up that morning just like I had on countless others before it, so wrapped up in going from one moment to the next that I hadn't stopped to consider just how precious normal, everyday, routine life could be.

By that afternoon, when Olivia called to tell me about Mum's stroke, my world crumbled. There was no comeback from that moment in time, no way to wipe the slate clean. From then on, life became a wild, unpredictable hurricane of emotions and heartbreak, awash with tears and bittersweet laughs and filled with loss.

But while the word 'loss' highlights that something has been taken, experiencing it can also add to you. I like to think of it as grief's secret gift.

Gradually, over time, instead of holding me back, my pain has paved the way for my success. In a strange quirk of fate, I found that the things that were once *holding me back* became the exact same things that *pushed me ahead*. The daily stresses I once feared might make me have a *breakdown*, became the fuel that powered my *breakthroughs* in years to come. What I was once embarrassed *at what made me different* is now what *makes me different* when it comes to job applications and even securing the publishing deal for this book. Stuff I used to worry about which made me *stand out* for all the wrong reasons, now makes me *stand out* for all the right reasons.

That is why now, the Rochelle who has emerged from this pain goes through life very differently:

I am better at brushing aside other people's expectations of me. Better at ignoring people who presume I want a life just like theirs and who offer unrequested advice. Better at reminding myself that I am free to live my life the way I see best, even if it's not the same as everyone else. I am stronger and braver in walking away from people and places that no longer feel a good fit for me. I am not afraid to leave a job, move cities, or up sticks to another country. I am not afraid to start over or do something I have never done before, because I now know that I can do those things and do more than I ever expected of myself.

I have come to realise that if my whole world could fall apart in a split second then my whole world can come together in an instant, too. Just like a game of snakes and ladders, you never know where the next throw of the dice will take you in life. You could be sitting proudly at the top of the board, just a few squares away from the gold cup on '100', only to land on a snake and slide right back to the very start. But if that does happen, remember that you don't know how quickly your fortunes could turn once more. Your next throw could lead you up the longest ladder on the entire board, taking you straight to victory. Just when you think you have lost the game for good and there's no point in carrying on, give life one more throw of the dice.

*It might be the one that changes everything.*

That 'one last go' could be all you need to get further ahead than you ever were before you fell. That's something I've had to remind myself a lot as I've tried to get on with life after losing Mum. It's helped to keep me going when all I wanted to do was to give up. When sisterly squabbles started, family rifts appeared and legal matters dragged on, I kept telling myself that the same morning you wake up thinking all is lost could be the very same morning that your dreams start coming true.

If you feel as though you've just slid down a snake, remember that a ladder could be waiting for you on the next roll.

# The Secret Code for Carers

There are no rules for being a carer, but maybe there should be? Not rules exactly, but perhaps a list of things to expect when you're caring for a loved one, so that when they happen you don't feel quite so alone or crazy.

There wasn't one when I was looking after my mum, so I decided to make my own. Here it is – a list of things that nobody tells you when someone you love is dying. The *If you know, you know* type stuff – The Secret Code for carers.

## 1. Always invest in decent tissues

With the amount you'll be wiping your eyes and blowing your nose, trust me when I say this bit of advice deserves to be *número uno* on the list. I learned this the hard way. In the early days, I used to wipe my eyes with my sleeve, kitchen roll, or anything else that was nearby when the floodgates opened. It wasn't long before it felt as if someone had grated the skin from my eyelids and I had to walk around with half a tub of Vaseline smeared over my face for weeks.

### 2. Nobody has the answers

You tell yourself that if you look on one more website, read one more book, get one more opinion, or phone one more charity helpline, you'll find that miracle cure or someone will tell you that vital piece of missing information that will magically make it all OK. You won't. They can't. There comes a point when you have to accept that sometimes there is no solution and simply start taking one day at a time.

### 3. You'll get frustrated that you can't make things better

You will pray to take the pain and illness on yourself just so that the person you love doesn't have to go through it anymore, but however many stars you wish upon, that's one wish that never comes true.

### 4. There will be times you want it to be over

However much you love them, however much you hope for a miracle, there will come a point where you want their suffering, your suffering – everyone's suffering – to be over. This is totally normal. You are *not*, I repeat *not*, a horrible person.

### 5. You do need to shower and you do need to wash your hair

I know you don't feel like it, but I promise a shower and hair wash will make you feel slightly more human. You can only get away with using dry shampoo for so long.

### 6. 'Why?' will become your new favourite word

Why me? Why the person I love? Why not someone else?

Why now? You will question why but may never get any answers. Somehow you need to learn to accept there are some things you just can't change.

### 7. Take lots of photos and videos

Record random bits of everyday life because it will be those little moments of normality that you will miss the most – the sound of their voice, the way they laugh and their funny expressions.

### 8. You will be eternally grateful for the invention of the smartphone

If you're hardcore you might be able to make it through a week of radiotherapy sessions by memorising the posters on the wall, playing I Spy and reading copies of *Country Living* from May 1994. But I am near certain that any more than a week without your own form of entertainment is beyond the limit of endurance for any normal human. Your phone will help you pass the ridiculous amounts of hours spent in hospital waiting rooms.

### 9. Wave bye-bye to your personality

However much you resist, daytime TV, staying in the house and lack of a social life will mean you forget how to have a conversation which doesn't revolve around hospital appointments, medication or symptoms. Fear not, this is only temporary. You can grow a personality back – trust me, I've done it. So, for now, take full advantage of having an excuse to forget birthdays, mix up people's names and not get things done on time.

### 10. *You will become a recluse*

Even if you were a social butterfly in your pre-carer days, there will now be times when you cannot face talking to anyone. Somehow saying things out loud make them all the more real. Plus, your new lack of personality (see point 9) will mean you no longer know how to keep conversation flowing without saying, *'Yeah... umm... yeah'* a lot.

### 11. *Sometimes you will feel OK and, dare I say it... happy*

When this happens, you will immediately feel guilty and wonder if this makes you heartless, evil and/or totally delusional. You are not any of those things. I promise. You're allowed to be happy even during sad times.

### 12. *Sometimes a hug is the answer*

It's that simple, although the science to back it up is quite complex. Studies show skin-to-skin contact helps regulate the nervous system and calm us down, which is why a hug can feel like it fixes so much.

### 13. *You'll experiment with every known alternative therapy*

You will spend hours researching a whole host of alternative therapies – then spend a small fortune on getting your loved one to try them all. Reiki, apricot kernels, homeopathy, an alkaline diet, CBD oil, crystals, bathing your feet in water blessed by Colombian fairies on a full moon (maybe not the last one, but some of the things Mum tried came pretty close).

### 14. *Something's gotta give*

Stop fretting that you're getting too much or too little sleep, that you're eating more or less than usual, or that you can't make it through the day without crying. Obviously, none of these things are ideal (and keep an eye on them in case they get out of control), but beating yourself up over how you think you 'should' be reacting doesn't help either. You are going through an *abnormal* situation – you can't expect yourself to be normal.

### 15. Adverts and soap storylines will suddenly all be about cancer, death and funerals

I swear TV planners do it on purpose! You can count on your favourite character being diagnosed at the same time as your loved one. You'll watch TV to unwind, but things end up being a little too close to home and you'll become skilled at subtle channel changing.

### 16. Friends come and go

The people you think will be there, won't. Yet the girl on your Facebook you haven't spoken to since primary school will step up and help you in ways you never expected.

### 17. A trip to 'big Tesco' will feel like a wild adventure

After spending so long at home, the highlight of your social calendar will be a trip to the superstore on the edge of town. The thought of clothes, homeware *and* food all in one place will bring you a worrying level of excitement that you once reserved for nights out and holidays with friends.

### 18. You will start to understand all the long words they use in medical dramas

After spending so long in hospitals and GP surgeries you'll start picking up all the long medical jargon – tachycardia, atrial fibrillation – you name it, you'll soon know it. If you're like me, you'll secretly feel quite smug – like you're an extra in *Holby City*.

### 19. 'How are you?' becomes the world's most difficult question
Forget trying to decide whether the chicken or the egg came first, when someone you love is dying, often you don't even know *who* you are let alone *how* you are.

### 20. Stock up with a variety of beverages to rival Starbucks
So many different people from different places will pop in that you'll need an array of tea bags, coffee, herbal teas, sugar, sweeteners, oat milk and squash to make sure you can cater for every surprise guest's beverage needs.

### 21. Staying at home all day is not fun
Despite what you thought when you were eight years old and faked the flu the night before sports day, spending day after day at home gets really boring, really quickly.

### 22. Your fashion sense will disappear
All praise the elasticated waistband! You will start living in PJs, trackies and leggings. For hospital appointments you might push the fashionista boat out and wear one of the three 'proper' outfits you have on constant rotation.

### 23. There's only person you consistently see, outside of your family...
... the postman.

### 24. *However much you sleep you will still be tired*

Or maybe you won't be able to doze off at all. Either way, don't be alarmed if you find yourself in a daze, putting your phone in the fridge and trying to text on a tub of Philadelphia.

### 25. *You'll spend the GDP of a small European nation on pillows to prop up your loved one in bed*

We're talking six pillows, two big scatter cushions, a bolster and then five to ten small ones for good measure. Dunelm is gonna love you.

### 26. *You're never going to eat hot food again*

Learn to accept that your food will go cold while you're cutting up and feeding the person who is poorly.

### 27. *No place or time is sacred*

On the loo? In the bath? The middle of the night? It doesn't matter. Cancer doesn't keep office hours so, in the words of Shakira, be ready to be called upon 'Whenever, Wherever'.

### 28. *You can identify the carers by their footsteps*

The way they walk down the path. The way they knock on the door. You'll know which carer is on shift that day before they've even set foot inside.

### 29. *Your phone battery will never die*

The panic of seeing a red battery with 5 per cent next to it will become but a distant memory, because you're always at home with your charger.

### 30. *You will become a font of knowledge on random topics*

Watching so much daytime TV means you will acquire a bizarre mix of very random and mostly useless knowledge. You hope to one day impress a hot guy at a pub quiz with facts such as the Spice Girls' video for 'Wannabe' being banned in some countries because you can see Mel B's nipples through her top. Or that *objectum sexuality* is the term for falling in love with inanimate objects, like the Swedish woman who married the Berlin Wall. Unfortunately, the whole pub quiz thing is highly unlikely.

### 31. *The receptionist at the GP surgery recognises your voice*

You don't even have to introduce yourself on the phone any more; she greets you straight away like an old friend.

### 32. *Your to-do list is a self-generating creature*

It's never-ending. Tasks will continue to be added to that list even after you yourself have died. Stop thinking it is possible to do everything that's on there. Split your list into *Must Do*, *Nice To Do* and *Can Wait To Do* and focus on the first group – anything else is a bonus.

### 33. *You'll wash out fancy jam jars and exotic-looking tins to use as vases*

Sending flowers is lovely but how does everyone always do it at the same time, as if they've coordinated a bulk Interflora delivery? You'll soon run out of vases and find yourself rummaging at the back of kitchen cupboards to find makeshift containers. Star finds will include a neglected Guinness pint glass from the 1999 Rugby World Cup and a plastic jug you got with a BBQ set.

### 34. *You will want to run away...*

... but you don't know where you would go, and you'd never forgive yourself if you did. Instead you'll just google 'remote forest retreats' and stare longingly at the photos.

### 35. *You will feel useless*

You will feel very useless, very often. At the precise moment that you start to feel this way, immediately re-read the next sentence: **You are not at all useless. You're doing an amazing thing right now.**

And finally ...

### 36. *You will get through it.*

There's no doubt about it. I promise.

# Acknowledgements

**Mum and Dad** – Looks like all those pens and notebooks I made you buy me growing up have paid off now that I'm an author! All I've ever wanted is to make you both proud. So, here's hoping that you are. Not just of me, but of Hannah and Olivia too, because this really has been a team effort. Thank you for the sacrifices, thank you for showing me anything is possible, and thank you for believing in me so much that I learned to believe in myself. Even though you're not around, I know that you're always around. Onwards and upwards…

**Hannah and Olivia** – What the hell? How did we survive all that? Nobody else will ever fully understand what we've been through (and they probably wouldn't want to), but it means we've got a Bugg-Bond™ so strong, it can never be broken – even when we do each other's heads in. You two have been my reason to keep going on my darkest days when all I wanted to do was give up. Thank you for the love, thank you for the laughs, oh and thank you for letting me use some of the awful family photos in this book. Thank you for being my *hermanas*, still, after it all. If we've come this far, then we really can do anything.

**Nosa** – Bad luck that I Wray & Nephew-ed my way into your life just in time for you to see me through writing this book. But your loss has been most definitely been my gain. Thank you for the 3,752 phone calls when I thought I'd never finish writing this, thank you for forcing me to take breaks in the Hyperbolic Time Chamber, but most of all, thank you for teaching me to *Protect My Peace*.

**Leisha, Maggie, Andy L, Andy F and Harps** – Kintsugi is the Japanese art of mending broken pottery by gluing it back together with gold. They say that by embracing the flaws and imperfections, you create something even stronger and more beautiful. Thank you to each of you for giving me the gold to piece myself back together when I was broken.

**Becky at Johnson and Alcock and all the team at John Blake Publishing** – To everyone who has had a hand in bringing this book into the world, what can I say, except a million thank yous? Thank you for believing this story needed to be told and thank you for guiding me through the process of doing just that.

And to everyone I haven't mentioned, you are far from forgotten. Thank you, thank you, thank you. I will forever be grateful.

# Resources

## GOING TO THERAPY

### *You can't heal if you pretend it never hurt you*

There is no shame in going to therapy either during or after your loved one's illness – or both! Being a carer and the loss of a loved one is going to affect you. There's no getting away from it. There's nothing wrong with needing help getting over something so traumatic – it would be more worrying if it didn't affect you at all.

### *If it's under the rug, it's still in the house*

Emotional trauma can leave you with lingering beliefs. Think of them as your body's receipts for the major life event(s) you've been through – proof your brain has to register the trauma and you now 'own' those experiences. But just as with receipts, those beliefs are only meant to be valid for a specific period, they are supposed to have an expiry date.

So, while it may have served you to be hyper-aware when

your loved one was ill (just in case they needed you), that way of thinking isn't so useful after they have gone. There comes a time when you need to spring-clean your mental clutter and get rid of anything that is no longer serving you.

### Therapy can't change what's happened – so what's the point?

Therapy, for me, has been like finally sitting down to read the instruction manual for my brain, after years of pressing any button and hoping for the best. It's not only helped me understand why I work the way I do – it has shown me shortcuts, explained why *that* particular error message always comes up, and allowed me to use the full range of features of my life.

There are lots of different types of therapy available, but here are five that I have tried and found to be particularly helpful.

### 1. Talking Therapy

People say it's good to talk, and that's true – but only if someone is listening. Before starting professional counselling, I had already spoken about being a carer and losing my parents hundreds of times, but my words had generally been met with offers of advice, the sharing of stories similar to mine or reassurance that it would all work out. But counselling sessions were different.

Helpful and healing, talking therapy was far more than just the comfy couch and aromatherapy sprays I had expected. My counsellor witnessed my pain, held space for my stories and validated my feelings. I never realised until then how powerful it is to have someone to mirror back to you what you already know.

*Yes, it really was that bad.*

*Yes, it really is unfair.*

*Yes, your responses are normal.*

## 2. Somatic Experiencing®

It is no exaggeration to say that Somatic Experiencing® sessions have changed my life. This intuitive approach focuses on felt senses in the body to overcome shock and trauma and heal the nervous system.

Doing this work has helped to free me from parts of myself that I thought had been permanently altered because of trauma. I am not *back* to my old self, I am *forward* to a new, improved self and, for me, that has been something far more valuable.

## 3. Eye Movement Desensitization and Reprocessing (EMDR)

During this interactive therapy, an EMDR practitioner will help you gently and carefully relive traumatic experiences while they either direct your eye movements, or you hold alternating buzzers in your hands. This method has been shown to help lessen the impact your traumatic memories have on you.

EMDR is great because it works even if you have little to no memory of certain events, for example if you don't remember anything from the night your loved one died or the period when you found out their diagnosis was terminal.

## 4. Tension Trauma Release Exercises (TRE®)

This series of exercises helps the body release deep muscular patterns of trauma and stress. Sometimes also known as 'Therapeutic Tremoring' because of the way the tension is released, this technique can look quite strange at first, but I've found it to be a great 'quick fix'. I use it now after any particularly 'charged' moments to immediately let go of any stress, instead of holding onto it and letting it fester.

## 5. Emotional Freedom Technique (EFT)

Another great 'emergency technique', you can practice EFT out and about as and when you need with no specialist equipment. It is also known as 'tapping' because you quite literally 'tap' on a set sequence of acupressure points to reduce physical and emotional pain while talking through a particular issue you are having. If you're interested, there are some great guided EFT sessions on YouTube.

### *The perfect match*

Finding the right therapist is often just as important as the therapy itself. Don't be afraid to shop around and go with your gut instincts about whether the practitioner is a good fit for you. Many offer a free introductory session to see if you think you would 'gel'.

# Charities & Organisations

**Cancer Research UK**

https://www.cancerresearchuk.org/

Cancer Research UK is a research and awareness charity, working on the prevention, diagnosis and treatment of the disease. It also develops evidence-based policy to inform Government decisions related to cancer and research.

**Carer's Allowance Information**

https://www.gov.uk/carers-allowance

https://www.citizensadvice.org.uk/

https://www.turn2us.org.uk/

These sites will be useful for navigating the financial aspects of being a carer. You can also seek guidance and advice from organisations supporting carers, such as the Carers Trust and Carers UK (see below).

**Carers' Charities**

http://www.careforcarers.org.uk/

https://www.carersuk.org/

https://carers.org/

These organisations are great for talking to people who 'get' what it's like to be a carer and can walk you through available help. As well as these national charities, there are hundreds of local charities supporting carers across the UK.

**Lobbying Organisations**

Organisations such as Carers UK and the Carers Trust also lobby alongside other organisations for better support for people caring for loved ones with life-limiting and terminal illnesses.

**Local Hospices**

Your local hospice may provide a range of support for carers (reflexology, massage etc.) as well as for the person that's ill. Many hospices offer daytime drop-in sessions as well as space for longer stays, a telephone helpline, and are often able to loan you specialist equipment.

**Macmillan Cancer Support**

https://www.macmillan.org.uk/

Macmillan was my first port of call for advice on everything from benefits to blue badges.

**Marie Curie**

https://www.mariecurie.org.uk/

Marie Curie provides help when living with someone with a terminal illness towards the end of their life. They also have nine hospices across the UK.

**Patient Advice and Liaison Service (PALS)**

https://www.nhs.uk/common-health-questions/nhs-services-and-treatments/what-is-pals-patient-advice-and-liaison-service/

The Patient Advice and Liaison Service (PALS) offers confidential advice, support and information on health-related matters.

They provide a point of contact for patients, their families and their carers. You can find officers from PALS in your local hospital.

**Targeted Charities**

https://www.thebraintumourcharity.org/

The Brain Tumour Charity was fantastic to us when Mum was ill, helping with tailored information and understanding the specific struggles of Mum's illness when I couldn't find support from other more general cancer charities. Whatever your loved one's illness, there will be amazing people dedicated to giving specialist advice and support, so be sure to seek them out.

# MENTAL HEALTH & BEREAVEMENT SUPPORT

**Blurt**

https://www.blurtitout.org

Blurt is a social enterprise dedicated to helping anyone affected by depression.

**Cruse Bereavement**

https://www.cruse.org.uk/

Cruse Bereavement Care is the UK's largest bereavement charity, which provides free services to support the bereaved, including a helpline and web chat service.

**Hope Support Services**

http://www.hopesupport.org.uk

A youth-led support service available to anybody aged 11–25 when a close family member is diagnosed with a life-threatening illness.

## Hub of Hope
https://hubofhope.co.uk/
The Hub of Hope is a mental health support database created by Chasing the Stigma. It is the UK's most comprehensive national mental health support database. You can download the free app, visit the website, or text HOPE to 85258 to find help fast.

## Let's Talk About Loss
https://letstalkaboutloss.org
Let's Talk About Loss provides a safe space to talk through taboos and address the reality of losing someone close to you when you are young.

## Mind
https://www.mind.org.uk/
0300 123 3393
Mind is a charity providing advice and support to empower anyone experiencing a mental health problem. They also campaign to improve services, raise awareness and promote understanding.

## PAPYRUS
https://www.papyrus-uk.org/
0800 068 41 41
Papyrus is an organisation supporting teenagers and young adults who are feeling suicidal.

## Samaritans
https://www.samaritans.org/
116 123
Samaritans operates a 24-hour service available every day of the year. If you prefer to write down how you're feeling, or if you're worried about being overheard on the phone, you can email Samaritans at jo@samaritans.org

**Shout**

https://www.giveusashout.org/get-help/

Shout 85258 is a free, confidential 24/7 text messaging support service for anyone who is struggling to cope. The service is there for anyone feeling anxious, stressed, depressed, suicidal or overwhelmed and who needs immediate support.

# BOOKS

Bessel van der Kolk, MD – *The Body Keeps the Score: Mind, Brain and Body in the Transformation of Trauma*, Penguin Books Ltd (2015), London

Eckhart Tolle – *The Power of Now*, Hodder & Stoughton (2005), London

Elisabeth Kübler-Ross – *On Death and Dying*, Routledge (2009), Abingdon, Oxon

Glennon Doyle – *Untamed*, Vermilion (2020), London

Mitch Albom – *The Five People You Meet in Heaven*, Time Warner Paperbacks (2004), London

Mo Gawdat – *Solve For Happy* (Hardcover), North Star Way (2017), New York

Peter A. Levine – *Waking the Tiger: Healing Trauma*, North Atlantic Books (1997), Berkeley, California

Rebecca Solnit – *A Field Guide to Getting Lost*, Canongate Books (2006), Edinburgh

Sandy Newbigging – *Mind Calm*, Hay House UK Ltd (2014), London

# PODCASTS

*Grief is My Superpower* – Mark Lemon

*Griefcast* – Cariad Lloyd

HANDLE WITH CARE

*Happier* – Gretchen Rubin
*Terrible, Thanks for Asking* – Nora McInerny
*Unlocking Us* – Brené Brown
*Who Cares Wins* – Kyro Brooks & James Townsend

# SOCIAL MEDIA

**YouTube**
Brad Yates (look for his videos specifically for caregivers)
Crappy Childhood Fairy
Jason Stephenson
Michael Sealey

**Instagram**
@anxiety_wellbeing
@bymariandrew
@carers.trust
@charliemackesy
@griefkid
@grief_guide
@medicineformoderntimes
@modernloss
@peopleiveloved
@something_to_look_forward_to
@thatgoodgrief
@thedinnerparty
@twinpowerment